PRISM

LISTENING AND SPEAKING 4

Jessica Williams

with
Angela Blackwell
Christina Cavage
Laurie Frazier

CAMBRIDGE
UNIVERSITY PRESS

University Printing House, Cambridge CB2 8BS, United Kingdom

One Liberty Plaza, 20th Floor, New York, NY 10006, USA

477 Williamstown Road, Port Melbourne, VIC 3207, Australia

314–321, 3rd Floor, Plot 3, Splendor Forum, Jasola District Centre, New Delhi – 110025, India

103 Penang Road, #05–06/07, Visioncrest Commercial, Singapore 238467

Cambridge University Press is part of the University of Cambridge.

It furthers the University's mission by disseminating knowledge in the pursuit of education, learning and research at the highest international levels of excellence.

www.cambridge.org
Information on this title: www.cambridge.org/9781009251334

First published 2017
Update published 2022
20 19 18 17 16 15 14 13 12 11 10 9 8 7 6 5 4 3 2 1

Printed in Mexico by Litográfica Ingramex, S.A. de C.V.

A catalogue record for this publication is available from the British Library

ISBN 978-1-009-25133-4 Student's Book with Digital Pack 4 Listening and Speaking
ISBN 978-1-316-62546-0 Teacher's Manual 4 Listening and Speaking

CONTENTS

SCOPE AND SEQUENCE

UNIT	WATCH AND LISTEN	LISTENINGS	LISTENING SKILLS	PRONUNCIATION FOR LISTENING
1 CONSERVATION *Academic Disciplines* Agriculture / Economics / Environmental Studies	Pelicans Threatened by Oil	1: A lecture about whether sustainable agriculture is a viable option 2: A panel discussion about how to assign responsibility for climate change	*Key Skills* Listening to introductions Rhetorical questions as signals *Additional Skills* Understanding key vocabulary Using your knowledge Listening for main ideas Taking notes Listening for opinion Listening for details Synthesizing	Intonation of complete and incomplete ideas
2 DESIGN *Academic Disciplines* Design Technology / Manufacturing / Marketing	The Appeal of Large Cell Phones	1: A presentation on current and future uses for 3D printing 2: A student presentation about planned obsolescence	*Key Skills* Using a graphic organizer to capture main ideas and details Reviewing and organizing notes *Additional Skills* Using your knowledge Understanding key vocabulary Predicting content using visuals Listening for main ideas Listening for details Listening for opinion Summarizing Synthesizing	Word stress
3 PRIVACY *Academic Disciplines* Information Technology / Law / Political Science	Security Breaches at Big-Box Stores	1: A public presentation about Internet security and privacy 2: A moderated forum on individual privacy and national security	*Key Skills* Listening for opinions Listening for facts and supporting information *Additional Skills* Using your knowledge Understanding key vocabulary Taking notes Listening for main ideas Listening for details Synthesizing	Sentence stress
4 BUSINESS *Academic Disciplines* Business / Finance / Management	A New Chapter for Independent Bookstores	1: A lecture about disruptive innovation 2: An overview of the business model of a nonprofit organization	*Key Skills* Listening for definitions Understanding figurative language *Additional Skills* Understanding key vocabulary Using your knowledge Listening for main ideas Listening for details Making inferences Synthesizing	Thought groups

	LANGUAGE DEVELOPMENT	CRITICAL THINKING	SPEAKING	ON CAMPUS
	Parallel structure in comparisons Language for blame and responsibility	Analyzing issues	***Speaking Skill*** Challenging other points of view ***Pronunciation*** Intonation of complete and incomplete ideas ***Speaking Task*** Have an informal debate about the mission of national parks. Is their primary purpose to protect the natural world from human activity or to encourage responsible human interaction with nature? Is it possible to accomplish both of these goals?	***Life Skill*** Volunteering and community service
	Using cause-and-effect phrases Degree expressions	Evaluating pros and cons	***Speaking Skill*** Acknowledging other arguments ***Pronunciation*** Stress in compound nouns and noun phrases ***Speaking Task*** Give a group presentation about a product that you believe was designed for obsolescence. Discuss the reasons, both positive and negative, why it was designed in this way.	***Presentation Skill*** Incorporating visuals
	Subject-verb agreement with quantifiers Collocations: online activity; legal terms	Eliciting information via surveys	***Speaking Skills*** Explaining data from graphics Presenting conclusions from research ***Pronunciation*** Question intonation ***Speaking Task*** Present data that you have collected from a survey and the conclusions that you have drawn from it.	***Study Skill*** Adapting to teaching styles
	Extreme comparisons and contrasts Academic alternatives	Brainstorming and narrowing	***Speaking Skills*** Crafting a pitch ***Speaking Task*** Make a pitch to get a venture started. Your goal is to get funding (investment or donations) for your peer-to-peer business or nonprofit organization.	***Communication Skill*** Participating in group discussions

UNIT	WATCH AND LISTEN	LISTENINGS	LISTENING SKILLS	PRONUNCIATION FOR LISTENING
5 PSYCHOLOGY *Academic Disciplines* Biology / Neuroscience / Psychology	Modern Shock Therapy	1: A planning session for a group presentation on first impressions 2: A lecture on navigation techniques and the brain	***Key Skills*** Listening for generalizations and summaries Listening for dependency relationships ***Additional Skills*** Using your knowledge Understanding key vocabulary Listening for main ideas Listening for details Taking notes Summarizing Synthesizing	Emphasis within thought groups
6 CAREERS *Academic Disciplines* Business / Education / Human Resources	Returnships: Hiring Moms	1: A special presentation by a career counselor for computer science majors 2: A workshop about job interview skills	***Key Skills*** Listening for pros and cons Making inferences ***Additional Skills*** Using your knowledge Understanding key vocabulary Listening for main ideas Listening for details Taking notes Summarizing Synthesizing	Reduction of auxiliary verbs
7 HEALTH SCIENCES *Academic Disciplines* Environmental Sciences / Health Sciences / Medicine	Water Pollution in West Virginia	1: A talk about environmental health and the increase of asthma 2: A community meeting about water quality	***Key Skills*** Taking unstructured notes as you listen Identifying persuasive appeals ***Additional Skills*** Using your knowledge Predicting content using visuals Understanding key vocabulary Listening for main ideas Listening for details Taking notes Summarizing Synthesizing	Contrastive stress
8 COLLABORATION *Academic Disciplines* Business / Political Science / Sociology	Are Office Meetings Useful?	1: A training session on group dynamics and the "bad apple" effect 2: Class discussion about two systems for decision making	***Key Skill*** Using anecdotes and proverbs to illustrate larger ideas ***Additional Skills*** Using your knowledge Understanding key vocabulary Summarizing Listening for main ideas Listening for details Taking notes Synthesizing	Contracted forms of *will*

	LANGUAGE DEVELOPMENT	CRITICAL THINKING	SPEAKING	ON CAMPUS
	Noun clauses with *wh-* words and *if/whether* Academic word families	Synthesizing information from multiple sources	***Speaking Skills*** Talking about research Incorporating visual support ***Speaking Task*** Give a group presentation about research on some aspect of human behavior. Support your presentation with slides.	***Study Skill*** Staying motivated
	Degree expressions with *so ... that; such a ... that* Emphatic expressions	Understanding job descriptions	***Speaking Skills*** Body language Preparing for a job interview ***Speaking Task*** Participate in a mock job interview.	***Study Skill*** Preparing for tests
	Establishing cohesion with *so* and *such* Adjectives of strong disapproval	Understanding motivation	***Speaking Skill*** Inclusive language ***Pronunciation*** Emphasis for emotional appeal ***Speaking Task*** Participate in a community meeting about a local environmental health crisis.	***Life Skill*** Seeking medical treatment
	Wh- clefts Collocations: prepositions	Cost-benefit analyses	***Speaking Skill*** Steps for consensus building Collaborative language: suggestion and concession ***Speaking Task*** Participate in a consensus-building decision-making task to decide on future food service operations at your school.	***Presentation Skill*** Handling audience questions

HOW *PRISM* WORKS

1 Video

Setting the context

Every unit begins with a video clip. Each video serves as a springboard for the unit and introduces the topic in an engaging way. The clips were carefully selected to pique students' interest and prepare them to explore the unit's topic in greater depth. As they work, students develop key skills in prediction, comprehension, and discussion.

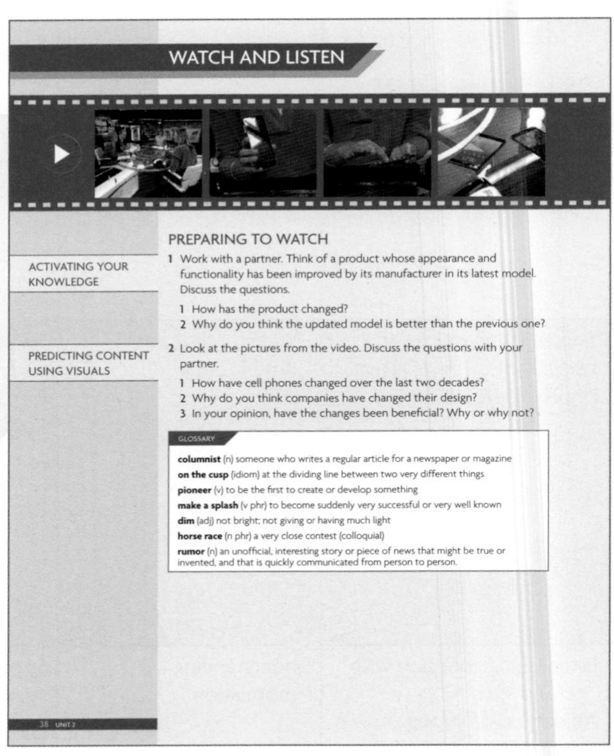

WATCH AND LISTEN

PREPARING TO WATCH

ACTIVATING YOUR KNOWLEDGE

1 Work with a partner. Think of a product whose appearance and functionality has been improved by its manufacturer in its latest model. Discuss the questions.

1 How has the product changed?
2 Why do you think the updated model is better than the previous one?

PREDICTING CONTENT USING VISUALS

2 Look at the pictures from the video. Discuss the questions with your partner.

1 How have cell phones changed over the last two decades?
2 Why do you think companies have changed their design?
3 In your opinion, have the changes been beneficial? Why or why not?

GLOSSARY

columnist (n) someone who writes a regular article for a newspaper or magazine
on the cusp (idiom) at the dividing line between two very different things
pioneer (v) to be the first to create or develop something
make a splash (v phr) to become suddenly very successful or very well known
dim (adj) not bright; not giving or having much light
horse race (n phr) a very close contest (colloquial)
rumor (n) an unofficial, interesting story or piece of news that might be true or invented, and that is quickly communicated from person to person.

38 UNIT 2

2 Listening

Receptive, language, and analytical skills

Students improve their listening abilities through a sequence of proven activities. They study key vocabulary to prepare them for each listening and to develop academic listening skills. Pronunciation for Listening exercises help students learn how to decode spoken English. Language Development sections teach grammar and vocabulary. A second listening leads into synthesis exercises that prepare students for college classrooms.

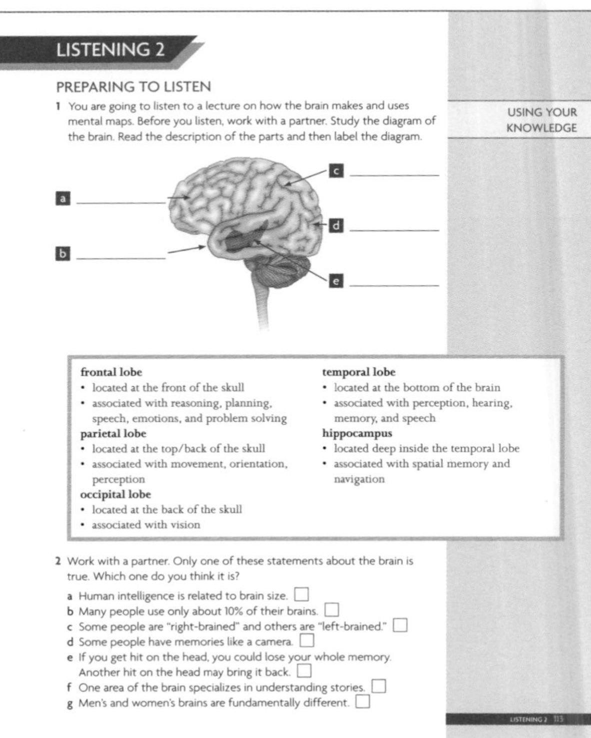

LISTENING 2

PREPARING TO LISTEN

USING YOUR KNOWLEDGE

1 You are going to listen to a lecture on how the brain makes and uses mental maps. Before you listen, work with a partner. Study the diagram of the brain. Read the description of the parts and then label the diagram.

frontal lobe
- located at the front of the skull
- associated with reasoning, planning, speech, emotions, and problem solving

parietal lobe
- located at the top/back of the skull
- associated with movement, orientation, perception

occipital lobe
- located at the back of the skull
- associated with vision

temporal lobe
- located at the bottom of the brain
- associated with perception, hearing, memory, and speech

hippocampus
- located deep inside the temporal lobe
- associated with spatial memory and navigation

2 Work with a partner. Only one of these statements about the brain is true. Which one do you think it is?

a Human intelligence is related to brain size. ☐
b Many people use only about 10% of their brains. ☐
c Some people are "right-brained" and others are "left-brained." ☐
d Some people have memories like a camera. ☐
e If you get hit on the head, you could lose your whole memory. Another hit on the head may bring it back. ☐
f One area of the brain specializes in understanding stories. ☐
g Men's and women's brains are fundamentally different. ☐

LISTENING 2 115

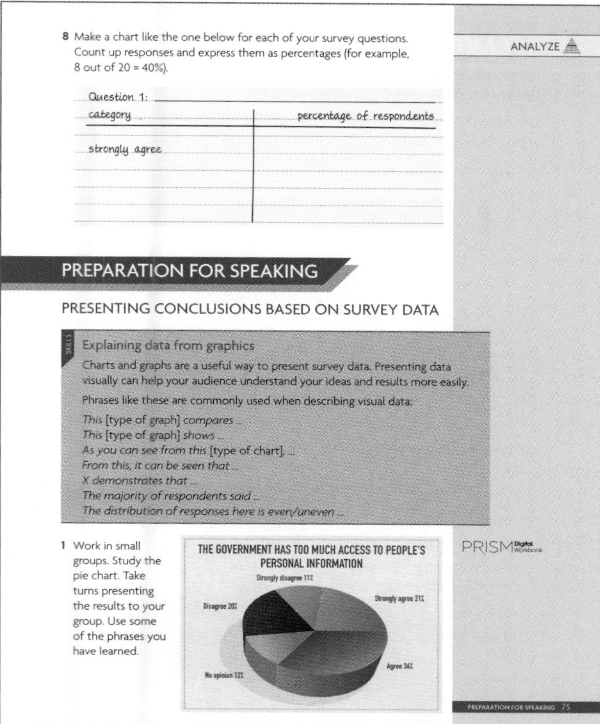

ANALYZE

8 Make a chart like the one below for each of your survey questions. Count up responses and express them as percentages (for example, 8 out of 20 = 40%).

Question 1:

category	percentage of respondents
strongly agree	

PREPARATION FOR SPEAKING

PRESENTING CONCLUSIONS BASED ON SURVEY DATA

SKILLS

Explaining data from graphics

Charts and graphs are a useful way to present survey data. Presenting data visually can help your audience understand your ideas and results more easily.

Phrases like these are commonly used when describing visual data:

This [type of graph] *compares* ...
This [type of graph] *shows* ...
As you can see from this [type of chart], ...
From this, it can be seen that ...
X demonstrates that ...
The majority of respondents said ...
The distribution of responses here is even/uneven ...

1 Work in small groups. Study the pie chart. Take turns presenting the results to your group. Use some of the phrases you have learned.

PREPARATION FOR SPEAKING 75

3 Speaking

Critical thinking and production

Multiple critical thinking activities begin this section, setting students up for exercises that focus on speaking skills, functional language, and pronunciation. All of these lead up to a structured speaking task, in which students apply the skills and language they have developed over the course of the entire unit.

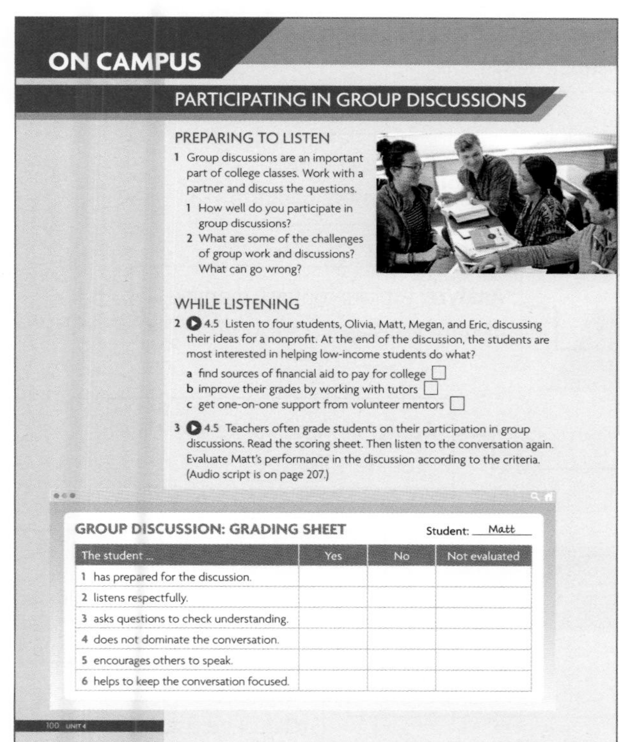

ON CAMPUS

PARTICIPATING IN GROUP DISCUSSIONS

PREPARING TO LISTEN

1 Group discussions are an important part of college classes. Work with a partner and discuss the questions.

1 How well do you participate in group discussions?
2 What are some of the challenges of group work and discussions? What can go wrong?

WHILE LISTENING

2 4.5 Listen to four students, Olivia, Matt, Megan, and Eric, discussing their ideas for a nonprofit. At the end of the discussion, the students are most interested in helping low-income students do what?

a find sources of financial aid to pay for college ☐
b improve their grades by working with tutors ☐
c get one-on-one support from volunteer mentors ☐

3 4.5 Teachers often grade students on their participation in group discussions. Read the scoring sheet. Then listen to the conversation again. Evaluate Matt's performance in the discussion according to the criteria. (Audio script is on page 207.)

GROUP DISCUSSION: GRADING SHEET Student: Matt

The student ...	Yes	No	Not evaluated
1 has prepared for the discussion.			
2 listens respectfully.			
3 asks questions to check understanding.			
4 does not dominate the conversation.			
5 encourages others to speak.			
6 helps to keep the conversation focused.			

100 UNIT 4

4 On Campus

Skills for college life

This unique section teaches students valuable skills beyond academic listening and speaking. From asking questions in class to participating in a study group and from being an active listener to finding help, students learn how to navigate university life. The section begins with a context-setting listening, and moves directly into active practice of the skill.

WHAT MAKES *PRISM* SPECIAL: CRITICAL THINKING

Bloom's Taxonomy

In order to truly prepare for college coursework, students need to develop a full range of thinking skills. *Prism* teaches explicit critical thinking skills in every unit of every level. These skills adhere to the taxonomy developed by Benjamin Bloom. By working within the taxonomy, we are able to ensure that your students learn both lower-order and higher-order thinking skills.

Critical thinking exercises are accompanied by icons indicating where the activities fall in Bloom's Taxonomy.

SPEAKING

CRITICAL THINKING

At the end of this unit, you are going to do the Speaking Task below.

Participate in a consensus-building decision-making task. Your goal is to choose one of three options for future food service operations at your school.

SKILLS

A cost-benefit analysis

Important decisions require a careful analysis of the pros (benefits) and cons (costs) of every option.

The benefits of biking to work, for example, might include a savings in transportation expenses and some good exercise; costs might include longer commute times and the discomfort of riding in bad weather.

In considering options, also consider the "winners and losers." Which stakeholders will get the greatest benefit from each of the options? Who will suffer the greatest costs?

UNDERSTAND

1 Work in small groups. Talk about your dining experiences.

1 What are the dining options on your campus or near your school?
2 Do you ever eat at fast-food restaurants? If so, what do you like about them? If not, why not?
3 Describe your experience eating in "institutional" dining facilities, for example, in a hospital, school, or government building.

182 UNIT 8

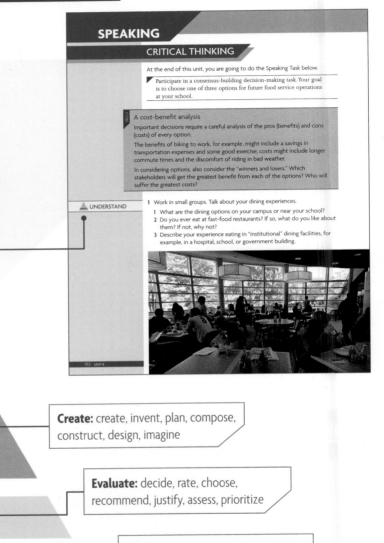

Create: create, invent, plan, compose, construct, design, imagine

Evaluate: decide, rate, choose, recommend, justify, assess, prioritize

Analyze: explain, contrast, examine, identify, investigate, categorize

Apply: show, complete, use, classify, illustrate, solve

Understand: compare, discuss, restate, predict, translate, outline

Remember: name, describe, relate, find, list, write, tell

WHAT MAKES *PRISM* SPECIAL: CRITICAL THINKING

3 With your group, consider the value of PO from the business side. Read the market scenarios for a consumer product. In which scenarios are the companies likely to build obsolescence into the design of their product as a way of encouraging repeated purchases?

EVALUATE

a One company is completely dominant in the market. There is no effective competition. If consumers want the product, they must buy it from that company.

b There are several companies that produce roughly equivalent products. Consumers have choices.

c There are several companies that produce roughly equivalent products. Consumers have choices. However, switching from one company to another has costs. For example, a consumer who buys from company X typically also purchases numerous accessories, which are not compatible with the equivalent product from company Z.

4 With your group, make a table like the one below. Choose two or three products that you have been considering for the speaking task. For each product, decide if obsolescence is, or could be

- entirely for the benefit of the producer – purely to increase revenue.
- a plan to increase revenue but also of some benefit to the consumer.
- a side effect rather than an intentional act.

For some products, multiple scenarios are possible.

product/feature	scenario 1	scenario 2	scenario 3
Cell phone: Consumers cannot access/ replace battery. Battery has a limited lifespan.	Consumers will have to buy a new phone when the battery dies. They have no choice.	Consumers will need to replace frequently. (good for company) Keeps costs down. (good for consumers) Consumers will want a new phone every few years anyway.	The design allows for a more attractive product. The inaccessible battery is smaller and lighter than a replaceable battery.

CRITICAL THINKING 51

Higher-Order Thinking Skills

Create, **Evaluate**, and **Analyze** are critical skills for students in any college setting. Academic success depends on their abilities to derive knowledge from collected data, make educated judgments, and deliver insightful presentations. *Prism* helps students get there by creating activities such as categorizing information, comparing data, selecting the best solution to a problem, and developing arguments for a discussion or presentation.

SPEAKING

CRITICAL THINKING

At the end of this unit, you are going to do the Speaking Task below.

Make a pitch to get a venture started. Your goal is to get funding (investment or donations) for your peer-to-peer business or nonprofit organization.

1 Work in small groups. Read the descriptions. Discuss the potential for success for each venture.

UNDERSTAND

group A: ideas for P2P businesses

1 *The Full Closet:* a service to help women with a lot of clothes generate income by renting out their clothing to others.

2 *Proud City:* a service that connects visitors and tourists with city residents who can act as guides and helpers, giving visitors a richer, more interesting city experience.

3 *Angel for a Day:* a service that connects individuals with certified, reliable, and affordable caregivers for family members.

group B: ideas for nonprofits working for social good

1 *Rain To Go:* a group that works with private companies to develop portable water purifiers and distribute them in poor countries.

2 *Safe Hangout:* a service that provides food and shelter for homeless teens.

3 *Reset:* a service that provides job training for nonviolent ex-prisoners in major cities around the country.

CRITICAL THINKING 95

Lower-Order Thinking Skills

Apply, **Understand**, and **Remember** provide the foundation upon which all thinking occurs. Students need to be able to recall information, comprehend it, and see its use in new contexts. *Prism* develops these skills through exercises such as taking notes, mining notes for specific data, demonstrating comprehension, and distilling information from charts.

WHAT MAKES *PRISM* SPECIAL: ON CAMPUS

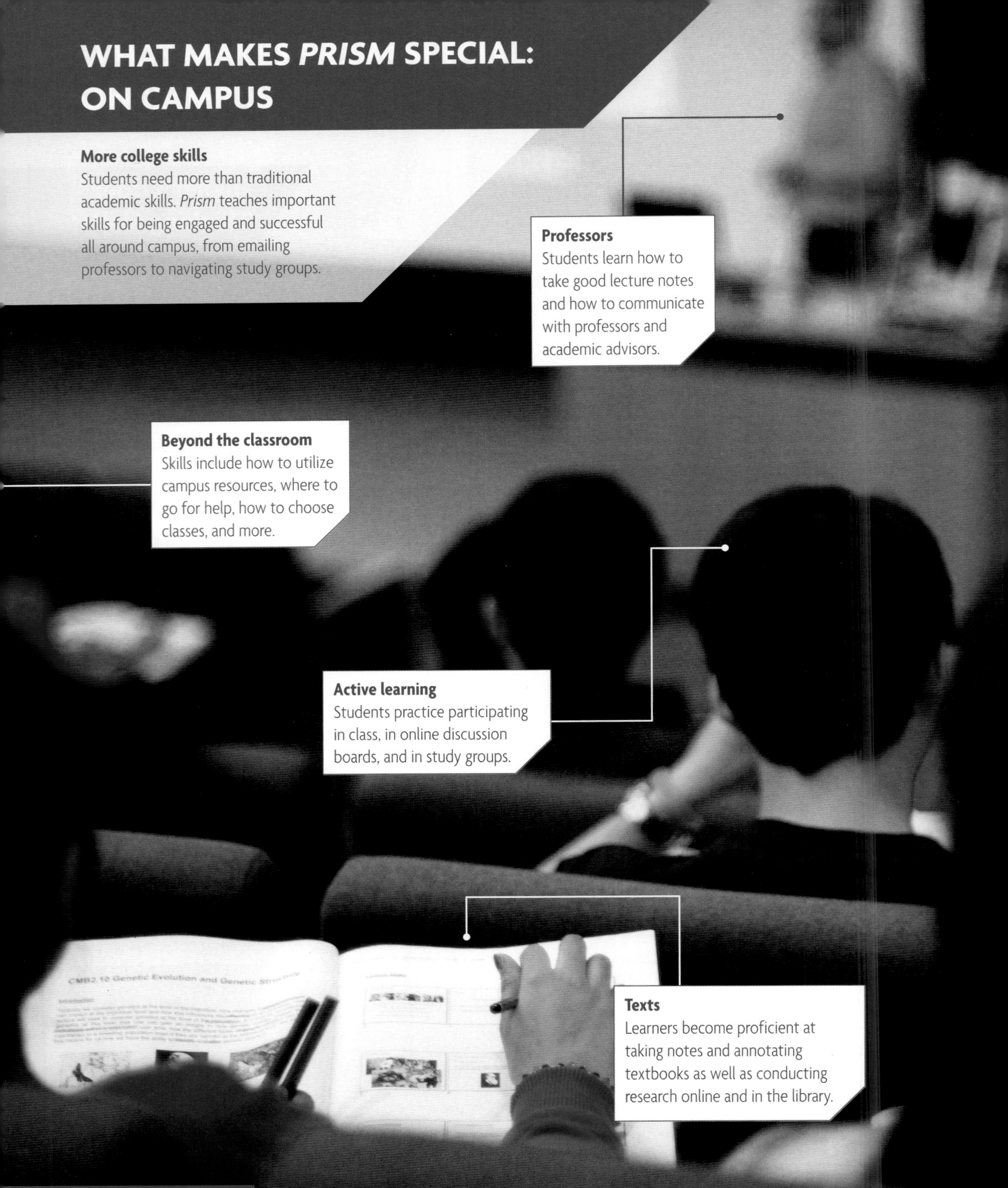

More college skills
Students need more than traditional academic skills. *Prism* teaches important skills for being engaged and successful all around campus, from emailing professors to navigating study groups.

Professors
Students learn how to take good lecture notes and how to communicate with professors and academic advisors.

Beyond the classroom
Skills include how to utilize campus resources, where to go for help, how to choose classes, and more.

Active learning
Students practice participating in class, in online discussion boards, and in study groups.

Texts
Learners become proficient at taking notes and annotating textbooks as well as conducting research online and in the library.

WHAT MAKES *PRISM* SPECIAL: RESEARCH

ACADEMIC ALTERNATIVES

LANGUAGE

Academic communication often includes lower-frequency words with the same or similar meaning as everyday vocabulary. Often, however, these academic words have more specific or specialized meaning than their higher-frequency counterparts. This allows speakers and writers to be more precise.

PRISM Digital Workbook

2 Work in small groups. What are the differences in meaning between these high (everyday) and low (academic) frequency word pairs? Use a dictionary to help you.

high	low	high	low
business	venture	main	primary
choice	option	sign (n)	trace
come out	emerge	sort (v)	sift
kind (n)	breed	stop using	abandon
large	massive		

3 Complete the sentences with the correct form of an academic word or phrase from Exercise 2.

1 The police will have to ________ through all the evidence to find clues to solve the crime.
2 A lot of people have ________ books completely and do all their reading on mobile devices.
3 There are no ________ of yesterday's celebration. Everything has been cleaned up.
4 Today there is a new ________ of tourist – one who wants to leave a small environmental footprint.
5 Several innovative ideas ________ during our discussion yesterday. We just need to decide which one to pursue.
6 My brother and I started this ________ in 1995. At the time, we were not sure it would ever be a success.
7 My ________ reason for using an online service is the lower cost.
8 I think we should look at some other ________. This apartment is too small and dark.
9 The company headquarters is ________. It has five multistory buildings and covers several acres.

4 Choose four of the academic words from the box above. Write a sentence in your notebook for each one that is relevant to its meaning.

90 UNIT 4

Vocabulary Research

Learning the right words

Students need to learn a wide range of general and academic vocabulary in order to be successful in college. *Prism* carefully selects the vocabulary that students study based on the General Service List, the Academic Word List, and the Cambridge English Corpus.

PRONUNCIATION FOR LISTENING

SKILLS

Contracted forms of *will*

Both speakers and writers use the contracted form of *will* with personal pronouns. In spoken English, however, this contraction is used much more often and with many different types of nouns, proper nouns, and pronouns.

John'll do that tomorrow. There'll be time to do that tomorrow.
It'll be done tomorrow. What'll we do tomorrow?

PRISM Digital Workbook

8 8.3 Listen to the sentences. Write out the words that the speaker contracts. Compare answers with a partner.

1 ________ 5 ________
2 ________ 6 ________
3 ________ ________
4 ________ ________

9 8.4 With a partner, underline the instances in these sentences where a speaker could and probably would contract *will*. Circle the instances where *will* wouldn't be contracted. Then listen and check.

1 My car will be in the repair shop for at least a week, but it's OK. I will just ride my bike to work.
2 There will be times in your life when you will want to give up. But things will get better if you just stay strong.
3 There is no doubt that the Internet has had and will continue to have a profound effect on the way we communicate.
4 Most experts agree that it will be a long time before we see any major change in transportation technology.
5 We formed four groups. Each group researched and will report on a different phase of the project.
6 I don't know if my mom and dad will join us, but my sister and her husband definitely will.
7 The products that company invented will go down in history.

DISCUSSION

10 With your partner, discuss the questions.

1 What is the best way to deal with each type of bad apple?
2 Why do you think negative behavior and attitudes spread so easily? Do you think positive behavior spreads as easily? Why or why not?
3 Does the bad apple principle change your perspective on difficult group dynamics you have experienced? Will you behave differently in the future if you are in a group with a bad apple?

176 UNIT 8

Pronunciation for Listening

Training your ears

This unique feature teaches learners to listen for specific features of spoken English that typically inhibit comprehension. Learners become primed to better understand detail and nuance while listening.

LEARNING OBJECTIVES	
Listening skills	Listen to introductions; rhetorical questions as signals
Pronunciation	Intonation of complete and incomplete ideas
Speaking skill	Challenge other points of view
Speaking Task	Have an informal debate
On Campus	Volunteering and community service

CONSERVATION UNIT 1

ACTIVATE YOUR KNOWLEDGE

Work with a partner. Discuss the questions.

1 How is human activity changing the world? Are these changes for the better or for the worse?

2 Is it possible for humans to live in harmony with nature, or does any type of human activity upset the balance of nature?

3 Are there places on Earth that should be off-limits to humans? If so, where?

WATCH AND LISTEN

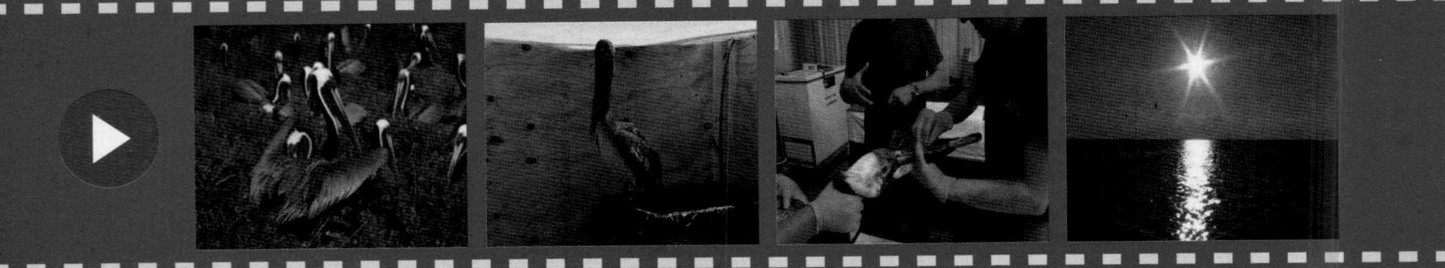

PREPARING TO WATCH

ACTIVATING YOUR KNOWLEDGE

1 Work with a partner. Discuss the questions.

1 What environmental problems exist with our oceans, seas, rivers, and lakes today? Are these problems man-made or a result of nature?
2 How do man-made problems affect the sea and animal life living in and around water?
3 What can be done to resolve these issues and better protect sea life?
4 What can governments do to ensure the protection of our waterways?

PREDICTING CONTENT USING VISUALS

2 Look at the pictures from the video. Discuss the questions with your partner.

1 What is the problem?
2 What animal is affected by this problem?
3 What is being done to help the animal?
4 Where do you think this problem is occurring?

GLOSSARY

pelican (n) a large, fish-eating bird with a long beak and a throat that is like a bag

lurk (v) to wait somewhere secretly, especially before doing something bad

decimate (v) to destroy large numbers of people, animals, or other creatures, or to harm something severely

marshland (n) an area of ground near a lake, a river, or the sea that often floods and is always wet

predator (n) an animal that hunts and kills other animals for food

mullet (n) a small sea fish that can be cooked and eaten

rehabilitation (n) the process of returning to a healthy or good way of life

WHILE WATCHING

UNDERSTANDING MAIN IDEAS

3 Watch the video. Write *T* (true) or *F* (false) next to the statements. Correct the false statements.

_____ 1 The pelicans are in danger due to the shrinking of the marshlands and oil-polluted water.
_____ 2 Coastal Louisiana used to be made up of 60% water and 40% land.
_____ 3 Oil-polluted water affects the pelicans' food source.
_____ 4 Pelicans with oil-saturated feathers are insulated from the cold.
_____ 5 It is unlikely that the pelicans will leave the area they are nesting in.

SUMMARIZING

4 Watch again. Complete the summary.

Coastal Louisiana is changing. Each year it loses more (1)__________ . The disappearance of the (2)__________ is affecting brown pelicans. However, it is not the only threat. (3)__________ is another danger. When oil spills into the water, it (4)__________ the pelicans' food supply. It also poses a danger because the birds are no longer able to insulate themselves or float. Many pelicans are rescued and (5)__________ back to health at a bird rehabilitation center. They ensure the pelicans are oil free and healthy.

MAKING INFERENCES

5 Work with a partner. Discuss the questions.

1 How else do you think the pelican population in Louisiana is suffering as a result of the disappearance of the marshlands?
2 What other species might also be affected by the disappearance of the marshlands? By oil spills?
3 After a pelican has been nursed back to health at the rehabilitation center, what do you think happens to it?

DISCUSSION

6 Work with a partner. Discuss the questions.

1 What other regions of the world have similar problems? Describe them.
2 Whose responsibility should it be to preserve animals and their natural habitats?
3 Are there times when human interests are more important than preserving animal habitats? Explain your answer.
4 What can we do to protect endangered natural habitats on our planet?

LISTENING

LISTENING 1

PREPARING TO LISTEN

UNDERSTANDING KEY VOCABULARY

1 Read the sentences and write the words in bold next to the definitions.

1 A poor diet left much of the population **vulnerable** to disease.
2 Technology has allowed farmers to get much higher **yields** from their crops than in the past.
3 The farmers were able to increase their **revenue** by selling their products directly to the public.
4 Dark-green leafy vegetables are full of important **nutrients** that are difficult to get from other sources.
5 In warm, tropical climates, both flowers and insects are **abundant**.
6 We need to find a **viable** alternative to fossil fuels for our energy needs.
7 The shift of population from the countryside to the city has resulted in the **conversion** of farmland into suburbs.
8 After the car accident, he required lengthy and **intensive** therapy.

a ____________ (adj) using a lot of effort or energy
b ____________ (adj) more than enough; plentiful
c ____________ (n) the process of changing from one thing to another
d ____________ (n) money that a business receives regularly
e ____________ (n) the amount of something, such as a crop, that is produced
f ____________ (adj) able to succeed
g ____________ (adj) easy to hurt or attack
h ____________ (n) healthful substances that plants and animals get from food

USING YOUR KNOWLEDGE

2 You are going to listen to a lecture on whether sustainable agriculture is a viable option. Before you listen, work with a partner.

1 What do you think the term *sustainable agriculture* means?
2 Read the statements and try to work out the meaning of the terms in italics. Use a dictionary or look online to check your ideas.

If fields are not designed well, wind and rain can cause *erosion* of the soil. The top layer of soil may completely disappear.

erosion: ____

One way to improve the *retention* of nutrients in the soil is to *diversify* crops. For example, a farmer can grow different crops in a particular field every year, instead of only corn or wheat year after year.

retention: ____

diversify: ____

SKILLS

Listening to introductions

The introduction to a lecture can provide valuable information. Speakers often give a preview of what they plan to talk about (the topic) and the order in which they will discuss the points (the structure).

3 ▶ 1.1 Listen to the introduction to the lecture. Choose **all** the correct answers to each question.

PRISM Digital Workbook

1 What details about high-yield agriculture are presented?
  a the need for chemical fertilizers
  b the use of irrigation systems to bring water to the crops
  c the use of heavy equipment
  d the use of pesticides to kill insects
  e reduced labor costs
  f an increase in wheat production

2 What have been the benefits of the green revolution?
  a high crop yields
  b better soil
  c more food for more people
  d conservation of resources

3 What do you think the speaker will discuss next?
  a more benefits of intensive agriculture
  b the negative impact of intensive agriculture
  c how we can improve agricultural practices
  d who deserves credit for the green revolution

WHILE LISTENING

Rhetorical questions as signals

A rhetorical question is usually followed by important information. The speaker may expand on a point, provide an explanation or reasons, or give examples.

4 ▶ 1.2 Read the questions and then listen to the rest of the lecture. Complete the notes about main ideas.

LISTENING FOR MAIN IDEAS

PRISM Digital Workbook

1 So what is intensive farming, and what happens when we farm intensively?
  Intensive farming involves ______
  The good thing about intensive farming is that ______
  The bad thing about intensive farming is that ______

2 What are the most important resources in agriculture?
  ______

3 Now, what are some other advantages of practices like crop rotation and the use of cover crops? ______

4 So why doesn't everyone just switch to sustainable practices?
  ______

TAKING NOTES ON DETAILS

5 1.2 Listen again and complete the student's notes.

I. Soil

1 Original quality of the soil declines because ____________

____

2 To replace lost nutrients, farmers use ____________

3 Three alternative approaches:

____

____

____

4 Another problem with soil quality is ____________

5 Causes:

____

____

____

II. Water

6 Agriculture uses ________ percent of the nation's water.

7 The two main sources of water:

____________ and ____________

8 Two approaches to conserving water / reducing erosion:

____

____

POST-LISTENING

LISTENING FOR OPINION

6 Which statement best expresses the speaker's opinion about each topic?

1 Intensive farming
   a It's been a huge success. With future technological advances, we can make it even more successful.
   b It's been beneficial, but it is not worth the environmental cost.
   c It's been very successful, but it's time to consider its pros and cons.
2 Farming that specializes in one crop
   a It's very efficient.
   b It's not sustainable.
   c It's not very practical.

3 Water
   a Agriculture uses too much water.
   b Agricultural use of water is likely to increase.
   c Rain will never provide enough water for agriculture.
4 Sustainable farming
   a It's a better option than conventional farming.
   b It's just as practical as conventional farming.
   c It will replace conventional farming.

PRONUNCIATION FOR LISTENING

SKILLS

Intonation of complete and incomplete ideas

Intonation is the pitch, or rise and fall, of the voice. In English, intonation that falls to a low level shows that an idea is complete. Intonation that rises or falls slightly can show that an idea is incomplete and that the speaker intends to say more.

7 1.3 Listen and write *I* (incomplete) or *C* (complete).

PRISM Digital Workbook

1 I want to talk about some issues __I__
2 Let's start by talking about natural resources ______
3 I'm a professor of agricultural science now ______
4 These farmers are using animal waste ______
5 They're also rotating crops ______
6 Diversifying crops can reduce the number of pests ______
7 It's hard to talk about one critical resource ______
8 This practice is not sustainable ______

DISCUSSION

8 Work with a partner. Discuss the questions.

1 Would you be willing to pay more for food if it was grown using sustainable agricultural practices? Why or why not?
2 The U.S. population has been moving away from farming communities and into cities since the 1950s. What impact might this change have on the push for sustainable agriculture?
3 Do you think sustainable practices are more likely to be adopted in some parts of the world than in others? Give reasons for your answer.

LANGUAGE DEVELOPMENT

PARALLEL STRUCTURE IN COMPARISONS

LANGUAGE

When using comparisons in explanations and arguments, it is important to make sure that the items being compared follow the same grammatical pattern.

When the main verb is *to be*, we can omit it in the second part of the comparison, but other verbs need a verb after *than* to be clear:

Today, farmers **grow** more wheat than they **grew** in the past.

To avoid repetition, substitute the main verb with the correct form of the auxiliary *do*, or omit the main verb if there is already an auxiliary:

Today, farmers **grow** more wheat than they **did** in the past.

Chemical fertilizers **have caused** more damage than erosion **ever could**.

Comparisons of nouns inside a prepositional phrase require repetition or substitution of the full noun phrase to be clear:

~~**The costs of** sustainable agriculture are higher than conventional agriculture~~.

The costs of sustainable agriculture are higher than **the costs of / those of** conventional agriculture.

PRISM Digital Workbook

1 Which sentences contain parallel structure and which do not? Write *P* or *NP*. In your notebook, rewrite the NP sentences so that they are clear.

1 The use of chemical fertilizers has caused more damage to farmland than erosion. ______
2 The cost of labor in organic farming is higher than traditional farming techniques. ______
3 American farms have higher yields than many other countries. ______
4 Some people say farmers should not grow almonds because they need more water than wheat and other grains. ______
5 The profits from nut trees, such as almonds and pistachios, are higher than those from grains. ______
6 The rivers in the south flood more frequently than rivers in the north do. ______
7 Wind causes more erosion than rain. ______
8 In 2014, China grew almost three times as much wheat as France. ______

2 In your notebook, write three comparison sentences using the information in the table. Make sure each sentence has parallel structure. Compare your sentences with a partner.

Farms in China produce more wheat than those in India do.

Wheat Production in Metric Tons			
	2012	2013	2014
European Union	134.5	143.3	157.2
China	125.6	121.7	126.2
India	94.9	93.5	94.5
United States	61.8	60	55.4

Source: Wikipedia/FAOSTAT

LANGUAGE FOR BLAME AND RESPONSIBILITY

LANGUAGE

Here are some common expressions that can be used to attribute credit, responsibility, or blame for something when making an argument.

	attribute	accept	avoid
credit	*credit (someone) with* *be credited with* *have (someone) to thank for*	*take (the) credit*	
responsibility	*responsibility falls (squarely) on the shoulders of* *hold to the same standard*	*step up* *bear responsibility*	*pass the buck* *duck responsibility*
blame	*point the finger / point fingers (at)* *drop the ball* *fall down on the job* *be the fault of*	*take the blame* *take the heat* *fall on (one's) sword*	

3 Use expressions from the table to complete the sentences logically. Be sure to check tense and agreement.

1 People often want to ___point___ ___fingers___ ___at___ the government for environmental problems, but we all __________ __________ for the situation.

2 The responsibility for the loss of habitat __________ on the __________ of the companies who profit from the extraction of resources.

3 This organization is __________ __________ increasing the popularity of organic foods across the nation.

4 You can't __________ __________ forever. At some point, you just have to __________ __________ and do whatever needs to be done.

5 Critics argue that the Environmental Protection Agency has really __________ __________ __________ when it comes to enforcing its own regulations.

6 If you are in a position of leadership, you need to be prepared to __________ __________ __________ for unpopular decisions.

7 Small businesses feel it's unfair to be __________ to the __________ __________ as large manufacturers when it comes to reducing emissions.

LISTENING 2

PREPARING TO LISTEN

USING YOUR KNOWLEDGE

1 You are going to listen to a panel discussion on the topic of assigning responsibility for climate change. Before you listen, work with a partner. Study the graph. Then answer the questions.

This graph compares the carbon emissions of countries in the OECD (Organisation for Economic Co-operation and Development) with non-OECD countries. OECD members are the countries of North America and Europe, as well as Australia, Chile, Israel, Japan, and Korea.

1 Why should we be concerned about CO_2 emissions?

2 What past change does the graph show?

3 What does it suggest for the future?

4 What do you think non-OECD countries could do to reduce their emissions?

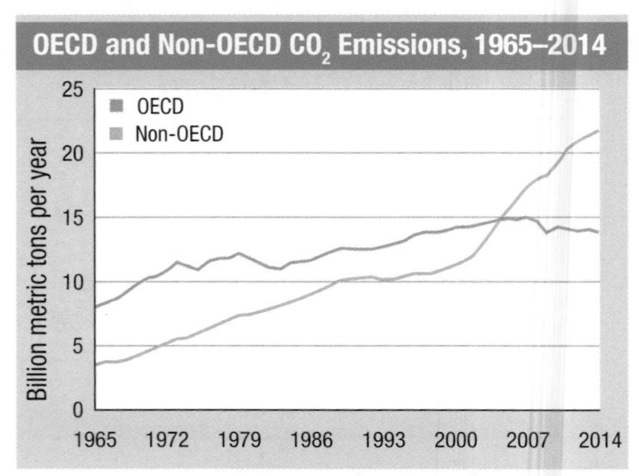

Source: BP Statistical Review of World Energy

2 Read the sentences and choose the best definition for the words in bold.

1 A committee has been appointed to decide how to **allocate** funds to each of the community projects.
   a to collect money
   b to give something as part of a total amount
   c to get the greatest benefit from

2 The World Health Organization has been working to **combat** malaria and other diseases all over the world.
   a to decrease
   b to find a cure for
   c to try to stop

3 Medical centers that use dangerous chemicals must have a plan to **dispose of** them properly.
   a to throw away
   b to label
   c to manage

4 The imprisonment of Japanese-Americans during World War II was one of the most **shameful** events in modern U.S. history. In 1988 the government made a formal apology.
   a morally wrong
   b guilty
   c misunderstood

5 Destruction of the forest has **accelerated** since the government relaxed the laws on logging.
   a to become more difficult
   b to happen more quickly
   c to enter a new stage

6 The little boy tried to **divert** his mother's attention while his sister slipped the bag of candy into her pocket.
   a to earn; to deserve
   b to maintain for a long time
   c to make something go in a different direction

7 The president has offered two journalists **unprecedented** access to his letters and other papers. Presidents have rarely allowed anything like this before.
   a without any restrictions; completely open
   b having never happened in the past
   c unlikely, unpredictable

8 The garbage that has been **accumulating** in the empty lot next door is now spilling into the street. The city has promised to clean it up.
   a to collect or increase over time
   b to be left
   c to create a problem

UNDERSTANDING KEY VOCABULARY

PRISM Digital Workbook

3 ▶ 1.4 Listen to the ad for the panel discussion. Answer the questions. Compare your answers with a partner.

1 What do you think you will be listening to?
   a a conversation between several professors
   b a meeting where the public can ask questions of experts
   c a presentation in which experts speak and respond to each other's points
2 What is the topic?
   a who should be held responsible for causing climate change
   b a scientific explanation of climate change
   c a look into the future of the planet
3 The ad mentions CO_2 and other damaging greenhouse gases. What are these things?
   a gases produced by rainforests that combat global warming
   b gases in the atmosphere that protect the earth from the sun's energy
   c gases produced by human activity that contribute to global warming
4 The speaker asks if we should use *boycotts* or *economic sanctions* to punish countries for their emission of harmful gases. What do these terms mean? Look them up if you're not sure or to check your ideas.

WHILE LISTENING

LISTENING FOR MAIN IDEAS

4 ▶ 1.5 Listen to the panel discussion. Match the people to their ideas about climate change and global responsibility.

Grace Chin (StepUp) ______
Russell Sanchez (Fair Share) ______
Dara Sinee (Citizens for Global Justice) ______
Vijay Gupta (Fund for the Environmental Future) ______

a All countries have to cut emissions immediately.
b Developing countries should pursue economic growth; developed countries should pay to combat climate change.
c Developing countries are driving climate change, so they should be held equally or even more responsible for it.
d Developing countries need help to pursue environmentally responsible development.

LISTENING FOR DETAILS

5 ▶ 1.5 Listen again. Choose **all** the correct answers to each question.

1 Why does Grace Chin think that developing countries should not be held responsible for curbing climate change?
   a The per capita emissions rate of most developing countries is not as high as that of developed countries.
   b Developing countries don't have the expertise to deal with such a complex issue.
   c Focusing on climate change would divert attention from economic development.
   d Slowing climate change would lead to political problems in many developing countries.
2 Why does Russell Sanchez disagree with Grace Chin?
   a He thinks the per capita figure is not as important as that for total emissions.
   b He doesn't think developed countries should be responsible for past behavior, which occurred at a time when they did not yet understand the science behind climate change.
   c He thinks developed countries should help replant forests that have been cut down in developing countries.
   d He believes that the developing world needs to demonstrate more leadership on environmental issues.
3 How does Dara Sinee's position differ from Grace Chin's?
   a Dara does not believe developing countries should be punished.
   b Dara believes that developing countries should be forgiven for harming the environment if it helps their economy.
   c Dara thinks that developing countries should contribute to the fight against climate change.
   d Dara wants developed countries to provide substantial economic aid to the developing world.
4 What are Vijay Gupta's concerns?
   a He thinks too much time is spent assigning blame.
   b Some communities are already underwater.
   c Time is running out.
   d He believes economic development is being ignored.

POST-LISTENING

SKILLS

Rhetorical questions to signal opinions

Speakers often use rhetorical questions to introduce their opinion about some piece of information they are presenting. Using rhetorical questions is somewhat less direct than expressing the same idea in a statement.

LISTENING FOR OPINION

PRISM Digital Workbook

6 Work with a partner. What opinion does each of these rhetorical questions indicate? Explain it in your own words.

1 So shouldn't the United States and other developed nations be the ones making changes, even if those changes are expensive?

____

2 Why not organize a global boycott of any products whose manufacture causes significant negative environmental effects?

____

3 How useful will economic development and resource extraction be to the people of Bangladesh then?

____

4 What good is pointing fingers and blaming one another?

____

DISCUSSION

7 Work in small groups. Discuss the questions.

1 Which figure do you think is more important: per capita emissions or total emissions?
2 If a country has to choose between allocating resources to economic development or environmental issues, which is the better course of action? Why?
3 Which of the speakers' positions to do you support? Why?

SYNTHESIZING

8 Look at your notes from Listening 1 and Listening 2. Work in small groups. Discuss the questions.

1 How can developing countries balance the need for increased food production and environmental protection when these needs are in conflict?
2 Should a country be forced to conserve its natural resources in order to help the rest of the world, or should each country be free to maximize those resources for its own people?

SPEAKING

CRITICAL THINKING

At the end of this unit, you are going to do the Speaking Task below.

Have an informal debate about the mission of national parks. Is their primary purpose to protect the natural world from human activity or to encourage responsible human interaction with nature? Is it possible to accomplish both of these goals?

SKILLS

Analyze the issues

Before you can take a stand, it is important to have some background information and to analyze the issues. The process of analysis can provide information to support your point of view.

ANALYZE

1 Work in small groups. Discuss the questions.

1. Think about a national park – a place you have visited or know about. Where is it? What did you do and see? What do you remember most about the visit?
2. Why do you think national parks were established?
3. Why do you think the government chooses particular places to become national parks?

APPLY

2 Read about some of the issues that national parks in the United States are facing today. What are the possible consequences of each?

Neighbors
Parks don't exist in isolation. They are often surrounded by residential areas, as well as commercial, agricultural, and industrial development. The wild species that live in a park do not recognize the park's boundaries, often moving in and out of it. As a result, what happens outside the park can have a significant impact on what happens inside.

Possible consequences:

____

____

Non-human visitors
Wild places like national parks are very attractive to all kinds of species, including those from other parts of the country or other parts of the world. They often arrive in the park with human visitors. These "invasive species," including insects, plants, and fish, pose a serious threat to a park's native species and its ecosystem.

Possible consequences:

____

____

Climate change
Weather conditions are getting more extreme every year. Parks in coastal and upland areas are experiencing accelerated soil erosion. Wetland parks are flooded to greater depths. In other areas, increased temperatures are causing rivers and streams to dry up.

Possible consequences:

____

____

Popularity
National parks in the United States have been called "America's best idea." Everyone loves them. More than 300 million people visit a U.S. national park each year. These visitors need roads and services. What happens when the visitors' needs and desires conflict with those of the natural inhabitants?

Possible consequences:

____

____

Natural resources
The parks are rich with natural resources, both on and under the land. These resources include trees, oil, gas, and minerals. There is great pressure on the parks to allow private companies to extract these resources.

Possible consequences:

____

____

3 Work in small groups. Answer the questions.

1 Which of the issues facing the national parks do you think represent the biggest challenges?
2 Which are the most important to resolve?

EVALUATE

4 1.6 Listen to a park ranger talk about the situation in Grand Canyon National Park. Then discuss the questions.

1 Which of the issues from Exercise 2 does the ranger mention in his description of Grand Canyon National Park?
2 In what ways is the Grand Canyon fulfilling the two potential missions of a national park (see chart below)?

UNDERSTAND

5 Work in small groups. Brainstorm some ideas that support and oppose both points of view. Write down all of your ideas.

CREATE

Mission A: National parks should protect the natural world from human activity	
points in favor (for)	points opposed (against)

Mission B: National parks should encourage responsible human interaction with the natural world	
points in favor (for)	points opposed (against)

6 Decide what your own position is on this issue. Consider the most important arguments that support your position.

My position: ______________________________

____

PREPARATION FOR SPEAKING

CHALLENGING OTHER POINTS OF VIEW

SKILLS

In discussing important issues, people often want to challenge an opinion or point of view presented. It is important to be able to express your views clearly, yet remain polite. There are many ways to do this.

I agree up to a point.
That's irrelevant.
Not necessarily.
I suppose, but ...
That doesn't follow.
Actually, ...
On the contrary, ...
How can you say that?
That's not (necessarily) true / the case.
You have a point. However, ...
That would be fine, except ...
That may be true, but ...
That might be the case if ...
And what happens if ...
That's not the point.
I would agree with you if ...

PRISM Digital Workbook

1 Complete the conversation with the signals of agreement, disagreement, or partial agreement from the box. There are two extras.

a Not necessarily. b That's not the point! c And what happens if d I suppose, but e I would agree with you if f Actually,

Sam: You're poisoning the groundwater by using those pesticides in your garden.
Mia: (1)_____ If you use pesticides carefully, they're totally safe. At least, that's what I've read.
Sam: (2)_____ there is no way to use these products safely. They should not be used under any circumstances.
Mia: (3)_____ there were any other options, but nothing works as well against the insects that ruin my flowers and vegetables.
Sam: (4)_____ So what if they work really well in your garden? It's irresponsible!
Mia: Well, then, maybe I should just give up gardening!

2 ▶ 1.7 Compare your answers with a partner. Then listen to the conversation to check your answers.

PRONUNCIATION FOR SPEAKING

INTONATION FOR COMPLETE AND INCOMPLETE IDEAS

3 With your partner, read the conversation in Exercise 1 using some of the other possible words and phrases from the explanation box. Be sure to use the appropriate intonation for complete and incomplete ideas.

SPEAKING TASK

Have an informal debate about the mission of national parks. Is their primary purpose to protect the natural world from human activity or to encourage responsible human interaction with nature? Is it possible to accomplish both of these goals?

PRISM Digital Workbook

PREPARE

1 Work in groups of four. Work with others who share your point of view.

2 Using the table from Exercise 5 and your notes from Exercise 6 in Critical Thinking, write a statement that presents your point of view. Share your statements for feedback. Revise your arguments if needed.

PRACTICE

3 Anticipate opposing points of view by preparing a list of arguments that you think the other side will make. Discuss how best to argue against these points. Practice responding within your group.

4 Refer to the Task Checklist as you prepare for your discussion.

TASK CHECKLIST	✔
Present a statement of your point of view.	
Offer supporting points for your position.	
Be sure that any comparisons you make are parallel.	
Use expressions of blame and responsibility where appropriate.	
Challenge other points of view with appropriate expressions.	

DISCUSS

5 Join a group of students who support a different point of view. One student from each side should begin with an opening statement. Then open the floor for a discussion of the topic. Each student should contribute the following:

- at least one statement arguing for your point of view
- at least one statement arguing against another point of view

ON CAMPUS

VOLUNTEERING AND COMMUNITY SERVICE

PREPARING TO LISTEN

1 You are going to listen to three students – Patrick, Bahar, and Yolanda – describing their volunteer experiences. Before you listen, work in small groups and discuss the questions.

   1 Have you ever volunteered or done community service? What kind of work did you do?
   2 What can be gained from volunteering? Why do it?

WHILE LISTENING

2 ▶ 1.8 Listen and check (✔) the boxes that apply to each person's experience.

	Patrick	Bahar	Yolanda
1 worked outdoors			
2 managed people			
3 worked in the local community			
4 got professional experience			

3 ▶ 1.8 Read the benefits of community service in the box. Then listen again and write two benefits that each student mentions.

Appreciate what you have   Become a more responsible citizen
Earn college credit   Gain confidence   Get exercise
Give back to your community   Learn about community resources
Learn useful skills   Make new friends

1 Patrick: ____________________   ____________________
2 Bahar: ____________________   ____________________
3 Yolanda: ____________________   ____________________

4 Compare answers with a partner. What other benefits can you think of?

PRACTICE

5 Look at the volunteer opportunities. What are the benefits of each one? Make a list in your notebook. Then compare answers with a partner. If you had to choose one to participate in, which would it be?

HOME | NEWS | SCHOOL | LEARNING | ACTIVITIES | CONTACT US

COMMUNITY SERVICE OPPORTUNITIES

Mentor, Welcome to College Program

Volunteers wanted to help new students make the transition to college. Meet with your assigned students regularly to identify problems and locate campus resources to help with academic, financial, or social needs. Organize campus tours for visitors.

Organizer / Fundraiser, Help the Homeless Program

Help homeless families in our community! Join in our fundraising efforts: collect used clothes and furniture, solicit donations from local businesses, help organize and host campus movie nights and talent shows. Lots of ways to get involved!

Community Farm Worker: Earn College Credit!

Learn the principles of sustainable, organic farming and water management. Plant and harvest crops; sell crops at local farmers markets. This is a live-in position for one semester. College credit is available.

REAL-WORLD APPLICATION

6 Research opportunities for volunteer work on your campus or in your community. Choose an organization that interests you and make notes.

- what the organization does ______________________________
- what volunteers do ______________________________
- how often volunteers are needed ______________________________
- what skills are needed ______________________________

7 Present the results of your research to the class.

LEARNING OBJECTIVES

Listening skills	Use a graphic organizer to capture main ideas and details; review and organize notes
Pronunciation	Word stress; stress in compound nouns and noun phrases
Speaking skill	Acknowledge other arguments
Speaking Task	Give a group presentation
On Campus	Incorporate visuals

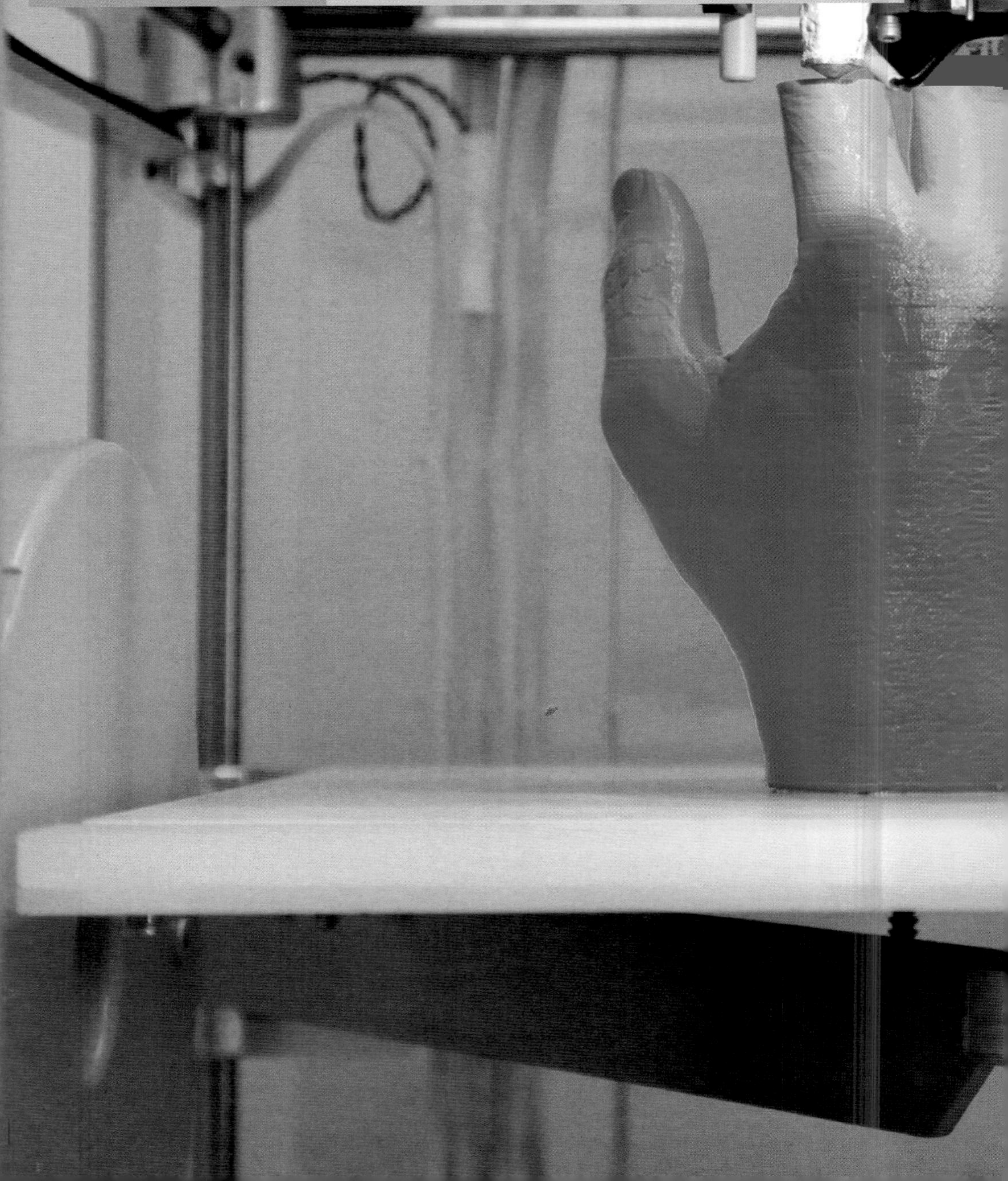

DESIGN

UNIT 2

ACTIVATE YOUR KNOWLEDGE

Work with a partner. Discuss the questions.

1 What is happening in this picture? Do you think this is the most important technological advance in recent years? Why or why not?
2 Do you think that the products we use every day are better now than in the past? Is there any way in which products in the past were superior?
3 What types of shopping (clothes, shoes, electronics, household items, etc.) would you avoid doing if you could? How much extra would you be willing to pay to avoid it?

WATCH AND LISTEN

PREPARING TO WATCH

ACTIVATING YOUR KNOWLEDGE

1 Work with a partner. Think of a product whose appearance and functionality has been improved by its manufacturer in its latest model. Discuss the questions.

1 How has the product changed?
2 Why do you think the updated model is better than the previous one?

PREDICTING CONTENT USING VISUALS

2 Look at the pictures from the video. Discuss the questions with your partner.

1 How have cell phones changed over the last two decades?
2 Why do you think companies have changed their design?
3 In your opinion, have the changes been beneficial? Why or why not?

GLOSSARY

columnist (n) someone who writes a regular article for a newspaper or magazine
on the cusp (idiom) at the dividing line between two very different things
pioneer (v) to be the first to create or develop something
make a splash (v phr) to become suddenly very successful or very well known
dim (adj) not bright; not giving or having much light
horse race (n phr) a very close contest (colloquial)
rumor (n) an unofficial, interesting story or piece of news that might be true or invented, and that is quickly communicated from person to person.

WHILE WATCHING

UNDERSTANDING MAIN IDEAS

3 Watch the video. Write *T* (true) or *F* (false) next to the statements. Correct the false statements.

_____ 1 Samsung led the industry by designing larger cell phones.
_____ 2 The number of people using smaller devices to browse the Internet has increased.
_____ 3 Carrying a laptop, a tablet, and a phone is convenient when traveling for business.
_____ 4 Most people prefer to only carry one device.
_____ 5 At the time of the video, it seemed unlikely that Apple would reveal anything other than the new phone model.

SUMMARIZING

4 Watch again. Fill in the blanks with words and phrases from the Glossary on page 38 to complete the summary.

Samsung is a design-oriented company. They have been known to (1)__________________ many new ideas in cell phone design. At the time of the video, the company's latest release was an updated model of one of its large-screen cell phones. It had a number of elements that would help the product (2)__________________ in the market. According to the tech (3)__________________ Molly Wood, Samsung wanted to take this opportunity to reveal its product because there was a (4)__________________ that Apple was (5)__________________ of making an announcement. There were, and continue to be, several companies in the (6)__________________ to design the latest and greatest cell phone, and Samsung wanted to finish first.

MAKING INFERENCES

5 Work with a partner. Discuss the questions. Give reasons for your answers.

1 Why do you think Samsung updated its phone with two touchscreens?
2 How do you think companies like Samsung and Apple learn about each other's new products before they are released?
3 What do you think the process is for determining market needs?

DISCUSSION

6 Work in a small group. Discuss the questions.

1 What features or functionalities are important to you in a cell phone?
2 Is having the latest design important to you? Why or why not?
3 Are Samsung and Apple still the cell phone industry leaders? How are their latest models different from the ones in the video?
4 In your opinion, what other industries are involved in a "horse race" when it comes to new product designs?

LISTENING

LISTENING 1

PREPARING TO LISTEN

USING YOUR KNOWLEDGE

1 You are going to listen to a presentation on current and future uses for 3D printing. Before you listen, work with a partner. Discuss which of these items you think were produced by a 3D printer.

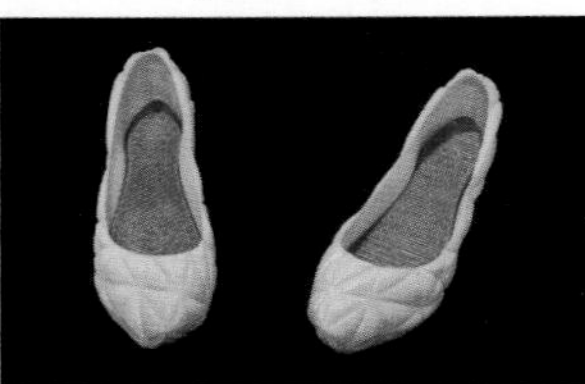

1 All of these items were made with a 3D printer. Does that surprise you? Why or why not?
2 What kinds of objects cannot be created with a 3D printer today?

UNDERSTANDING KEY VOCABULARY

2 Read the definitions. Complete the sentences with the correct form of the words in bold.

assembly (n) the process of putting parts together to create one thing
customize (v) to make or change something to fit a user's needs
downside (n) disadvantage
drastically (adv) severely; with very noticeable effect
foundation (n) the thing on which other things are based
mass production (n) the process of producing large numbers of one thing in a factory
scenario (n) a description of possible events
shift (v) to change position or focus

1 You can __________ the software so that it only includes the functions that you need.
2 On my new phone plan, I get service everywhere. The __________, however, is that it is much more expensive than my old plan.
3 Furniture that you buy online often comes in several pieces and requires __________ at home.
4 The math skills that you acquire in high school provide a __________ for the more advanced work you'll do in college.
5 Public attention usually __________ to economic issues and away from international issues during an election year.
6 The consultant outlined three different __________ for the company's future depending on how well it does this year.

7 The state has __________ cut the education budget for the coming year, so schools will no longer be able to provide music or art classes.
8 Before the apparel industry adopted __________ , each item of clothing people wore was made by hand just for them.

PREDICTING CONTENT USING VISUALS

3 Work with a partner. Study the diagram of a supply chain. Discuss what happens at each stage.

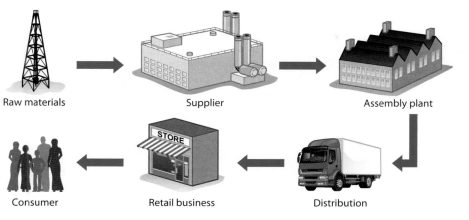

Raw materials → Supplier → Assembly plant → Distribution → Retail business → Consumer

WHILE LISTENING

LISTENING FOR MAIN IDEAS

4 2.1 Listen to the presentation. Check (✔) the five main ideas that you hear.

a 3D printing will allow us to create and replace objects on demand. ☐
b 3D printing is no longer expensive. ☐
c 3D printers can be used to create human organs. ☐
d 3D printers can customize clothing. ☐
e 3D printing is likely to be used much more in the developing world. ☐
f 3D printing will drastically change the manufacturing process. ☐
g 3D printing has already been widely accepted and adopted. ☐
h 3D printing does have some potential negative consequences. ☐

LISTENING FOR DETAILS

5 2.1 Listen again. Write *T* (true), *F* (false), or *DNS* (does not say).

______ 1 3D printing is a very new technology.
______ 2 3D printing is a more precise way of creating human organs.
______ 3 3D printers use cotton and other fibers to print clothing.
______ 4 Most 3D fashions will probably be printed in developing countries.
______ 5 The cost of 3D printing goes down as the number of items produced goes up.
______ 6 3D printing will reduce the need for companies to keep a large inventory on hand all the time.
______ 7 3D printing may allow criminals to operate more freely.
______ 8 There has been a lot of opposition to 3D printing from manufacturers.

SKILLS

Using a graphic organizer to capture main ideas and details

When a speaker makes the structure of upcoming information clear, it can be helpful to use the same structure as you take notes.

PRISM Digital Workbook

6 ▶ 2.2 Listen to an excerpt from the presentation and complete the chart.

AM = additive manufacturing

disrupts two elements of mftg in several ways:

(1) ______	(2) ______
parts made as a single piece	(5) ______
(3) ______	fabricated on demand
stronger	(6) ______
(4) ______	short supply chains

POST-LISTENING

SKILLS

Reviewing and organizing your notes

After a lecture, while the information is still fresh in your mind, rewrite your notes in an outline structure. This helps you understand the main ideas and details of the lecture.

TAKING NOTES ON MAIN IDEAS AND DETAILS

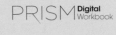

PRISM Digital Workbook

7 ▶ 2.1 Use your answers from Exercises 4, 5, and 6 to make a set of notes. Start by listing the main ideas (1–5) and supporting details for each main idea (a, b, c, etc.). Listen to the complete talk again to check that your notes are accurate and to add more details.

1.
   a.
   b.
   c.
2.
   a.
3.
4.
5.

8 Work with a partner. Complete the task.

SUMMARIZING

1. Use your notes from Exercise 7 to recap the talk on 3D printing. Include only the main points and important details. Present it aloud to your partner.
2. As you listen to your partner's presentation, write down any important details they included that you missed. Add them to your notes.
3. Whose recap do you think was more accurate and complete? Does the order of main points make a difference? Were the details presented with the relevant main points?

PRONUNCIATION FOR LISTENING

Word stress

In words with more than one syllable, one syllable is stressed more than the others. A stressed syllable is longer, louder, and higher in pitch than an unstressed syllable.

down-side (n)   ad-vance (v)   con-sum-er (n)

Though stress is sometimes difficult to predict, there are some rules. For example, always stress the syllable that precedes these suffixes: *-ical, -ion, -ity, -logy*.

bi-o-lo-gy   bi-o-log-i-cal

9 Read the words and underline the syllables that should be stressed.

	a	b	c
1	tech-no-lo-gy	pro-cess	ob-ject (n)
2	com-pu-ter	soft-ware	sce-nar-i-os
3	dra-ma-tic	bi-o-med-i-cal	re-search
4	at-tracts	pos-si-bil-i-ty	cus-tom-iz-ing
5	pro-duc-tion	fa-cil-i-ties	in-dus-try
6	el-e-ments	foun-da-tion	man-u-fac-tur-ing
7	en-tre-pre-neur	fac-to-ries	as-sem-bled

10 2.3 Listen to the excerpts from the talk to check your answers.

DISCUSSION

11 Work with a partner. Discuss the questions.

1. The speaker mentions the disruptive power of AM several times. What do you think the long-term consequences might be on the apparel industry? For example, what would happen if all clothing could be printed at home?
2. Use your imagination to think of an application of 3D printing that was not discussed by the speaker. Share your ideas with another pair of students or the class.

LANGUAGE DEVELOPMENT

USING CAUSE-AND-EFFECT PHRASES

LANGUAGE

To express a cause using a phrase

By using digital locks, manufacturers limit consumers' ability to repair their own phones.
Manufacturers limit consumers' ability to repair their own phones by using digital locks.

Notice that, although the subject is not expressed in the causal phrase, you can infer it. Such phrases can only be used if the inferred subject is the same as the subject of the whole sentence – in this case, *manufacturers*.

To express an effect using a phrase

The blouses appear on shelves the following week, encouraging the trend.

This is a reduction of a nonidentifying relative "comment" clause:

The blouses appear on shelves the following week, which encourages the trend.

PRISM Digital Workbook

1 Complete the sentences with a phrase that explains the cause.

1 ______________________, manufacturers ensure that consumers buy new products on a regular basis.
2 ______________________, clothing companies encourage people to buy new clothes often.
3 ______________________, the team completed the project just before the deadline.
4 ______________________, they were able to find a better design for the product.
5 ______________________, AM has disrupted manufacturing.

2 Rewrite each nonidentifying relative clause as a phrase expressing the effect.

1 Clothing can be made very cheaply today, which makes it psychologically easier to throw things away.

____

____

2 AM makes it easier to complete all production steps in one place, which leaves assembly plants in developing countries out of the process.

____

____

3 Complete the sentences with your own phrase that expresses a result.

1 Clothing companies respond immediately to consumer preferences, ______________________________________ .

2 Thousands of people throw away their cell phones every year, ______________________________________ .

3 Many consumers have made their own repairs, ____________________ ______________________________________ .

4 The cost of consumer electronics has dropped significantly, ______________________________________ .

4 Write three sentences using phrases for the cause and/or effect of a situation in your own life. The sentences can be on any topic.

By working on my paper last weekend, I was able to hand it in on time.

____

____

____

DEGREE EXPRESSIONS

LANGUAGE

Sometimes you need to measure the amount or degree of something against a standard. When the amount or degree does not match the standard, use the adverb *too* + an adjective or adverb for the degree and the infinitive form of the verb for the standard.

He is too young to drive.
DEGREE (too young) STANDARD (to drive)

The cost of 3D printing is too high to make this practical.
DEGREE (too high) STANDARD (to make)

When the amount or degree does match the standard, use an adjective, adverb, or verb + *enough* for the degree and the infinitive form of the verb for the standard.

He is old enough to drive.
DEGREE (old enough) STANDARD (to drive)

The cost of 3D printing has fallen enough to open up many new possibilities.
DEGREE (has fallen enough) STANDARD (to open up)

5 Complete the sentences with your own ideas.

PRISM Digital Workbook

1 The phone I bought last year is too old ____________________ .
2 Some consumer electronics are cheap enough ____________________ .
3 ____________________ to be used with the latest software.
4 ____________________ are comfortable enough to wear all day long.
5 Some video games are too complicated ____________________ .

LISTENING 2

UNDERSTANDING KEY VOCABULARY

PRISM Digital Workbook

1 Read the sentences and write the words in bold next to the definitions.

1 The protests were seen as an angry public **backlash** against the new increase in taxes.
2 Their first meeting went on far too long, so they agreed that all **subsequent** meetings would last no longer than two hours.
3 The employees **resent** the fact that they only get two weeks of vacation while their boss gets six weeks.
4 Computer hackers are very good at finding ways to **circumvent** passwords and other security protocols.
5 The company has **devised** a system to keep track of all their customers and the purchases they make.
6 The percentage of college students who are women just keeps increasing. No one has been able to provide a complete explanation for this **phenomenon**.
7 The biggest **obstacle** to our success is a lack of funds.
8 We only have a **finite** amount of money, so we need to spend it wisely.

a __________ (v) to feel angry or hurt at being treated unfairly
b __________ (n) something happening that is noticeable because it is new or unusual
c __________ (adj) next; happening after something else
d __________ (v) to avoid something by going around it
e __________ (v) to create a plan or system using intelligence and creativity
f __________ (n) a strong negative reaction
g __________ (adj) limited; set and fixed
h __________ (n) something that blocks forward movement

PREPARING TO LISTEN

PREDICTING CONTENT USING VISUALS

2 Work with a partner. Answer the questions.

1 What is in the photo?
2 How did all of these devices end up there?
3 What are the possible consequences if this continues?

3 You are going to listen to a presentation about planned obsolescence. Before you listen, complete the table. Then compare tables with a partner and answer the questions.

How often do you replace these items? Add one more item to the list. Compare your habits with an older friend or family member.

item	me	older friend or family member
cell phone		
computer		
shoes/boots		
jeans		
car		

1 Why do you replace these items as often as you do?
2 Do you ever repair items to make them last longer? Why or why not?
3 Do you think you replace these items more or less often than other people replace them?

WHILE LISTENING

LISTENING FOR MAIN IDEAS

4 ▶ 2.4 Listen to the presentation. Check (✔) the topics that are mentioned in the listening.

a the inventor of planned obsolescence ☐
b an explanation of the concept of *planned obsolescence* ☐
c consumer responses to planned obsolescence ☐
d planned obsolescence in electronics ☐
e the use of technology to combat planned obsolescence ☐
f fast fashion ☐

5 For each of the topics that you checked in Exercise 4, write the main idea that the speaker expresses in your own words in your notebook.

Planned obsolescence is a deliberate policy to create products with a finite and usually short lifespan.

6 ▶ 2.4 Listen to the presentation again. Add supporting details for each main idea in your notes.

POST-LISTENING

LISTENING FOR OPINION

7 Work with a partner. Check (✔) how you would describe the tone toward planned obsolescence (PO) that the speakers used in their presentation. Consider *how* the speakers spoke, as well as *what* they said.

a strongly supportive of the advantages of PO ☐
b mostly objective, mildly negative attitude toward PO ☐
c neutral and objective ☐
d strongly negative attitude toward PO ☐
e mostly objective, but generally supportive of PO ☐

SUMMARIZING

8 Work with a partner. Complete the task.

1 Use your notes to create a brief recap of the presentation on planned obsolescence. Include the main points and important details. Present it aloud to your partner.
2 As you listen to your partner's presentation, write down any important details they included that you missed. Add them to your notes.
3 Whose presentation do you think was more accurate or effective? Does the order of main points make a difference? Were the details presented with the relevant main points?

DISCUSSION

SYNTHESIZING

9 Work in small groups. Read the information about Brooks Stevens, who invented the term *planned obsolescence* in 1954. Discuss the questions.

> Brooks Stevens defined *planned obsolescence* as "instilling in the buyer the desire to own something a little newer, a little better, a little sooner than is necessary. … When I design a 1961 model car, I am not styling it for the man who bought one in 1960. I'm styling it for the man next door who didn't buy it when his neighbor did."

1 How is Stevens' definition different from how the term is widely understood today?
2 Explain the analogy Stevens uses.
3 Can you think of another analogy to help explain the concept of planned obsolescence?

10 Work in your group. Consider the facts about the apparel industry in the United States as given in these graphs. Then answer the questions.

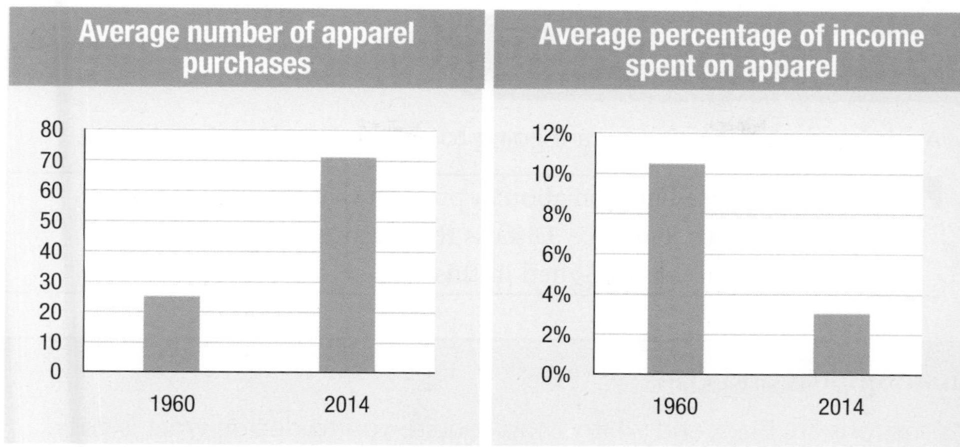

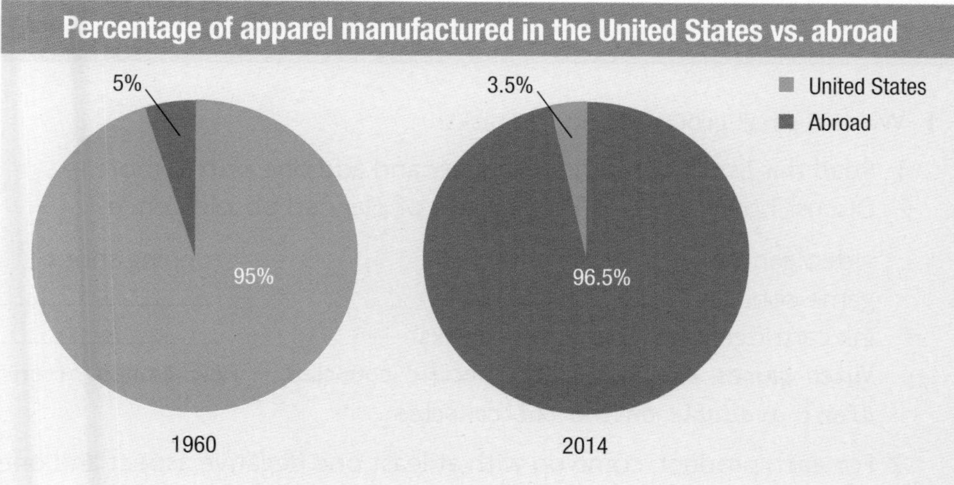

1 What does each of the graphs show?
2 How are the facts in the two sets of graphs related to one another?
3 How do these facts support the information in the presentation?
4 Do any of the facts surprise you? Explain your answer.
5 Think of some implications of this phenomenon for the United States, for the rest of the world, and for the environment.

11 Look at your notes from Listening 1 and Listening 2. Discuss the questions.

1 Look back at the table you completed in Exercise 3. Do you think your behavior will change now that you know more about planned obsolescence and fast fashion? Why or why not?
2 Review Listening 1. What impact do you think AM will have on planned obsolescence in general and fast fashion in particular?

SPEAKING

CRITICAL THINKING

At the end of this unit, you are going to do the Speaking Task below.

Give a group presentation about a product that you believe was designed for obsolescence. Discuss the reasons, both positive and negative, why it was designed in this way.

SKILLS

Evaluating pros and cons

Few situations are black and white. Most require you to decide what is good and what is bad about something – the "pros and cons." Remember, the pros and cons may not be the same for everyone involved in the situation.

APPLY

1 Work in small groups to do the tasks.

1 Read this list of consumer products and add one or two more. Discuss how each item is a product of planned obsolescence.

video games	cars	running shoes
game consoles	software	________
ink cartridges	textbooks	________

Video games are made for specific consoles – new games often aren't available on the old consoles.

2 For each product, come up with at least one negative aspect and one positive or neutral aspect of its short lifespan.

The graphics and game design keep getting better and better.

3 For each product, discuss how (or if) it could be made to last longer.

ANALYZE

2 With your group, study this list of reasons for buying something. Can you think of any others? What are some examples of products that people buy for these reasons?

- They have no choice. They need it.
- It is really useful. It makes their lives easier.
- It represents their aspirations. People they admire have it.
- It's new. It's cool.
- It's a good value.
- The company that makes it has a good reputation.
- It has some specific attractive quality (e.g., color for running shoes)
- They respond to it emotionally.

EVALUATE

3 With your group, consider the value of PO from the business side. Read the market scenarios for a consumer product. In which scenarios are the companies likely to build obsolescence into the design of their product as a way of encouraging repeated purchases?

a One company is completely dominant in the market. There is no effective competition. If consumers want the product, they must buy it from that company.

b There are several companies that produce roughly equivalent products. Consumers have choices.

c There are several companies that produce roughly equivalent products. Consumers have choices. However, switching from one company to another has costs. For example, a consumer who buys from company X typically also purchases numerous accessories, which are not compatible with the equivalent product from company Z.

4 With your group, make a table like the one below. Choose two or three products that you have been considering for the speaking task. For each product, decide if obsolescence is, or could be

- entirely for the benefit of the producer – purely to increase revenue.
- a plan to increase revenue but also of some benefit to the consumer.
- a side effect rather than an intentional act.

For some products, multiple scenarios are possible.

product/feature	scenario 1	scenario 2	scenario 3
Cell phone: Consumers cannot access/ replace battery. Battery has a limited lifespan.	Consumers will have to buy a new phone when the battery dies. They have no choice.	Consumers will need to replace frequently. (good for company) Keeps costs down. (good for consumers) Consumers will want a new phone every few years anyway.	The design allows for a more attractive product. The inaccessible battery is smaller and lighter than a replaceable battery.

5 As a group, decide on the product you will present. Brainstorm ideas related to these points:

- How will you describe the product?
- Why and how was it designed for obsolescence?
- What are the pros and cons of its obsolescence?
- Who benefits from its obsolescence? Who does not benefit?
- Why do consumers continue to buy this product?

PREPARATION FOR SPEAKING

PRONUNCIATION FOR SPEAKING

LANGUAGE

Stress in compound nouns and noun phrases

In compound nouns, the stress is usually on the first word in the compound.

software upgrade dishwasher

In two-word compound nouns, the first word gets more stress, but syllable stress still applies within each word.

department store **software** upgrade

In adjective + noun phrases, both words are stressed equally, but syllable stress still applies within each word.

planned obsolescence **social media**

PRISM Digital Workbook

1 2.5 Mark the stress in these compound nouns and noun phrases. Then listen and check your answers.

1 apparel industry
2 complex devices
3 backlash
4 design policy
5 digital locks
6 fast fashion
7 finite lifespan
8 runway
9 tech sector

2 2.6 Work with a partner. Practice saying these compound nouns using the correct stress patterns. Listen to check your work.

1 dishwasher
2 video game
3 game console
4 textbook
5 ink cartridges
6 gym shoes

3 With your partner, make sentences with the words in Exercise 2 and add an adjective. Make any necessary changes to the stress pattern.

My parents just bought an **energy-efficient dishwasher**.

ACKNOWLEDGING OTHER ARGUMENTS

When you are assessing the pros and cons of a situation, it is useful to step back and examine other perspectives. You may still favor one side, but you can also concede the merit of other arguments.

Several phrases are commonly used to express this even-handed approach:

On the one hand, ... on the other hand, ...
Granted, ... , but ...
Many people think that ... , some others say that ...
There are two points of view / ways of looking at ...
There are two sides to / ways of looking at this question/issue/situation:
That said, ...
Having said that, ...

Expressions of concession follow several patterns:

position A + concession expression + position B

Planned obsolescence clearly benefits manufacturers; that said, it can also be seen as providing some consumer benefits.

concession introduction + position A + position B

There are two different ways of looking at planned obsolescence: either it is for the exclusive benefit of manufacturers, or it can be seen as beneficial to both buyers and sellers.

concession introduction + position A + concession expression + position B

Granted, planned obsolescence is a huge benefit to manufacturers, but consumers also benefit from the constant variety of new products on the market.

4 Write three sentences about planned obsolescence that address both sides of the issue.

PRISM Digital Workbook

position A + concession expression + position B

____

____

concession introduction + position A + position B

____

____

concession introduction + position A + concession expression + position B

____

____

5 Work with a partner. Check each other's sentences in Exercise 4. Make any necessary corrections based on your partner's feedback.

SPEAKING TASK

PRISM Digital Workbook

Give a group presentation about a product that you believe was designed for obsolescence. Discuss the reasons, both positive and negative, why it was designed in this way.

PREPARE

1 In your group, follow these steps to prepare your presentation.

Step 1: Assign roles

Decide on roles for your presentation: Who will:

- explain the concept of planned obsolescence?
- introduce the product?
- explain its obsolescence?
- explain the pros and cons?
- explain who benefits from its obsolescence and who does not?

Think about how to make transitions from one speaker to another. For example, one speaker could briefly say the next speaker's role.

Step 2: Review

Review all of your notes and brainstorming as well as the phrases and expressions you will need to make your presentation.

Step 3: Prepare notes

Prepare some talking points, but don't write out what you will say. If you read from your notes, you will not sound natural.

PRACTICE

2 Take turns presenting your parts of the presentation within your group. Give your classmates feedback on their parts of the presentation and consider the feedback they give you. Revise your notes as needed.

3 Refer to the Task Checklist as you prepare for your discussion.

TASK CHECKLIST	✔
Briefly explain the concept of planned obsolescence.	
Introduce the product you have built your presentation around.	
Explain the pros and cons of its obsolescence.	
Discuss who is affected by the planned obsolescence and whether these effects are positive or negative.	
Acknowledge other points of view with appropriate expressions.	
Make smooth transitions between speakers.	
Use correct word and syllable stress with compound nouns and adjective + noun phrases.	

PRESENT

4 Give your presentation.

REFLECT

5 In small groups or as a class, discuss these questions.

1 Which presentation was the most interesting? Why do you think so?
2 How well did you present your part of the presentation?
3 What could you do better next time?

ON CAMPUS

INCORPORATING VISUALS

PREPARING TO LISTEN

1 Match the types of visual aids with their usual function.

1 bar chart ______
2 bulleted list ______
3 diagram ______
4 graph ______
5 pie chart ______

a to show measurable change over time
b to show percentages
c to compare data
d to summarize main points
e to illustrate a process

WHILE LISTENING

2 2.7 Listen to the excerpts from a group presentation on e-waste. Number the topics in the order they are presented.

______ a Computers and energy use
______ b Introduction to the presentation
______ c The increase in e-waste
______ d The increase in recycling
______ e The problem of e-waste

3 2.7 Listen again. For each excerpt, circle the type of visual aid that would be more appropriate.

1 bulleted list / bar chart
2 graph / photograph
3 graph / pie chart
4 bar chart / pie chart
5 diagram / pie chart

PRACTICE

4 Look at the presentation slides. Which one is more effective? Why?

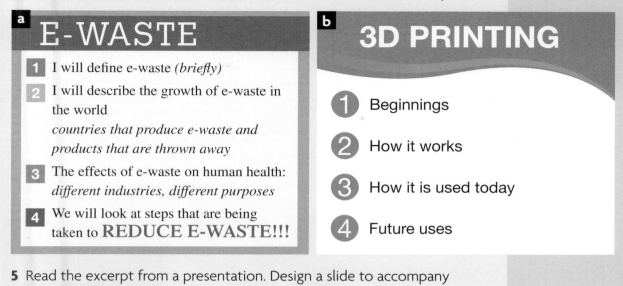

a

E-WASTE

1 I will define e-waste *(briefly)*

2 I will describe the growth of e-waste in the world
countries that produce e-waste and products that are thrown away

3 The effects of e-waste on human health:
different industries, different purposes

4 We will look at steps that are being taken to **REDUCE E-WASTE!!!**

b

3D PRINTING

1 Beginnings

2 How it works

3 How it is used today

4 Future uses

5 Read the excerpt from a presentation. Design a slide to accompany this information.

There are many good reasons to recycle your electronics. First of all, recycling saves energy. Did you know that the energy saved by recycling 273 laptops could produce enough power for one home in a year? Not only that, but e-waste contains toxic chemicals such as lead and mercury. These are harmful when they are not recycled properly. So recycling helps the environment. It also helps conserve resources. The kinds of rare earth minerals used in electronic goods are expensive and difficult to produce. Finally, you can help your community by allowing another person to use your refurbished cell phone or laptop.

6 Work in small groups and compare your slides. Which one is the most effective? Why?

When using visuals in presentations:

- keep visuals simple and clear
- use words and phrases, not sentences
- use large font (at least 30-point)
- simplify data

REAL-WORLD APPLICATION

7 Work in groups of five. Read the transcript for track 2.7. Each person designs one visual aid for each excerpt – a chart, a graph, a slide, etc.

8 Present your visual aid to your group and summarize the information in it. Choose the most effective slides to share with the class.

LEARNING OBJECTIVES	
Listening skills	Listen for opinions; listen for facts and supporting information
Pronunciation	Sentence stress; question intonation
Speaking skills	Explain data from graphics; present conclusions from research
Speaking Task	Present survey data and conclusions
On Campus	Adapt to teaching styles

UNIT 3

PRIVACY

ACTIVATE YOUR KNOWLEDGE

Work with a partner. Discuss the questions.

1 What steps do you take to protect your privacy and avoid identity theft?
2 Who do you think is responsible for protecting individual privacy?
3 How much access do you think the government or businesses should have to information about what you like and what you do?

WATCH AND LISTEN

PREPARING TO WATCH

ACTIVATING YOUR KNOWLEDGE

1 Work with a partner. Discuss the questions.

1 Do you regularly use a debit card or credit card when you go to a store? Why or why not?
2 Do you think paying with a card is safe? Why or why not?
3 Do you think shopping online with a card is safe? Why or why not?

PREDICTING CONTENT USING VISUALS

2 Look at the pictures from the video and read the quote below. Then discuss the questions with your partner.

> "Protecting our customers' information is something we take extremely seriously ..."
>
> Paula Drake, Home Depot Spokesperson

1 What do you think happened to Home Depot and their customers?
2 What dangers exist with online banking?
3 What technology do you think you are going to hear about in the video?

GLOSSARY

breach (n) an act of breaking a rule, law, custom, or practice
wake-up call (n phr) a shocking event that changes the way people think
market cap (n phr) the total value of a company's shares on the stock market
plummet (v) to fall very quickly and suddenly
dual verification (n phr) the process of testing or finding out if something is true, real, or accurate through two methods

WHILE WATCHING

UNDERSTANDING MAIN IDEAS

3 Watch the video. Circle the correct answer.

Which statement best summarizes the main idea of the video?

a If Home Depot hadn't ignored its technology problems, this security breach could have been prevented.

b Security breaches occur, but new technology has been developed to prevent more breaches.

c While new technology has been developed to prevent large breaches, Target was reluctant to invest in it.

UNDERSTANDING DETAILS

4 Watch again. Answer the questions.

1 How many shoppers were affected by Target's security breach? ______

2 How much money was stolen at that time? ______

3 By how much did Target's market cap fall as a result of the breach? ______

4 What were two other consequences of the breach? ______ ______

5 What is the new card-reader technology to prevent such breaches called? ______

6 Of the companies in the video, which was the first to adopt this technology? ______

7 How much is it likely to cost to implement the new card-reader technology everywhere in the United States? ______

MAKING INFERENCES

5 Work with a partner. Discuss the questions. Give reasons for your answers.

1 Who do you think repaid consumers for charges they incurred due to the security breach? How do you know?

2 Why do you think some companies are unprepared for the new technology?

3 Do you think cyberthieves will find a way around the new technology? Why or why not?

DISCUSSION

6 Work in small groups. Discuss the questions.

1 Would you continue to shop at a store that had had a large security breach? Why or why not?

2 If there is a breach, who should be responsible for the financial loss?

3 Have you or anyone you know ever experienced security issues like the ones in the video? Describe the circumstances and results.

LISTENING

LISTENING 1

PREPARING TO LISTEN

USING YOUR KNOWLEDGE

1 You are going to listen to a presentation about Internet security and privacy. Before you listen, think about what kinds of activities you do online. Complete the survey. Then compare answers with a partner.

activity	once in a while	regularly
shop; check prices and products		
read news, features, or blogs		
comment on websites, blogs, or online forums		
check social media		
send and receive messages, images, or videos		
do research		
watch videos		
upload content (e.g., videos to YouTube)		
play games		
manage your finances		
take care of healthcare related needs or business		

2 With your partner, answer the questions.

1 When you engage in these online activities, what kind of information is stored online (for example, your search history, passwords, mailing address)?
2 Do you actively control what gets stored? How?
3 Do you always click "agree" or "yes" when a website asks for permission? Why or why not?
4 What is *identity theft*? Has this ever happened to you or someone you know?

3 Read the sentences and write the words in bold next to the definitions.

UNDERSTANDING KEY VOCABULARY

1 The university is planning to **counter** recent claims of racism with diversity seminars that all students and staff must attend.
2 Our laws have not **caught up with** advances in technology.
3 Law enforcement officials are using email messages to find someone who stole five million dollars. They have **traced** the messages to a computer on a Caribbean island.
4 Doctors have an **arsenal** of medications for fighting this disease.
5 I never told him my address, so it was kind of **creepy** when he knocked on my door.
6 This website is **targeted** at young women between 15 and 20.
7 He was not very well **informed** about the election, so he read several news articles before he voted.
8 I use an app to **track** how many steps I walk. My goal is 10,000 per day.

a ____________ (v) to follow and collect data on a person's activity
b ____________ (v) to defend against or respond to
c ____________ (adj) causing discomfort because of being strange or unnatural
d ____________ (v) to direct something at someone
e ____________ (adj) having a lot of knowledge about something
f ____________ (phr v) to reach the same level or get in sync
g ____________ (n) a collection of weapons
h ____________ (v) to find the origin of something

WHILE LISTENING

Using a T-chart to take notes

There are many different ways to take notes. A T-chart allows you either to write down separate main ideas as you hear them and then add details about each idea later, or note down related details in each box as you hear them and connect them to main ideas later.

TAKING NOTES ON MAIN IDEAS AND DETAILS

4 3.1 Listen to the presentation. In your notebook, make a T-chart like the one below and take notes on main ideas and details.

main ideas	details

LISTENING FOR DETAILS

5 3.1 Listen again. This time, listen for these key terms. Write a definition or explanation of each.

1 behavioral targeting ____________
2 cookie ____________
3 third-party cookie ____________
4 secure cookie ____________
5 surfing incognito ____________
6 flash cookies ____________
7 web beacon ____________

POST-LISTENING

6 Update your notes with the key terms from Exercise 5. Review all of the details you have written in your chart. Do any of them suggest additional main ideas? Add them to your notes.

7 Circle **all** the answers that are correct according to the information in the presentation. For some items, there is more than one correct answer.

1 Retail businesses target customers by ...
  a tracking consumer behavior and preferences.
  b creating special advertisements.
  c sending cookies to potential customers' accounts.
2 Cookies store information about ...
  a financial records.
  b consumers and their browsing behavior.
  c consumer purchases.
3 Identity theft may occur when ...
  a a third-party cookie is created.
  b a nonsecure cookie is transmitted.
  c a flash cookie is stored.
4 You can prevent online retailers from building a profile about you by ...
  a browsing incognito. b disabling cookies. c clicking "agree."
5 Online retailers use techniques other than cookies to try to monitor your browsing. They also use ...
  a web beacons. b alternate browsers. c business profiles.

SKILLS

Listening for opinions

Informational presentations consist mostly of facts. However, even primarily objective presentations may include a presenter's opinions and beliefs. Signals of speaker opinion include the following:

expressions of belief
I think ...
I believe ...
In my view, ...
In my opinion, ...
Let's be honest, ...

words that express likelihood or doubt
probably
likely
maybe
clearly
no doubt

modals of suggestion or inference
You should ...
This should ...
We all should ...

evaluative expressions
These are the best / most valuable ...

8 Work with a partner. Are these statements from the presentation facts, opinions, or neither? Write *F*, *O*, or *N*.

PRISM Digital Workbook

1 You're reading an online newspaper or blog and then, bam! An ad for that lens you want flashes onto your screen. ______
2 Companies track your browsing activity and use it to send you advertisements that target you specifically. ______
3 The primary tool that companies use to track and remember you is the cookie. ______
4 So cookies are clearly useful. ______
5 Every time you visit another site that has ads from the same company, the cookies can be traced back to you. ______
6 I think more sites will probably move to secure cookies in the future, but for now, only about half of all websites use secure cookies. ______
7 Maybe you're thinking you should stop using the Internet altogether! ______
8 You should say "no" if you don't want that company to store information about you. ______
9 If you take some of these steps, you will probably be OK – or at least less vulnerable. ______
10 No doubt, tech privacy experts will soon catch up with these developments and find ways to counter them as well. ______

PRONUNCIATION FOR LISTENING

SKILLS

Sentence stress

English sentences follow a rhythm of stressed and unstressed words. Stress helps listeners focus on the important words in a sentence.

Stressed words are louder, longer, and higher in pitch than unstressed words. They are often content words, such as nouns, adjectives, adverbs, main verbs, and negative auxiliary verbs.

Unstressed words are often grammar or function words, such as articles, pronouns, prepositions, and auxiliary verbs.

9 3.2 Listen and underline the stressed words in each sentence. The number of stressed words is given in parentheses for the first three sentences. Listen again to check your work.

1 Our speaker today is Casey Chan, who is an expert in the field. (6)
2 There is a new lens you really want, but it's kind of expensive. (6)
3 Their hope is that by understanding what you like and want, they can send you ads. (6)
4 Let's be honest, when a website tracks and remembers where you've been, it can be pretty useful, right?
5 Without cookies, the cart could not collect the items you select.
6 The creepy part starts when they cross over to other websites.
7 One final cookie issue that you should be aware of is that some cookies are transmitted over a secure network.
8 I'm going to give you some advice about a few easy ways to manage and protect your privacy without going offline.

DISCUSSION

10 Work with a partner. Discuss the questions.

1 Do you think you will change your browsing behavior after reading about behavioral targeting? Why or why not?
2 Do you think the convenience that cookies provide is more important than their negative impact? Why or why not?
3 What are some other positive aspects of electronic tracking technology? Could it be applied outside of retail? How?
4 Do you think there should be more control over the use of cookies and other electronic tracking methods? If so, who should regulate this activity?

LANGUAGE DEVELOPMENT

SUBJECT-VERB AGREEMENT WITH QUANTIFIERS

LANGUAGE

Many quantifiers appear in expressions with *of* when the noun or noun phrase is definite.

In these types of phrases, the verb agrees with the noun or noun phrase.

Some of the people in the survey **say** they use the password "12345."
Most of the time **was** spent discussing cybersecurity.

DEFINITE NOUN PHRASE

There are many phrases that can express quantity. These may be used with indefinite or definite noun phrases. As with quantifiers, the verb agrees with the noun or noun phrase.

fractions	percentages	other expressions of quantity
half of	*fifty percent of*	*a majority of*
a quarter of	*25% of*	*a number of*

1 Complete the sentences with the correct form of the verb in parentheses.

PRISM Digital Workbook

1 The majority of online retailers ___________ (offer) a secure form of payment.
2 Some of the cookies ___________ (be) stored outside of the browser.
3 Half of the information that you read online ___________ (contain) factual errors.
4 Most of your online activity ___________ (be) visible to cybercriminals.
5 A number of critics ___________ (have) questioned the efforts made by social media sites to protect their members.

LANGUAGE

Expressions of quantity can be used as pronouns. The noun phrase that the expression refers to must be inferred. The verb agrees with the inferred noun phrase.

Many said they wanted Wi-Fi in the dorms, but few were willing to pay for it.

2 Circle the correct word or form for each sentence.

1 I didn't have much time and half *was / were* spent trying to log on!
2 There were a lot of speakers at the conference. A fairly large number *teach / teaches* at the local university.
3 Most people gave this app favorable reviews, but a minority *say / says* it takes too long to load.

4 Our respondent pool was about 250 people. Almost 35%, or about one-third, *prefer / prefers* to shop at a mall or department store.
5 We had about 70 participants in the study, but a number of them *has / have* had to cancel since then.
6 It took hours to fix my computer! A little of the time *was / were* spent upgrading the system, but most *was / were* taken up with deleting cookies and adware.

COLLOCATIONS

PRISM Digital Workbook

3 Complete the paragraph using the correct collocations for online activity. There are two extras. Make sure that verbs and nouns are in the correct form.

clear (your) cookies	surf the Internet/the web/the net
enable/disable cookies	secure network
search engine	search terms

Whenever you provide private information online, or even if you are just (1)____________________ , you should make sure you are using a (2)____________________ . If you don't want any personal information to be stored, you should use a (3)____________________ that allows you to browse anonymously. And you should always (4)____________________ after you have finished working online.

4 Complete the paragraph using the correct collocations for legal terms. There is one extra. Use a dictionary if needed. Make sure that verbs and nouns are in the correct form.

combat crime	violate/enforce laws
commit a crime	law-abiding (adj)
obey/break the law	law enforcement (noun)

I am a (1)____________________ citizen, and I spend a lot of time online. I believe that the majority of people who do business online are honest and they (2)____________________ . However, there are an increasing number of exceptions. (3)____________________ needs to do a better job of (4)____________________ that occurs online and (5)____________________ that exist to protect people from cybercriminals and identity thieves.

LISTENING 2

PREPARING TO LISTEN

USING YOUR KNOWLEDGE

1 You are going to listen to a moderated public forum about privacy issues in modern society. Before you listen, work in small groups and discuss the questions.

1 How much information do you think the government has about individuals? About you?
2 How do you think the government collects this information?

UNDERSTANDING KEY VOCABULARY

PRISM Digital Workbook

2 Read the sentences and choose the best definition for the words in bold.

1 This law was passed **in the interest of** protecting public health.
a as one option for b for the purpose of c to limit the cost of
2 The teacher said she would only accept late papers from students with a **legitimate** excuse for missing the deadline.
a true and reasonable b legal c medical
3 The senator was **compelled** to resign because he had broken the law.
a forced or pressured b asked or begged c wrongly advised
4 Our website has **encryption** software that protects customer data from identity theft.
a the process of stealing data through cookies in the computer code
b the process of destroying dangerous data instantly
c the process of protecting data by changing it into code
5 The musician's decision to sell her music directly to the public set a **precedent** that others soon followed.
a an action or decision that proves to be unwise
b an action or decision that justifies later actions or decisions
c an action or decision that is an immediate success
6 The speaker gave a **convincing** argument for why the government should support human rights.
a based on history and experience
b easy to follow; open and accessible
c able to make you believe that something is true or right
7 Because of her experience and **expertise** in information sciences, she was hired to direct the university library.
a advanced knowledge
b advanced degree
c previous employment
8 You can spend less money and buy the cheaper version, but the **tradeoff** is that it will probably wear out sooner than the better brand.
a a close relationship
b a situation in which one thing increases the value of the other
c a balance between two opposing but desirable things

3 ▶ 3.3 Listen to the introduction. Then answer the questions.

1 What will you be listening to?
   a a conversation among acquaintances
   b a debate between experts
   c a radio interview with ordinary people
2 What issue will be discussed?
   a recent threats to national security
   b the tradeoff between privacy and national security
   c how people respond when they are in danger
3 Complete the two questions that will be discussed.
   Q1: Should communications companies have to give ____________________ about private individuals to the police?
   Q2: Should tech companies have to help the police ____________________ private individuals?
4 Predict one point of view or opinion that you think will definitely be presented. After you listen, check to see if your prediction was correct.

____

WHILE LISTENING

TAKING NOTES ON MAIN IDEAS

4 ▶ 3.4 Listen to the forum. In the *answer* column, write *Y* (yes), *N* (no), or *X* (not stated) for each of the questions from the interviewer.

speaker	answer	facts or opinions	type of support
Joel	Q1 ______		
	Q2 ______		
Lauren	Q1 ______		
	Q2 ______		
Drake	Q1 ______		
	Q2 ______		
Karina	Q1 ______		
	Q2 ______		
Tony	Q1 ______		
	Q2 ______		
Sunjoo	Q1 ______		
	Q2 ______		

SKILLS

Listening for facts and supporting information

When speakers express their point of view, they are really talking about their beliefs and opinions. They often support their views with facts. These may include references to scientific research, information in published reports, expert statements, statistics, laws, and personal experience.

5 ▶ 3.4 Listen again, this time for facts and opinions. In the third column of the chart on page 70, write *F* (fact) or *O* (opinion). In the fourth column write information about the type of support the speakers offer.

PRISM Digital Workbook

POST-LISTENING

WORKING OUT MEANING

6 Circle the best answer to explain the expressions.

1 Joel says, "We've learned that lesson the hard way." He means ...
  a we had a bad experience in the past.
  b it was something that was very challenging.
  c at first we didn't understand, but now it's clear.

2 Joel says that asking tech companies to break into devices would be "crossing the line." He means ...
  a it would be justified.
  b it would be going too far.
  c it would be open to debate.

3 Lauren starts her response to the second question by saying, "Don't get me started." This means ...
  a she doesn't want to talk about it now or anytime in the future.
  b she has strong feelings and could talk about it for a long time.
  c she doesn't need any help from the interviewer to state her ideas.

DISCUSSION

SYNTHESIZING

7 Work with a partner. Using your notes from Listening 1 and Listening 2, discuss the questions.

1 Which of the guests' positions in Listening 2 do you think makes the most sense? Why?
2 What are some possible positive and negative outcomes if the government had full access to the information on private devices?
3 What are some possible positive and negative outcomes if private businesses were able to access private information on mobile devices?
4 Who bears the responsibility for protecting private data on mobile devices – the government, private companies, or individuals?

SPEAKING

CRITICAL THINKING

At the end of this unit, you are going to do the Speaking Task below.

Present data that you have collected from a survey and the conclusions that you have drawn from it.

SKILLS

Eliciting information via surveys

In some forms of research, surveys can be a helpful tool. In contrast to interviews, which focus on individual responses, survey research focuses on trends across a whole group of respondents.

Surveys are particularly good for eliciting information of two types:

opinions/beliefs: *Should tech companies be obliged to help the government find out about the activities of private individuals?*

behavior: *What do you do to protect your information online?*

When you develop a survey, you need to have a specific question or issue as the goal and build your survey items around it. Items should be neutral in tone so that respondents can answer honestly and comfortably.

CREATE

1 Work in small groups. Consider the two issues that are explored in this unit. Brainstorm questions related to these issues that you could use in a survey. Mark "opinion" questions with an *O* and "behavior" questions with a *B*.

privacy and security (review Listening 2)

_____ ______________________________

_____ ______________________________

_____ ______________________________

_____ ______________________________

_____ ______________________________

_____ ______________________________

Internet use and protecting personal information (review Listening 1)

_____ ______________________________

_____ ______________________________

_____ ______________________________

_____ ______________________________

_____ ______________________________

_____ ______________________________

2 With your group, discuss which of these questions would work well in a survey. Give reasons for your choices.

1 How many Internet-enabled devices do you use at least once per day?
2 Do you ever disable cookies when you surf the Internet?
3 How do you protect your information on the Internet?
4 Do you think tech companies should help the government?
5 How often do you click "I agree" when a website asks permission to send you something?
6 "The government should have to get permission from a judge before obtaining an individual's private information." Do you agree, disagree, or have no opinion?

Scales

Many surveys use some sort of a scale in order to make it easier to categorize responses. This also makes it easier to spot and report on trends.

The scale you offer your respondents should be appropriate to the survey item. Scales can take many different forms. Here are some examples:

Assign a number between one and ten, where one is the worst and ten is the best.

Choose the phrase that best matches your opinion: yes, no, no opinion.

Generally speaking, how often do you X per week – every day, a few times, several times, never?

3 Circle the type of scale that is more appropriate for each survey item.

1 I believe that the university library provides good service.

a	1 (best)	2	3	4	5 (worst)
b	strongly agree	agree	no opinion	disagree	strongly disagree

2 How often do you eat green vegetables?

a	1	2	3	4	5
b	every day	several times a week	once a week	hardly ever	never

3 How many forms of transportation do you use on an average day?

a	0	1	2	3	more than 3
b	none	a few	some	many	too many

4 How often do you consult Wikipedia for your research?

a	1 (most)	2	3	4	5 (least)
b	all the time	frequently	sometimes	rarely	never

5 How important is your teacher's feedback?

a	1	2	3	4	5
b	very important	important	somewhat important	not important	no opinion

CREATE

4 With your group, follow the steps to write your survey.

1 Choose an issue from Exercise 1 as the topic of your survey.
2 Write five questions that you feel will give you the information you need to address the issue.

Q1: ______

Q2: ______

Q3: ______

Q4: ______

Q5: ______

3 Choose a five-point scale for each of your five questions. You can use scales from Exercise 3 or come up with your own. Consider whether a "don't know" or "no opinion" option is appropriate for each scale.

APPLY

5 Exchange surveys with another group. Take their survey in order to give feedback on these points:

- clarity of questions: Are they easy to understand?
- appropriateness of scale: Can you answer the questions with the scale provided?
- neutrality of tone: Are the questions comfortable to answer?

PRONUNCIATION FOR SPEAKING

SKILLS

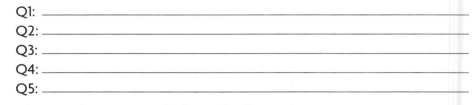

Question intonation

Intonation rises at the end of *yes/no* questions, and it falls at the end of *wh-* (information) questions. Using the correct intonation helps listeners understand the type of question you are asking.

Should companies have to hand over information about their customers? ↗

Lauren, what do you think? ↘

PRISM Digital Workbook

6 ▶ 3.5 Listen to the questions and decide whether each one ends with rising intonation or falling intonation. Circle the appropriate arrow.

1	a ↗	b ↘	5	a ↗	b ↘
2	a ↗	b ↘	6	a ↗	b ↘
3	a ↗	b ↘	7	a ↗	b ↘
4	a ↗	b ↘			

7 Conduct your survey. Gather answers from at least 20 respondents either by distributing the survey in written form or by conducting the survey in person and marking the responses. You may ask friends and acquaintances or people you do not know.

ANALYZE

8 Make a chart like the one below for each of your survey questions. Count up responses and express them as percentages (for example, 8 out of 20 = 40%).

Question 1: ____________________

category	percentage of respondents
strongly agree	

PREPARATION FOR SPEAKING

PRESENTING CONCLUSIONS BASED ON SURVEY DATA

SKILLS

Explaining data from graphics

Charts and graphs are a useful way to present survey data. Presenting data visually can help your audience understand your ideas and results more easily.

Phrases like these are commonly used when describing visual data:

This [type of graph] *compares* ...
This [type of graph] *shows* ...
As you can see from this [type of chart], ...
From this, it can be seen that ...
X demonstrates that ...
The majority of respondents said ...
The distribution of responses here is even/uneven ...

1 Work in small groups. Study the pie chart. Take turns presenting the results to your group. Use some of the phrases you have learned.

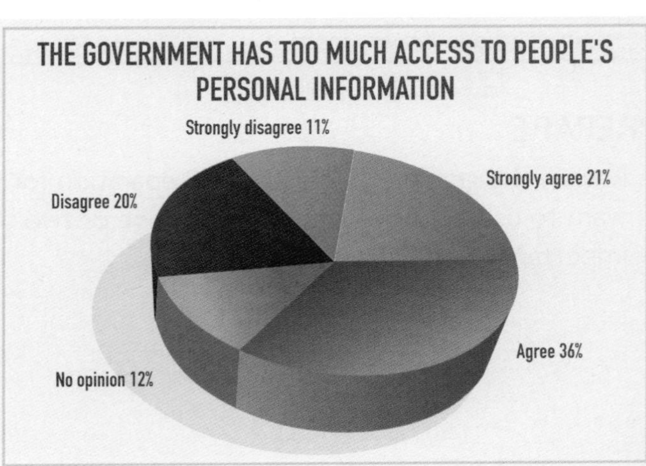

PRISM Digital Workbook

2 With your survey group, review your data analysis from Critical Thinking, Exercise 8. What kind of graph(s) would work best to display your results: a pie chart (for data that adds up to 100%), a bar graph (with a bar for each kind of response), or some other type? Create your graph(s).

3 Take turns presenting your graphs to each other. Use some of the phrases for explaining data from graphics. Give feedback to your group members.

4 Work with your group. Look back at the issue you chose as the topic of your survey (Critical Thinking, Exercise 4) and the analysis charts of your survey questions (Critical Thinking, Exercise 8). Answer the questions.

1 Does the data you gathered in your survey address well the issue you chose?

2 Looking at all the graphs and data together, what conclusions can you draw about the topic?

SKILLS

Presenting conclusions from research

Here are some phrases that are commonly used when presenting conclusions that have been drawn from survey data or other forms of research:

Survey results indicate that …
This stands in contrast to …
It can be concluded that …
Taking all of the results into account, …
It is clear that …
It follows that …
We can conclude that …

5 Take turns presenting your conclusions to others in your group. Use phrases from the explanation box. Listen carefully to the others and offer feedback. Consider the feedback that they give you and revise your conclusions if needed.

SPEAKING TASK

PRISM Digital Workbook

Present data that you have collected from a survey and the conclusions that you have drawn from it.

PREPARE

1 Review the graphs you created in Preparation for Speaking. Do you want to use all of the graphs, or just one or two that present the most important results?

2 Prepare talking points, but don't write out what you will say. Be sure to include the following:

- a description of your survey and data collection process
- an explanation of your results, including any graphics you wish to use, as well as the conclusions you have drawn from the data

3 If you are doing a group presentation, assign roles. Who will ...

- introduce your presentation?
- provide background on your survey?
- present your graphs?
- present your conclusions?

How will you make transitions from one speaker to the next?

4 Refer to the Task Checklist as you prepare your presentation.

TASK CHECKLIST	✔
Describe your survey process.	
Use an effective visual.	
Explain your results.	
Use appropriate expressions to refer to your results.	
Make smooth transitions between speakers.	
Draw conclusions based on your results.	

PRACTICE

5 Practice your presentation or your part of the presentation in your group.

PRESENT

6 Deliver your presentation to another group or to the class.

REFLECT

7 In small groups or as a class, discuss these questions.

1 Which presentation was the most interesting? Why do you think so?
2 How well did you present your part of the presentation?
3 What could you do better next time?

ON CAMPUS

ADAPTING TO TEACHING STYLES

PREPARING TO LISTEN

1 What kind of learner are you? Choose the option that best describes you. Then discuss your answers with a partner.

1 In class, I usually prefer to *listen to the teacher / take part in discussions*.
2 I usually prefer teachers who are *formal and serious / informal and friendly*.
3 I learn best when I *study alone / work in a group*.
4 I like teachers who *have specific guidelines for assignments / allow students to approach assignments in different ways*.
5 When I get an assignment, I usually *get started early / procrastinate*.
6 I usually prefer teachers who give *one final paper or exam / several short assignments*.
7 I am most motivated when *I understand how a subject is relevant to me / the subject interests me*.
8 Feedback from the teacher *is / is not* very important to me.

WHILE LISTENING

2 ▶ 3.6 Listen to the interview. What is the main point that Dr. Huang makes?

a Students should be ready to adapt to teachers' teaching styles.
b Teachers should adapt to students' learning preferences.
c Students should choose teachers whose style matches their learning preferences.

3 ▶ 3.6 Listen again and complete the notes.

1 Definition of *learning preferences*:
____
2 Examples: ______________ ______________ ______________
3 Conflict arises because of
____
4 Advice:
____
____
____
____

PRACTICE

4 Work in small groups. Read the problems. What advice would you give to a student in each situation?

1 We never have class discussions. The professor just lectures all the time. It's so boring!
2 My friend is taking this class with a different teacher, and they aren't doing this assignment. Why should I have to do it?
3 This class is really hard for me. The teacher never tells us anything about our progress, so I don't know how I'm doing. I'm really scared I'm not doing well.
4 My teacher asks questions and always calls on the same people to answer. I never get a chance to participate.
5 My teacher doesn't give very clear directions for our assignments, but she leaves really quickly right after class because she has to go to a different building for her next class. How can I find out what I need to know?

REAL-WORLD APPLICATION

5 Work with a partner to do a role play.

Choose either teacher or student.
Read the information for **your role only**. Plan your talking points.
Role-play the conversation. Work to resolve the situation in a way that is acceptable to both of you.
Switch roles and repeat the task. What will you do differently from your partner?

Student:
For the first time in your life, you are getting low grades in English composition. The reason seems to be that you are not using the correct punctuation and formatting when you cite ideas from a different source. You feel that the teacher is too picky – the content of your papers is what should matter, not the punctuation.

Teacher:
A major goal of this class is for students to learn the correct formatting in their papers. Professors in the other departments will insist on this when students start to write research papers. This is clearly set out in the class syllabus and in the directions provided for the assignment.

LEARNING OBJECTIVES

Listening skills	Listen for definitions; understand figurative language
Pronunciation	Thought groups
Speaking skill	Craft a pitch
Speaking Task	Make a pitch to get funding for a new venture
On Campus	Participate in group discussions

BUSINESS

UNIT 4

ACTIVATE YOUR KNOWLEDGE

Work with a partner. Discuss the questions.

1 How have retail businesses changed the way they interact with their customers in the past twenty years?
2 How have customers changed what they expect from businesses?
3 Consider some charitable organizations that you know (e.g., the Red Cross, Greenpeace). In what ways are they like businesses?

WATCH AND LISTEN

Sales of e-books increased from $78 million in 2008 to $1.7 billion in 2011.
2008

PREPARING TO WATCH

ACTIVATING YOUR KNOWLEDGE

1 Work with a partner. Discuss the questions.

1 Do you usually buy books at a bookstore or online? Do you prefer small, independent bookstores or large chain stores? What are the advantages and disadvantages of each?
2 Do you prefer a physical book or a digital book? Why?
3 How has the development of e-books changed book purchasing?
4 Do you think physical books will exist in 10 or 20 years? Why or why not?

PREDICTING CONTENT USING VISUALS

2 Look at the pictures from the video. Discuss the questions with a partner.

1 Why do you think people like to shop at a bookstore?
2 What might the challenges be of owning a bookstore today?
3 Only one in five Americans read an e-book in the previous year. Does that statistic surprise you? Why or why not?

GLOSSARY

no-brainer (n) something that is very simple to do or to understand, or a decision that is very easy to make

page-turner (n) a book that is so exciting that you want to read it quickly

algorithm (n) a list of instructions for solving a problem in mathematics

done deal (n phr) a final decision or agreement (colloquial)

advent (n) the beginning of an event or an invention, or the arrival of a person

WHILE WATCHING

UNDERSTANDING MAIN IDEAS

3 Watch the video. Write three reasons Ann believes a physical bookstore is important.

1 ______________________________
2 ______________________________
3 ______________________________

UNDERSTANDING DETAILS

4 Watch again. Complete the notes below with the missing words.

Ann Patchett = author / owner Parnassus Books
- Two huge (1) ________________ bookstores closed; so thought small bookstore could work
- at first, didn't care about selling bks – called it her (2) ________________

Staff
- people who (3) ________________
- staff good at (4) ________________ based on other books you like – not like (5) ________________

Physical book vs ebook
- ebooks make us (6) ________________ to phys bks

Independent bkstr
- landscape very different for aus now
- independent bkstr
  - (7) ________________ new aus
  - give aus a place to (8) ________________ with readers; talk to them
  - ebooks are popular but phys bks are not (9) ________________!

MAKING INFERENCES

5 Work with a partner. Discuss the questions.

1 How do you think the people in Ann's community feel about her bookstore? How do you know?
2 Do you think Ann's bookstore appeals to people of all ages? Why or why not?
3 What might online stores not consider when making recommendations to their consumers?

DISCUSSION

6 Work in a small group. Discuss the questions.

1 Would you visit a bookstore like Ann's? Why or why not?
2 Do you think it is important for authors to have an online presence through social media? Why or why not?
3 What benefits do small independent businesses bring to a community?
4 How has the increase in online shopping affected the stores in your town or city?
5 The video suggests that customers sometimes resist new technology for various reasons. Can you think of any other examples of this?

LISTENING

LISTENING 1

PREPARING TO LISTEN

UNDERSTANDING KEY VOCABULARY

1 Read the sentences and choose the best definition for the words in bold.

1 The plans for the building are so **elaborate** that very few people can understand them.
   a late and rushed b old and out of date c richly detailed
2 The new smart transit card will **facilitate** travel around the city.
   a make easier b make cheaper c increase the use of
3 Although it's a writing class, she's **effectively** teaching critical thinking because the students have to analyze data and make inferences.
   a in a manner that is reliable c in a predictable way
   b in reality but not officially
4 I have been dealing with an email **overload**, but I think I have finally cleared out my inbox.
   a too much of something c something that is too heavy
   b an unsafe situation
5 The bank charges a small fee for each international **transaction**.
   a an activity that requires legal permission
   b an activity that involves hiring or firing someone
   c an activity that involves the movement of money
6 I used to check a lot of different websites for traffic information, but I found an **aggregator** for my area that I use exclusively now.
   a a tool that collects and organizes information
   b a tool that publishes new information
   c a tool that investigates whether information is accurate
7 She was so tired that she just **dumped** all of her books on the floor and didn't pick them up until the next day.
   a threw in different directions
   b left behind
   c dropped without caring where
8 The speaker used all the right **buzzwords** for online marketing, but he really didn't say anything useful.
   a words and expressions that cause a lot of disagreement
   b popular words or expressions that are sometimes overused in a field
   c words or expressions that people outside a field often misunderstand

USING YOUR KNOWLEDGE

2 You are going to listen to a lecture about disruptive innovation. Before you listen, take the survey. Compare responses with a partner.

1 Where would you be most likely to buy a book?
   a at a bookstore
   b online
   c other: ____________________
2 How are you most likely to book a flight?
   a on an airline's website
   b with a travel agent
   c on an online site such as Expedia, Kayak, etc.
3 Where would you be most likely to buy car insurance?
   a at an agent's office
   b on an insurance company's website
   c other: ____________________
4 When you travel, how would you be most likely to book a room?
   a a hotel website
   b an online site such as Kayak or Hotels.com
   c Airbnb or similar service
5 Which of these sites have you used? Check (✔) all that apply.
   a Amazon ☐
   b eBay ☐
   c Uber ☐
   d Craigslist ☐
   e Etsy ☐
   f Mechanical Turk ☐

3 With your partner, answer these questions.

1 Do you think you (or someone like you) would have given the same answers to these questions five years ago? Ten years ago? Why or why not?
2 What *innovations* – new ideas or ways of doing business – are responsible for recent changes in how we get products and services?

4 ▶ 4.1 Listen to the beginning of the lecture. Check (✔) the questions you think this lecture will answer.

a What are some other examples of disruptive innovation? ☐
b How has the market changed forever? ☐
c What industries have been disrupted by this innovation? ☐
d What has happened to mainframe computers? ☐

WHILE LISTENING

LISTENING FOR MAIN IDEAS

5 ▶ 4.2 Listen to the lecture. Check your predictions in Exercise 4.

SKILLS

Listening for definitions

Speakers often provide a signal of definition either before or after giving the definition. Some signals of definition to listen for include:

X, which is ...	*In other words, ...*	*The word/term*
By X, I mean ...	*This means ... ,*	*for this is X.*
X, meaning ...	*The definition of X is ...*	*... is referred to as ...*
... , that is, ...	*We can define X as ...*	*X is the term for ...*

Speakers don't always use such obvious markers, however. Often, a definition is given in a more conversational way, simply linking the term and a definition with *is* or pausing briefly between the term and its definition.

In the current economy, it is difficult for many start-ups – new, fast-growing businesses – to survive.

LISTENING FOR DETAILS

PRISM Digital Workbook

6 ▶ 4.2 Listen again. Write the term that is being defined by the markers.

1 You may have heard the buzzword "____________________," which is when a new technology or business model fundamentally changes a market.
2 By ____________________ , I mean two things: first, suddenly, anyone with a computer and a network connection could access all kinds of information.
3 As a result, most people no longer bothered with these ____________________ – the middlemen.
4 First, we have ____________________ ; these are businesses, such as Amazon, that bring together every product imaginable.
5 In the second business model, referred to as ____________________ , there is more of a departure from the past.
6 Gates predicted that online markets might allow for "____________________"; in other words, the smooth and easy exchange of goods and labor, with no middleman and no transaction costs.
7 What they need is a middleman to sift through it all. ... The buzzword for this sifting activity is "____________________ ."
8 Wary eBay customers can now turn to what are often referred to as "____________________ ," participants who act as intermediaries on the site.
9 They want a middleman who will actually do everything for them. The buzzword for what these customers want is a "____________________ ," and yes, the Internet can provide this, too.

POST-LISTENING

SKILLS

Understanding figurative language

Figurative language includes words and expressions that do not have their usual or literal meaning. If you know the literal meaning of a word or expression, you can often infer the figurative meaning from the context.

7 Work with a partner. Complete the chart. Use a dictionary if needed.

PRISM Digital Workbook

excerpt	literal meaning	figurative meaning
"The Internet has become the **engine** of disruptive innovation in dozens of markets, from travel to publishing to insurance."		something that provides power or energy for a process
"... it has allowed the automation of transactions, reducing what Bill Gates referred to as '**friction**' in the market."	the force that makes it difficult for one object to slide past another	
"These new 'curators' have become experts at **harnessing** the power of the Internet."		
"A final **casualty** of the elimination of the middleman has been luxury."		

DISCUSSION

8 Work in small groups. Discuss the questions.

1 The presenter ends by saying, "And so disruptive innovation has brought us full circle." What do you think that means?

2 What services mentioned by the presenter (i.e., curation, concierges, power sellers) have you used? What do you think about them?

3 What do you think the speaker means by "the massive amount of information ... may lead to indecision, in some cases, even paralysis"? Have you ever experienced something like that?

PRONUNCIATION FOR LISTENING

SKILLS

Thought groups

Speakers often pause after important words, such as transition words, and after thought groups.

Thought groups are words that go together to form an idea. They are usually grammatical units such as clauses (noun + verb), noun phrases (article + noun), or prepositional phrases (preposition + noun).

Speakers connect words within thought groups and signal the end of a thought group with a slight change in intonation and a pause. This helps listeners to hear where one idea ends and another begins.

9 ▶ 4.3 Listen to the example sentence. Notice the change in intonation and pauses at the end of each thought group. Then, listen to the sentences and mark the end of each thought group that you hear.

The classic example / is the personal computer / which was pioneered by IBM / a company that had previously dominated the market / for large mainframe computers.

1 With IBM's new smaller model however computers became accessible to an entirely new group of customers.
2 The Internet has become the engine of disruptive innovation in dozens of markets from travel to publishing to insurance.
3 First suddenly anyone with a computer and a network connection could access all kinds of information that had previously only been available to professionals.
4 Travel sites such as Expedia and Kayak aggregate information on dozens of airlines and car rentals and hundreds of hotels allowing customers to compare and make their choices from a single site.
5 In online transactions there is no need for people no need for interaction which could slow things down.

10 Work with a partner. Read the paragraph and mark where you think you should pause. Then take turns reading it aloud. Give each other feedback.

Next, I'd like to talk about some successful nonprofits. One example is Kiva a nonprofit organization based in San Francisco. Its mission is to alleviate poverty by connecting people who need loans to people who donate money to them through Kiva's website. Through Kiva people can lend money to entrepreneurs and students from more than 80 countries around the world.

LANGUAGE DEVELOPMENT

EXTREME COMPARISONS AND CONTRASTS

LANGUAGE

There are many ways to make comparisons and contrasts more extreme.

even

When a comparison contains the word *even*, this suggests that the thing, event, or action is extreme – more than expected.

The massive amount of information a consumer encounters online may lead to indecision, in some cases, **even** paralysis.

Here, *paralysis* is an extreme form of *indecision*.

let alone

The phrase *let alone* also makes a comparison more extreme. It usually occurs in sentences that contain a negative. It can appear before a verb, noun, adjective, or adverb.

Customers no longer have to visit different websites, **let alone** different stores, to get everything they need.

Whatever follows *let alone* is the less probable, more extreme option.

not to mention

The phrase *not to mention* usually occurs after a list of at least two qualities, activities, or things. It introduces the most extreme, important, or surprising item in the list.

She is talented and athletic, **not to mention** beautiful.

1 Complete the sentences with *even*, *let alone*, or *not to mention*.

PRISM Digital Workbook

1 She didn't tell her own mother about what happened, ________ her colleagues at work.
2 I didn't learn computer programming until college, but today ________ young kids are building their own websites.
3 Any amount of exercise is helpful; ________ a ten-minute walk to work can make a difference.
4 It would have saved a lot of time and energy, ________ money, if you had planned this project better from the start.
5 It seems unlikely that the city government, ________ an individual, can change the way this process is done.
6 I'm so busy these days that I don't have time to go shopping, cook, clean, do laundry, ________ sleep!

ACADEMIC ALTERNATIVES

LANGUAGE

Academic communication often includes lower-frequency words with the same or similar meaning as everyday vocabulary. Often, however, these academic words have more specific or specialized meaning than their higher-frequency counterparts. This allows speakers and writers to be more precise.

PRISM Digital Workbook

2 Work in small groups. What are the differences in meaning between these high (everyday) and low (academic) frequency word pairs? Use a dictionary to help you.

high	low	high	low
business	venture	main	primary
choice	option	sign (n)	trace
come out	emerge	sort (v)	sift
kind (n)	breed	stop using	abandon
large	massive		

3 Complete the sentences with the correct form of an academic word or phrase from Exercise 2.

1 The police will have to __________ through all the evidence to find clues to solve the crime.
2 A lot of people have __________ books completely and do all their reading on mobile devices.
3 There are no __________ of yesterday's celebration. Everything has been cleaned up.
4 Today there is a new __________ of tourist – one who wants to leave a small environmental footprint.
5 Several innovative ideas __________ during our discussion yesterday. We just need to decide which one to pursue.
6 My brother and I started this __________ in 1995. At the time, we were not sure it would ever be a success.
7 My __________ reason for using an online service is the lower cost.
8 I think we should look at some other __________ . This apartment is too small and dark.
9 The company headquarters is __________ . It has five multistory buildings and covers several acres.

4 Choose four of the academic words from the box above. Write a sentence in your notebook for each one that is relevant to its meaning.

LISTENING 2

PREPARING TO LISTEN

UNDERSTANDING KEY VOCABULARY

PRISM Digital Workbook

1 Read the definitions. Complete the sentences with the correct form of the words in bold.

concisely (adv) clearly and using few words
fabulous (adj) great; wonderful
funding (n) money for a particular purpose
mission (n) goal or purpose, especially of an organization
oversight (n) supervision over; management of
overview (n) a short description or general idea of something
scope (n) the range that is covered by something
status (n) official position

1 The director gave us a(n) __________ of the new product line.
2 We tried a(n) __________ new Iraqi restaurant. We loved it!
3 He's here on a student visa, so his behavior may have a negative impact on his residency __________ in this country.
4 I'm afraid this matter is not within the __________ of my responsibility.
5 We need to find additional __________ to pay for the new project.
6 __________ for this project is provided by the New York office.
7 Your thesis is not clear at all. Please state it more __________ .
8 The __________ of the United Nations is to promote world peace.

USING YOUR KNOWLEDGE

2 You are going to listen to an informative presentation on nonprofit organizations. Before you listen, study the table and answer the questions.

A selection of the ranking of 145 countries for charitable behavior

COUNTRY	RANKING	COUNTRY	RANKING	COUNTRY	RANKING
Burma	1	Malaysia	10	Sierra Leone	54
U.S.A.	2	Kenya	11	South Korea	64
New Zealand	3	United Arab Emirates	14	Vietnam	79
Canada	4	Guatemala	16	Portugal	82
Australia	5	Thailand	19	Mexico	90
U.K.	6	Germany	20	Japan	102
Netherlands	7	Kuwait	24	Brazil	105
Sri Lanka	8	Costa Rica	36	Russia	129
Ireland	9	Saudi Arabia	47	Burundi	145

Source: Charities Aid Foundation, 2015

1 Which country is number 1 (the highest ranking)? __________
2 Which country has a ranking that surprises you? __________

3 In small groups, discuss the questions.

1 Share your answers from Exercise 2. Why does your answer to question 3 surprise you?
2 Do you think that donating money and volunteering time are the best ways to help people in need? What other ways are there to help?
3 Do you think that charitable organizations do a good job of helping people in need? Give an example of an organization that you are familiar with and the work it does.

WHILE LISTENING

LISTENING FOR MAIN IDEAS

4 ▶ 4.4 Listen to the talk. Write *T* (true), *F* (false), or *DNS* (does not say).

_____ 1 The purpose of the presentation is to give the students an introduction to nonprofit organizations.
_____ 2 The main difference between a for-profit business and a nonprofit organization is that a nonprofit has no revenue.
_____ 3 Donations to nonprofits cannot be used for administrative functions.
_____ 4 Nonprofit organizations have no owner.
_____ 5 Ninety percent of nonprofit revenue comes from fundraising.
_____ 6 Nonprofit organizations are not affected by market forces.

LISTENING FOR DETAILS

5 ▶ 4.4 Listen again. Define the terms as they relate to nonprofit organizations.

1 nonprofit organization: ____________________
2 mission: ____________________
3 revenue: ____________________
4 program: ____________________
5 equity: ____________________
6 board of directors: ____________________
7 fundraising: ____________________

6 Use the terms from Exercise 5 to complete the paragraph.

(1)____________________ differ from businesses that operate for a profit in that they cannot keep the money they raise or distribute it to owners or shareholders as (2)__________ . Instead, their (3)__________ , most of which is provided through (4)__________ , must be used to pay for the organization's (5)__________ . To ensure that the (6)__________ of the organization is protected, a (7)____________________ maintains oversight of all operations.

POST-LISTENING

One type of figurative language is personification, which is when speakers attribute human traits to something that is not human.

*The flames **danced** in the dark.*

*The waves **attacked** the shore.*

Speakers may also attribute the traits or treatment of animals.

*The storm raged like an angry **beast**.*

*The new economic policy is designed to **tame** inflation.*

This kind of imagery can be very powerful and can make descriptions more colorful and interesting.

MAKING INFERENCES

7 Work with a partner. Underline the figurative language in the expressions from the presentation. Explain why you think the speaker uses this figurative language.

1 I cannot stress enough that fundraising is the lifeblood of a nonprofit.

____

2 Running a nonprofit is like having a child that is always hungry!

____

3 They can't do those things on a starvation budget.

____

4 They are learning from the for-profit sector about how to harness market forces, but for social good.

____

5 But we also have a foot in the for-profit world.

____

8 With your partner, underline the figurative language in these excerpts from the presentation. Answer the questions.

> So that tells you about some of the nuts and bolts of running a nonprofit, but I know that all of you are more interested in how you can get started on turning your dreams into reality.

1 What type of imagery is used? _______________

2 What does the expression mean? _______________

> Money is what makes the wheels of commerce turn, and the same can be said of nonprofits.

3 What type of imagery is used? _______________

4 What does the expression mean? _______________

9 Write some sentences using imagery and figurative language on these topics. Then write two more on topics of your own. Share your sentences in a small group.

- sleep
- traffic
- growing up

1 ____
____

2 ____
____

3 ____
____

4 ____
____

5 ____
____

DISCUSSION

SYNTHESIZING

10 With your group, use your notes from Listening 1 and Listening 2 to discuss the questions.

1 How do you (or would you) choose an organization to donate your time or money?

2 A lot of people – especially donors – believe that the best charities are the ones that do the most with the least. They look for charities with low expenses and ones that pay their staff very little. Yet, the presenter advises the students to invest in administration. Why do you think he gives this advice?

3 What kinds of lessons do you think nonprofit organizations can learn from for-profit businesses?

4 Do you think an aggregator, a curator, or a concierge service could work in the nonprofit world? Why or why not?

SPEAKING

CRITICAL THINKING

At the end of this unit, you are going to do the Speaking Task below.

Make a pitch to get a venture started. Your goal is to get funding (investment or donations) for your peer-to-peer business or nonprofit organization.

1 Work in small groups. Read the descriptions. Discuss the potential for success for each venture.

UNDERSTAND

group A: ideas for P2P businesses

1 *The Full Closet:* a service to help women with a lot of clothes generate income by renting out their clothing to others.

2 *Proud City:* a service that connects visitors and tourists with city residents who can act as guides and helpers, giving visitors a richer, more interesting city experience.

3 *Angel for a Day:* a service that connects individuals with certified, reliable, and affordable caregivers for family members.

group B: ideas for nonprofits working for social good

1 *Rain To Go:* a group that works with private companies to develop portable water purifiers and distribute them in poor countries.

2 *Safe Hangout:* a service that provides food and shelter for homeless teens.

3 *Reset:* a service that provides job training for nonviolent ex-prisoners in major cities around the country.

EVALUATE

2 With your group, rank the ideas presented in Exercise 1.

1 If you were an investor, which start-up would you give your money to?
1 ______________ 2 ______________ 3 ______________

2 If you were a donor, which nonprofit would you contribute money to?
1 ______________ 2 ______________ 3 ______________

CREATE

3 With your group, follow the steps to select a venture.

step 1: Decide if you would like to do a presentation on a peer-to-peer business or a nonprofit organization.
step 2: Brainstorm ideas for your business or organization.
step 3: Narrow your list down to three possibilities. Make a chart listing the pros and cons of each.
step 4: Choose one business or organization for your presentation.

4 Focus on your idea and decide what exactly you want to accomplish. Discuss these questions to help you develop your pitch. Make notes.

for a nonprofit organization:
- What will your mission be?
- What kinds of programs will you offer?
- Who are your likely donors?
- How much money will you need?
- Will you have employees?

for a P2P business:
- Will you be "disrupting" a traditional business? If so, which one?
- Who will you be connecting?
- What does each party want?
- How much money will you need?
- Who will be working for you?

PREPARATION FOR SPEAKING

MISSION STATEMENTS

Every business or nonprofit organization has a mission statement. It usually consists of one or two sentences that communicate three basic pieces of information:
- why your organization exists
- who it serves
- how it serves them

"At eBay, our mission is to provide a global online marketplace where practically anyone can trade practically anything, enabling economic opportunity around the world."

"Team Rubicon unites the skills and experiences of military veterans with first responders to rapidly deploy emergency response teams."

An organization's mission statement is not a promotional or advertising slogan; rather it is the guiding principle for day-to-day operations.

1 Rewrite this mission statement more concisely. Then compare your new mission statement with a partner's.

> *Our mission is to empower teen youth from low-income families to aspire to higher education by offering educational assistance services and mentoring programs in a supportive community environment.*

PRISM Digital Workbook

2 Work with your group. Write a mission statement for your business or organization in a maximum of two sentences.

APPLY 

3 Practice saying your mission statement.

- Review your statement several times so that you can say it without sounding as if you are reading it.
- Speak with authority to show that you know what you are talking about and that the topic is important.

CRAFTING A PITCH

SKILLS

Businesspeople say that you should be able to make a pitch in the time it takes to ride to the top story of a building in an elevator. This means you need to communicate all of the most important ideas in just a few minutes:

- Demonstrate that you have a plan.
- Show that it is viable and practical.
- Offer a measurement for success.

4 Answer the questions to determine the substance of your pitch. Make notes but do not write out your answers.

1 What is your business plan? How can you describe it very briefly?
2 What will you actually do – what services will you deliver? Describe them very briefly.
3 How do you know it will work? Have you tested it on a small scale?
4 How will you (and your investors/donors) know when you have been successful?

SKILLS

Your pitch must also be persuasive and personal, so you need to talk to your listeners, not read something that you have prepared.

- Consider your audience. Show why this investment or donation is good for them.
- Grab their attention by telling a story. Use figurative language or imagery to help them understand the need or opportunity your venture will address. Be sure to keep the story very short.
- Appeal to their emotions.
- Make them feel special. (*You'll be ahead of everyone if you do this.*)
- Make them feel nervous. (*You'll be left out if you don't do this.*)
- Finish with a strong statement in support of your project and yourself.

PRISM Digital Workbook

5 Answer the questions to help you develop the style of your pitch. Make notes, but do not write out your answers.

1 Who is your audience (investors or donors)? What are their goals?
2 What story could you use to help illustrate the value of your idea?
3 What imagery could you use for your pitch?
4 How can you appeal to their emotions?
5 What could you say as a strong statement of support for your idea and yourself? Why should they invest in or donate to your venture?

SPEAKING TASK

PRISM Digital Workbook

Make a pitch to get a venture started. Your goal is to get funding (investment or donations) for your peer-to-peer business or nonprofit organization.

PREPARE

1 Look back at the notes you made in Critical Thinking, Exercise 4, and in the Preparation for Speaking section. Rewrite your notes so that they are clear and organized, but do not write full sentences.

____
____
____
____
____
____

2 Organize your team. If you will all participate in a single presentation, assign roles.

__________ : ____

__________ : ____

__________ : ____

__________ : ____

3 Refer to the Task Checklist as you prepare for your presentation.

TASK CHECKLIST	✔
Give a clear, concise mission statement.	
Include a story to illustrate the need for your venture.	
Explain how you will achieve your goals.	
Offer a measure of success.	
Appeal to the listeners' emotions.	
End with a strong statement of support for your venture and yourself.	

PRACTICE

4 Practice your pitch several times in your group until you can give it without reading from your notes. Be sure to make eye contact with your listeners.

PRESENT

5 Make your pitch to another group or to the class. Take notes as you listen to the other pitches. Ask questions at the end. Offer feedback to the others and listen to the feedback that they give you.

REFLECT

6 In small groups or as a class, discuss these questions.

1 Which presentation was the most persuasive? Why do you think so?
2 How well did you give your pitch?
3 What could you do better next time?

ON CAMPUS

PARTICIPATING IN GROUP DISCUSSIONS

PREPARING TO LISTEN

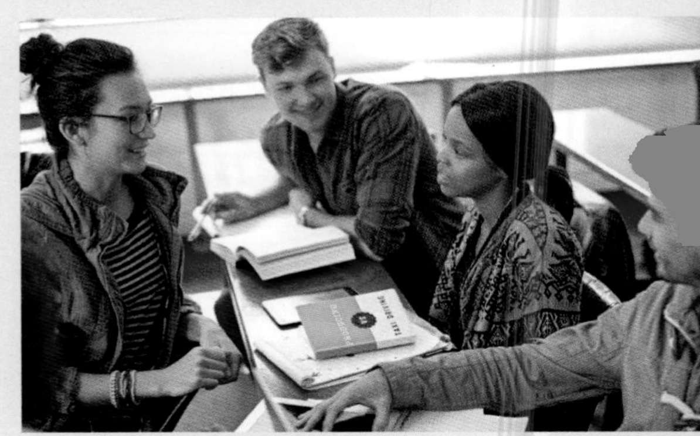

1 Group discussions are an important part of college classes. Work with a partner and discuss the questions.

1 How well do you participate in group discussions?
2 What are some of the challenges of group work and discussions? What can go wrong?

WHILE LISTENING

2 ▶ **4.5** Listen to four students, Olivia, Matt, Megan, and Eric, discussing their ideas for a nonprofit. At the end of the discussion, the students are most interested in helping low-income students do what?

a find sources of financial aid to pay for college ☐
b improve their grades by working with tutors ☐
c get one-on-one support from volunteer mentors ☐

3 ▶ **4.5** Teachers often grade students on their participation in group discussions. Read the scoring sheet. Then listen to the conversation again. Evaluate Matt's performance in the discussion according to the criteria. (Audio script is on page 207.)

GROUP DISCUSSION: GRADING SHEET Student: Matt

The student ...	Yes	No	Not evaluated
1 has prepared for the discussion.			
2 listens respectfully.			
3 asks questions to check understanding.			
4 does not dominate the conversation.			
5 encourages others to speak.			
6 helps to keep the conversation focused.			

4 With a partner, compare your evaluations of Matt's participation. Discuss the questions.

1 Do you disagree on any of the points? Why?
2 How could Matt improve?
3 Are the criteria fair?
4 Does the rating sheet give a full picture of Matt's participation? What criteria do you think should be added to or removed from a grading sheet like this?

PRACTICE

5 Read the list of functions, a–d. Then read the sentences and assign a function to each one.

a ask questions to check understanding
b respond to ideas of other group members
c keep the conversation on track
d encourage others to participate

1 **Are you suggesting that** we have employees? ______
2 **I like** Justin's idea for the website. ______
3 **I think we should talk about** how we're going to fund this project. ______
4 **I'd like to hear** what Brian thinks. ______
5 **Let's get back to** the subject of marketing. ______
6 **That's a good point.** ______
7 **What do you mean by** "disrupt"? ______
8 **What do you think**, Susanna? ______

REAL-WORLD APPLICATION

6 Work in small groups. Choose one of the topics and discuss it for five minutes. Each person should focus their comments around one of the functions in Exercise 5. At the end of the conversation, guess what function each person chose. Repeat the exercise, choosing different topics and functions.

Topics

1 What are some good ways to raise money for charity?
2 What peer-to-peer businesses are most useful for students?
3 Why should start-ups invest in administration and development?
4 How will shopping change in the future?
5 What kinds of nonprofits need our support the most?

LEARNING OBJECTIVES

Listening skills	Listen for generalizations and summaries; listen for dependency relationships
Pronunciation	Emphasis within thought groups
Speaking skills	Talk about research; incorporate visual support
Speaking Task	Give a group presentation synthesizing research
On Campus	Stay motivated

PSYCHOLOGY

UNIT 5

ACTIVATE YOUR KNOWLEDGE

Work with a partner. Discuss the questions.

1 What is your impression of the people in this picture? Are they people you think you would like? Why or why not?
2 What goes into making a judgment about something or someone new? Do you have complete control over the process? How much of it is automatic?
3 Are your first impressions of experiences and people usually proved right or wrong?

WATCH AND LISTEN

PREPARING TO WATCH

ACTIVATING YOUR KNOWLEDGE

1 Check (✔) the medical treatments you would consider for yourself. Share your ideas with a partner.

a Cryogenic chamber therapy (*standing in freezing air to relieve muscle and joint pain*) ☐
b Medicinal leeches (*attaching a small blood-sucking animal to your body to increase blood flow*) ☐
c Brain shock therapy (*shocking the brain with electrical current to improve memory*) ☐
d Deep brain stimulation (*implanting a device in the brain that sends out electric impulses to treat depression*) ☐

PREDICTING CONTENT USING VISUALS

2 Look at the pictures from the video. Discuss the questions with your partner.

1 What is the man being treated for?
2 Is it a physical or psychological condition?
3 How is he being treated?
4 What benefits do you think this treatment offers?

GLOSSARY

Alzheimer's disease (n phr) a disease that results in the gradual loss of memory, speech, movement, and the ability to think clearly; especially common among older people

intimidating (adj) making you feel frightened or nervous

electric eel (n phr) a bony, snake-shaped fish that can give a severe electric shock

hippocampus (n) a large part of the brain that is part of the limbic system and is important for memory

transcranial stimulation (n phr) a procedure that uses magnetic fields to stimulate parts of the brain

zap (n) an electric charge to a part of the body like the brain

orchestrate (v) to plan and organize something carefully

WHILE WATCHING

UNDERSTANDING MAIN IDEAS

3 Read the questions. Watch the video and take notes. Then discuss the questions with a partner.

1 How have doctors used electricity in the past?
2 What was the main finding of researchers at Northwestern University?
3 How painful is electrical stimulation?

UNDERSTANDING DETAILS

4 Watch again. Answer the questions.

1 What conditions does the device have the potential to treat? ____________
2 What condition is the device currently used to treat? ____________
3 What part of the brain does the device stimulate? ____________
4 How old were the subjects in the Northwestern study? ____________
5 During the study, how long did it take to see benefits? How long did these last? ____________
6 What are the key questions for further research? ____________

MAKING INFERENCES

5 Work with a partner. Discuss the questions. Give reasons for your answers.

1 How does Dr. Agus feel about the device?
2 If the device works in older people, what are the implications for the researchers? For people with Alzheimer's? For the population in general?

DISCUSSION

6 Work in a small group. Discuss the questions.

1 Would you consider having the device used on you, a family member, or a close friend? Why or why not?
2 What are the dangers of using new treatments without widespread testing?
3 What are other ways brain-related diseases and conditions can be treated?
4 Should medical devices or drugs be used to improve normal brain functions? Why or why not?

LISTENING

LISTENING 1

PREPARING TO LISTEN

USING YOUR KNOWLEDGE

1 You are going to listen to a group of students discussing an assignment on the topic of first impressions. Before you listen, answer the questions.

1 How important are the following elements when you meet someone for the first time? Rank them in order from 1 (most important) to 8 (least important). Then compare your rankings in small groups. Discuss the reasons for your ranking.

_____ facial expression
_____ voice
_____ handshake
_____ attractiveness
_____ clothing
_____ greeting
_____ hair
_____ eye contact

2 Which of the elements above help you decide if the person is friendly, distant, confident, nervous, etc.?

2 With your group, discuss the questions.

1 When you meet people, how long does it take you to decide if you like them?
2 How important is physical appearance in forming a first impression of someone? For example, can you tell if someone is trustworthy just by looking at the person?
3 What kind of behavior do you think is most important in making a first impression? What actions are likely to make a positive first impression? A negative one?
4 It is very common to change your mind about someone after you get to know the person better. So why do you think people have first impressions at all? What is the value of a first impression?

UNDERSTANDING KEY VOCABULARY

3 Read the sentences and write the words in bold next to the definitions.

1 I don't have enough information about the situation, so I am not going to **speculate** about why it happened.
2 He is an excellent jazz musician, but that doesn't necessarily make him **competent** to lead the school orchestra.
3 This type of dog is known for its **dominance** and aggressive behavior.
4 It is difficult to learn a new language as an adult just from **exposure** to it. You'll need to take some classes while you're in Mexico, too.
5 This new software will have many **applications**; for example, it is already being used in driverless cars.
6 For plants, the amount of daylight is a more important **cue** than temperature. Trees begin to lose their leaves when the days become shorter, not when they become colder.
7 I heard an **intriguing** story on the radio about a man who was in a coma after a car accident and just woke up after twenty years! Can you imagine?
8 Everyone told me that the boss was very serious and rather cold, but I found him very **approachable**.

a ____________ (adj) skilled; able to do things well
b ____________ (n) experiencing something by being in a particular place or situation
c ____________ (v) to guess when there is not enough information to be certain
d ____________ (adj) friendly and easy to talk to
e ____________ (n) a way in which something can be used
f ____________ (n) behavior that aims to control others
g ____________ (adj) very interesting because of being unusual or mysterious
h ____________ (n) a signal; something that causes a response

WHILE LISTENING

LISTENING FOR MAIN IDEAS

4 ▶ 5.1 Listen to the conversation. Check (✔) the topics that the students discuss.

a scientific studies ☐
b newspaper stories ☐
c their class readings ☐
d plans for their presentation ☐
e their professor ☐

SKILLS

Listening for generalizations and summaries

Speakers often help listeners understand their main ideas by providing signals that they are going to offer a generalization or summarize what they have said. Here are some signals to listen for:

In general, ... / Generally, ...
... a generalization ...
Overall, ...
A rule of thumb, ...
In short, ...
In a nutshell, ... (informal)
To conclude, ... / In conclusion, ...
We/They can conclude that ...
X leads us to conclude that ...
To summarize, ...
In summary, ...
To sum up, ...
The bottom line is ...
Bottom line – ...

5 5.1 Listen again. Write down the generalizations that you hear after these signal phrases, paraphrasing as needed.

1 OK, if I had to draw one **generalization** from all the readings, it would be ____________________ ____________________.

2 For first impressions, **in a nutshell**, it's ____________________.

3 The scientists who conducted the study speculate that, **in general**, ____________________ ____________________.

4 **Overall**, it turns out the judgments were pretty accurate. Most participants ____________________ ____________________.

5 Well, the authors of the study had an interesting explanation ... . **They conclude** that ____________________ ____________________.

6 Can you just summarize it? ____________________ ____________________ ____________________.

7 **Bottom line** – he was able to ____________________ ____________________ ____________________.

6 5.1 Answer the questions. Then listen to the conversation again to check your answers.

1 Participants in the studies described by the students had to make decisions about people's character based on their faces. What traits were mentioned in the studies? Check (✔) all the traits that were discussed.

a aggressive ☐
b approachable ☐
c attractive ☐
d competent ☐
e thoughtful ☐
f dominant ☐
g likeable ☐
h nervous ☐
i sincere ☐
j trustworthy ☐

2 Of these, which four traits were found to be the most consistent in the studies?

____________________ ____________________

____________________ ____________________

POST-LISTENING

7 Which of these are the main ideas (*MI*) of the studies the students read and which are supporting details (*D*)?

1 First impressions occur very quickly. _____
2 The primary cue in first impressions is physical appearance. _____
3 A specific part of the brain is responsible for first impressions. _____
4 Decisions about whom to trust may have provided an advantage to early humans. _____
5 First impressions are generally accurate. _____
6 One scientist broke down facial expressions into 65 separate features expressing different traits. _____
7 Judgments about facial expressions are consistent. _____
8 Smiles contribute to positive responses. _____

8 Work with a partner. Look at the computer-generated faces from the last study the students discussed. Which facial features (eyes, eyebrows, nose, smile, etc.) do you think were most important for decisions about each of the traits given?

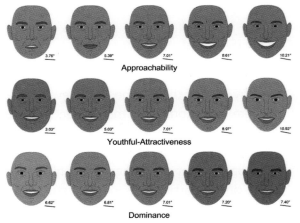

PRONUNCIATION FOR LISTENING

SKILLS

Emphasis within thought groups

Emphasis is the extra stress placed on the most important word in a thought group. Usually, the last content word in a thought group is emphasized, but sometimes other words, such as transition words or words signaling particular or new information, are emphasized because they are more important.

 5.2 Listen to these examples from Listening 1.

Eva: OK, / so has everyone read / all the material?
Leo: Yep. / So how do you think / we should organize it? / There is so much information.

9 ▶ 5.3 Listen to the excerpts from the conversation and underline the emphasized word(s) in each thought group.

1 **Eva:** So / what about some of the cues?
Leo: For first impressions / in a nutshell / it's physical appearance. / It's the most important cue.

2 **Leo:** In general / being able to decide if you can trust someone quickly / was really important / during early human evolution.
Eva: It probably still is! That's really interesting. I read another study / on a similar topic / but it was a little more specific.

3 **Alexa:** Some of the photos were of really attractive people / and all the participants pretty much agreed they were fours. / But there were some photos / that only a few people found attractive.

4 **Alexa:** Our first response / is to go for someone who is generally attractive, / what they call "a good catch."

5 **Alexa:** But the different preferences / suggest we also make judgments / about who would be "a good catch for me."

DISCUSSION

10 Work with a partner. Discuss the questions.

1 Why do you think some of the evaluations talked about in the studies were more consistent than others (e.g., trustworthiness)?
2 The authors of one of the studies speculated that there might be an evolutionary advantage to being able to make quick decisions about people. What advantage might it provide today?
3 All of the participants in these studies were educated and lived in Western countries. Do you think that makes a difference, or are the responses universally human?

LANGUAGE DEVELOPMENT

LANGUAGE

Noun clauses with *wh-* words and *if/whether*

Writers often introduce issues with *wh-* noun clauses. These clauses begin with *what, who, which, when, how, why, whether,* or *if* and occur most frequently as the object of a sentence. These clauses present questions inside of a larger sentence.

Let's talk about **what** we found in our readings and then plan the presentation.

The authors of the study discussed **how** useful this will be in computer-generated graphics in games and movies.

Participants had to decide **if** they would want to date the person in the picture, on a scale of one to four.

Notice that these noun clauses use statement word order.

Let's talk about what **we found** in our readings.

Let's talk about what ~~did we find~~ in our readings.

1 Combine each pair of sentences. Change the question into a noun clause in the new sentence.

PRISM Digital Workbook

1 Who would make a good life partner? This quiz can tell you.

____

2 What do people react to in first impressions? It's difficult to say.

____

3 Which facial features are particularly significant in first impressions? It's surprising.

____

____

4 Are initial judgments accurate? Researchers wanted to find out.

____

____

5 How fast do people make decisions about traits such as reliability and intelligence? One recent study looked at this.

____

____

2 Write three sentences about first impressions using *wh-* noun clauses.

1 ______________________________

2 ______________________________

3 ______________________________

LANGUAGE

Academic word families

Nouns that describe personality traits generally take the endings *-ness*, *-ity*, or *-ence/-ance*. Some noun forms require additional spelling changes.

adjective	noun
aggressive	aggressiveness
approachable	approachability
attractive	attractiveness
competent	competence
thoughtful	thoughtfulness
dominant	dominance
likeable	likeability

PRISM Digital Workbook

3 Complete the sentences with the correct form of an academic word in the explanation box above.

1 It was so ___________ of you to remember my birthday.
2 Be careful. That breed of dog is known for its strength and ___________ .
3 The main qualities we are looking for in candidates for this position are past experience and ___________ in several technical areas.
4 I saw Serena Williams at a restaurant once. I was nervous to talk to her, but she was surprisingly ___________ . She even gave me a signed tennis ball as a souvenir.
5 The physical ___________ of a job candidate should never be a factor in hiring decisions.

4 Write two sentences using words from the explanation box that were not used in Exercise 3.

1 ____
____
____

2 ____
____
____

LISTENING 2

PREPARING TO LISTEN

USING YOUR KNOWLEDGE

1 You are going to listen to a lecture on how the brain makes and uses mental maps. Before you listen, work with a partner. Study the diagram of the brain. Read the description of the parts and then label the diagram.

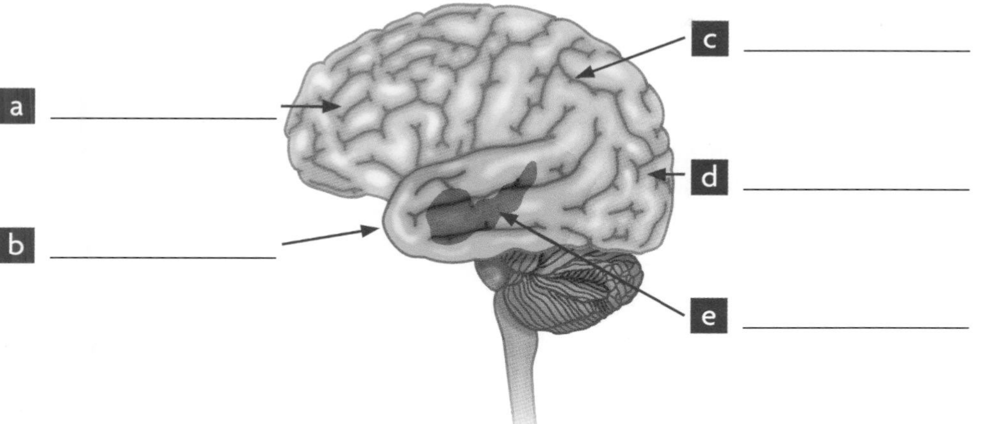

frontal lobe
- located at the front of the skull
- associated with reasoning, planning, speech, emotions, and problem solving

parietal lobe
- located at the top/back of the skull
- associated with movement, orientation, perception

occipital lobe
- located at the back of the skull
- associated with vision

temporal lobe
- located at the bottom of the brain
- associated with perception, hearing, memory, and speech

hippocampus
- located deep inside the temporal lobe
- associated with spatial memory and navigation

2 Work with a partner. Only one of these statements about the brain is true. Which one do you think it is?

a Human intelligence is related to brain size. ☐
b Many people use only about 10% of their brains. ☐
c Some people are "right-brained" and others are "left-brained." ☐
d Some people have memories like a camera. ☐
e If you get hit on the head, you could lose your whole memory. Another hit on the head may bring it back. ☐
f One area of the brain specializes in understanding stories. ☐
g Men's and women's brains are fundamentally different. ☐

UNDERSTANDING KEY VOCABULARY

PRISM Digital Workbook

3 Read the sentences and choose the best definition for the words in bold.

1 When her health began to **deteriorate**, she decided to move in with her daughter.
a improve
b worsen
c stabilize

2 After interviewing dozens of witnesses, the police began to **reconstruct** the crime.
a recreate
b investigate
c understand the reasons for

3 The **differentiated** functions of each lobe of the brain allow it to perform complex operations.
a advanced
b combined
c specialized

4 I use **landmarks**, such as parks and buildings, to help me figure out where I am.
a geographical features such as waterfalls and rock formations
b places or structures that are easy to recognize
c places in the community where people gather

5 Scientists proved **definitively** that we use 100% of our brains.
a eventually; after a lot of effort
b completely; without doubt
c unexpectedly; when researching something else

6 Pilots once depended on just their eyes to **navigate**, but now they use advanced technology.
a find one's way
b read instructions
c communicate with others

7 Both alcohol and lack of sleep can **impair** your ability to drive.
a change
b maintain
c damage

8 Sailors used to depend on the stars to **orient** themselves on voyages.
a establish one's location
b describe one's route
c create a sense of security for

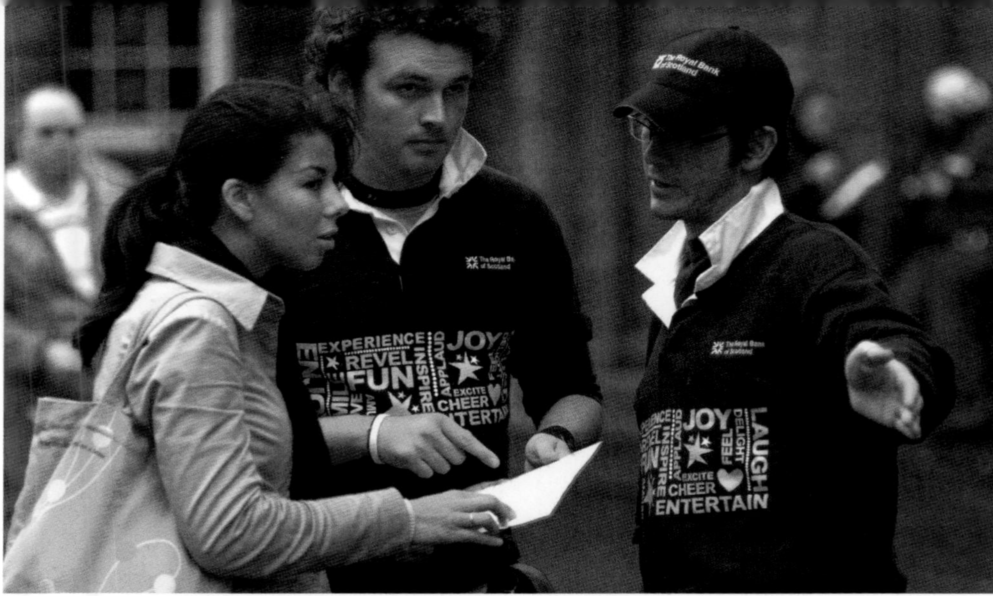

4 Work with a partner. Answer the questions.

1 How do you navigate when you are in an unfamiliar place?
2 Is this different from how your parents navigated when you were a child?
3 What do you do when you get lost? How do you find your way?
4 Do you know anyone who has suffered from dementia, that is, a loss of cognitive function as a person grows older? Describe what happened. For example, did the person begin to forget names or other words?

WHILE LISTENING

LISTENING FOR MAIN IDEAS

5 ▶ 5.4 Listen to the lecture. Check (✔) the questions that the lecturer answers in his presentation.

a How do humans navigate? ☐
b How do humans lose memory ability as they age. ☐
c How does memory loss relate to the hippocampus? ☐
d How does navigation experience affect the human brain? ☐
e How do maps impact human cognition? ☐

6 ▶ 5.4 Listen again and take notes. Then use your notes to complete these statements about the main ideas in the lecture. Compare your work with a partner.

1 Scientists have established that the hippocampus ____________________ ____ .
2 Humans use two forms of navigation: __________ and __________ .
3 Research results suggest that the __________ navigation strategy leads to the creation of mental maps.
4 Recent studies suggest that the constant creation of mental maps may result in ____ .

SKILLS

Listening for dependency relationships

Scientific research is filled with language describing dependency relationships. Some relationships are causal – one thing causes another. In other relationships, one element may be a contributing factor to another. Here are some common signals of dependency relationships.

causal	**dependence**	**partial causality or dependence**
X *causes ...*	X *relies on ...*	*is a factor*
X *is the cause of ...*	X *depends on ...*	*contributes to*
X *leads to ...*	X *is dependent on ...*	*has an impact/effect on*
X *is the result/ consequence of ...*	*reliance on ...*	*influences*
because	*dependence on ...*	*affects*
because of		*promotes*

LISTENING FOR DETAILS

PRISM Digital Workbook

7 5.4 Listen again. Listen for the dependency signals in bold and complete the information.

1 The lecture reports on research about our **increasing reliance** on ______________________________.
2 The hippocampus **plays a key role** in ______________________________.
3 The landmark strategy **relies on** ______________________________.
4 In the response strategy, your knowledge of the route **is the result of** ______________________________.
5 In Maguire's first study, MRI images strongly suggest that creating mental maps all the time **had affected** ______________________________.
6 In her second study, she was able to prove **a causal relationship** between ______________________________.

POST-LISTENING

SUMMARIZING

8 Work in groups of four. Each group member will give an oral summary of one of the studies described in the presentation. Other members of the group will ask questions.

DISCUSSION

SYNTHESIZING

9 Work with a partner. Using your notes from Listening 1 and Listening 2, discuss the questions.

1 Have you ever arrived somewhere "automatically" without remembering the journey? Describe the experience.
2 Which form of navigation do you use, landmark or response? Do you think there could be an evolutionary advantage to navigating one way or another? How might that work?

SPEAKING

CRITICAL THINKING

At the end of this unit, you are going to do the Speaking Task below.

Give a group presentation about research on some aspect of human behavior. Support your presentation with slides.

SKILLS

Synthesizing information from multiple sources

When you present a synthesis of research, first you must analyze individual studies and find common themes. Be sure that the sources you use are reliable and that the information can be verified. University and government organizations are often a good source of reliable information.

1 Work in groups of four. Read the information about some human behavior studies. Decide which topic your group would like to present or find another topic on your own.

ANALYZE

☐ **A PERCEPTUAL BLINDNESS**

Perceptual blindness refers to the failure to see or notice a stimulus that is in plain sight. However, this lack of attention has nothing to do with vision problems. A number of studies have tested this idea, especially when the stimulus is unexpected.

REFERENCES:
Invisible gorilla experiment
Clown on a unicycle experiment

☐ **B THE JUDGMENT OF OTHERS**

The halo effect describes the fact that people frequently extend their judgments of others in one area (e.g., physical attractiveness) to another area (e.g., intelligence). Experiments have documented this effect in many different contexts.

REFERENCES:
The halo effect
Beauty is talent

☐ **C OBEDIENCE TO AUTHORITY**

Obedience to authority experiments test the willingness of participants to inflict unpleasant or painful stimuli on other people when ordered to do so by someone in authority.

REFERENCES:
Milgram experiment
Shock the puppy experiment

☐ **D** ______________________

____
____
____
____
____
____

 ANALYZE

2 Use the references given to search online for two (or more) studies on your topic. Collect information about them in the chart.

	study 1	study 2
goal: What was the research question?		
participants: How were they chosen?		
study description: What were the participants asked to do?		
results: What did the study show?		
conclusions: What did the researcher(s) conclude from the results?		

EVALUATE

3 With your group, discuss the studies you have found. Answer the questions.

1 In what ways are the studies the same? In what ways are they different?
2 Does each study confirm, expand on, or conflict with the findings of the other(s)?

CREATE

4 Use the information in the table from Exercise 2 to synthesize the studies. Write notes for your presentation.

1 Why were these research studies conducted? What important questions do they address or answer?

The chameleon effect describes our tendency to mimic the gestures and body position of the person we are talking to. Both studies addressed different aspects of this phenomenon. The first study focused on facial expressions, whereas the second looked at hand movement.

2 What are the areas of overlap, similarity, or contrast?

Both of Maguire's studies used MRIs to investigate the impact of navigation strategies on the brain. Maguire's first study found a relationship between spatial navigation and larger hippocampi, but she could not conclude which was the cause and which was the effect. By controlling for the size of participants' hippocampi in the second study, she was able to provide stronger support for the claim that spatial navigation leads to a larger hippocampus.

3 Is it possible to conclude anything from the two sets of results?

There is a strong, possibly causal connection between the constant creation of mental maps and the size of the hippocampus.

PREPARATION FOR SPEAKING

TALKING ABOUT RESEARCH

SKILLS

Research presentations generally follow the same format as research papers:

- introduction
- research questions
- methods and participants
- results
- conclusions

Presenters prepare their talking points on these elements and refer to them as they speak; they do not write out whole sentences. You should never read a research presentation.

1 Follow this informal outline to prepare your talking points.

PRISM Digital Workbook

I. Explain the question(s) that the studies were investigating.
II. Explain why the question is important:
  A. Give an example of the question in a broader context.
  B. Explain how it could be relevant to your listeners.
III. Make a statement that brings together the two studies.
  Both studies examine __________ ; however, they took very different approaches.
IV. Explain briefly and concisely what happened in each study: How was the experiment set up? What did the participants do? How was their behavior measured?
V. Give a brief description of the results of the two studies.
VI. Compare the results of the two studies.
  Thus, both studies established the fact that ...
  The two studies present conflicting results ...
VII. Draw a conclusion or speculate about future possibilities.

INCORPORATING VISUAL SUPPORT

SKILLS

Most formal presentations include slides to provide visual support for what the speaker is saying.

Do …

✔ use just one type of background on all slides.

✔ include only the most important information.

Don't …

✘ use too many colors or complicated graphics.

✘ have too much information on each slide.

Effective presenters don't read their slides aloud. They face their audience and speak, referring to the talking points in their notes, and let the audience read the slides as they listen.

PRISM Digital Workbook

2 Create the slides that will accompany your talking points from Exercise 1. Be sure that the information on a slide relates closely to its talking point but does not duplicate it. Add notes to yourself about pausing or changing slides, if needed.

talking points	slides

SPEAKING TASK

PRISM Digital Workbook

Give a group presentation about research on some aspect of human behavior. Support your presentation with slides.

PREPARE

1 Assign roles for your presentation. Who will …

- introduce the presentation and the central question of the research?
- report on the first study?
- report on the second study?
- bring the results of the two studies together and offer a conclusion?

2 Review your talking points and slides.

3 Refer to the Task Checklist as you prepare for your presentation.

TASK CHECKLIST	✔
Synthesize the important points of two studies.	
Discuss points of similarity and contrast.	
Follow the formal format for presentation of a research study.	
Support your talking points with well-crafted slides.	
Add emphasis to the focus words in sentences.	

PRACTICE

4 Take turns presenting your parts of the presentation within your group. Give your teammates feedback and consider the feedback they give you. Revise your notes and slides as needed. Think about these things.

- Be enthusiastic.
- Don't speak too quickly. Take the time to say each word clearly. Some of the information you are providing is technical and will be new to your listeners.
- Don't read your presentation. Refer to your talking points and notes, but keep your head up and direct your presentation to the audience.
- Anticipate questions. What will you do if people raise their hands to ask questions while you are speaking? What will you do if you don't know the answer?
- Observe time limits. Find out how long the full presentation is allowed to be and make sure that your presentation does not run too long. Revise or trim parts if needed.

PRESENT

5 Give your presentation.

REFLECT

6 As a class, discuss these questions.

1 Which presentation was the most interesting? Give reasons for your answer.
2 How well did you present your part of the presentation?
3 What could you do better next time?

ON CAMPUS

STAYING MOTIVATED

PREPARING TO LISTEN

1 Take the quiz about your general motivation level for different tasks. For each task, circle a number from 1 (highly motivated) to 5 (not at all motivated).

a doing homework	1	2	3	4	5
b doing research	1	2	3	4	5
c going to class	1	2	3	4	5
d reading assigned material	1	2	3	4	5
e starting work on a paper	1	2	3	4	5
f studying for a test	1	2	3	4	5

2 Compare your results with a partner. Discuss the questions.

1 Why do you think you are motivated to do some tasks but not others? What factors affect your motivation?
2 When is your motivation weakest, at the start of a task, in the middle, or at the end?
3 Do you have any tricks to start or keep yourself motivated?

WHILE LISTENING

3 ▶ **5.5** Listen to the lecture. Complete the definitions, using your own words.

1 Intrinsic motivation: ____________________
2 Extrinsic motivation: ____________________

4 ▶ **5.5** Listen again. Check (✔) the statements that can be inferred from the information in the lecture.

1 If a student is not motivated, he/she may drop out. ☐
2 Intrinsic motivation is a common trait among artistic and creative people. ☐
3 Liking what you do is necessary for future job success. ☐
4 Intrinsic motivation is a constant force. ☐
5 Extrinsic motivators, like making a lot of money, are not as strong as intrinsic motivators. ☐
6 If you don't have a clear idea of what motivates you, school or work can be more of a struggle. ☐

5 Work with a partner. Discuss the questions.

1 Would you say that you are intrinsically motivated? Do you know people who definitely are? Describe them.
2 What do you think motivates most college students?

PRACTICE

Ways to stay motivated:

- Remind yourself of your goals and of what you have accomplished.
- Get support from others.
- Reward yourself for your hard work.

6 Match the pieces of advice to the specific examples.

1 Focus on your final goals. ______
2 Visualize your future after the task is done. ______
3 Get support from family, friends, and teachers. ______
4 Be proud of what you have already accomplished. ______
5 Think about the people in your life that are counting on you. ______
6 Reward yourself for your hard work. ______

a I ask my family to leave me alone while I study.
b I look at job opportunities in my field and think about which jobs I'll apply for.
c I study for three hours, and then I take a coffee break.
d I keep a picture of my grandmother on my desk. She wasn't able to go to college.
e I write a to-do list and cross off the jobs that I've done.
f I write a list of the reasons why I am in college.

7 Think of another example for each piece of advice (1–6).

REAL-WORLD APPLICATION

8 Answer the questions. Then, work in small groups to discuss your answers.

1 What is your ultimate goal? ______________________________
2 What have you accomplished towards this goal so far? ______________________________
____
3 Who supports you in this goal? ______________________________
4 How do you reward yourself? ______________________________
5 What motivates you the most? (Family? Grades? Getting a good job?)
____
6 How can you help yourself stay motivated in the future?
____

LEARNING OBJECTIVES	
Listening skills	Listen for pros and cons; make inferences
Pronunciation	Reduction of auxiliary verbs
Speaking skill	Prepare for a job interview
Speaking Task	Participate in a mock job interview
On Campus	Prepare for tests

UNIT 6
CAREERS

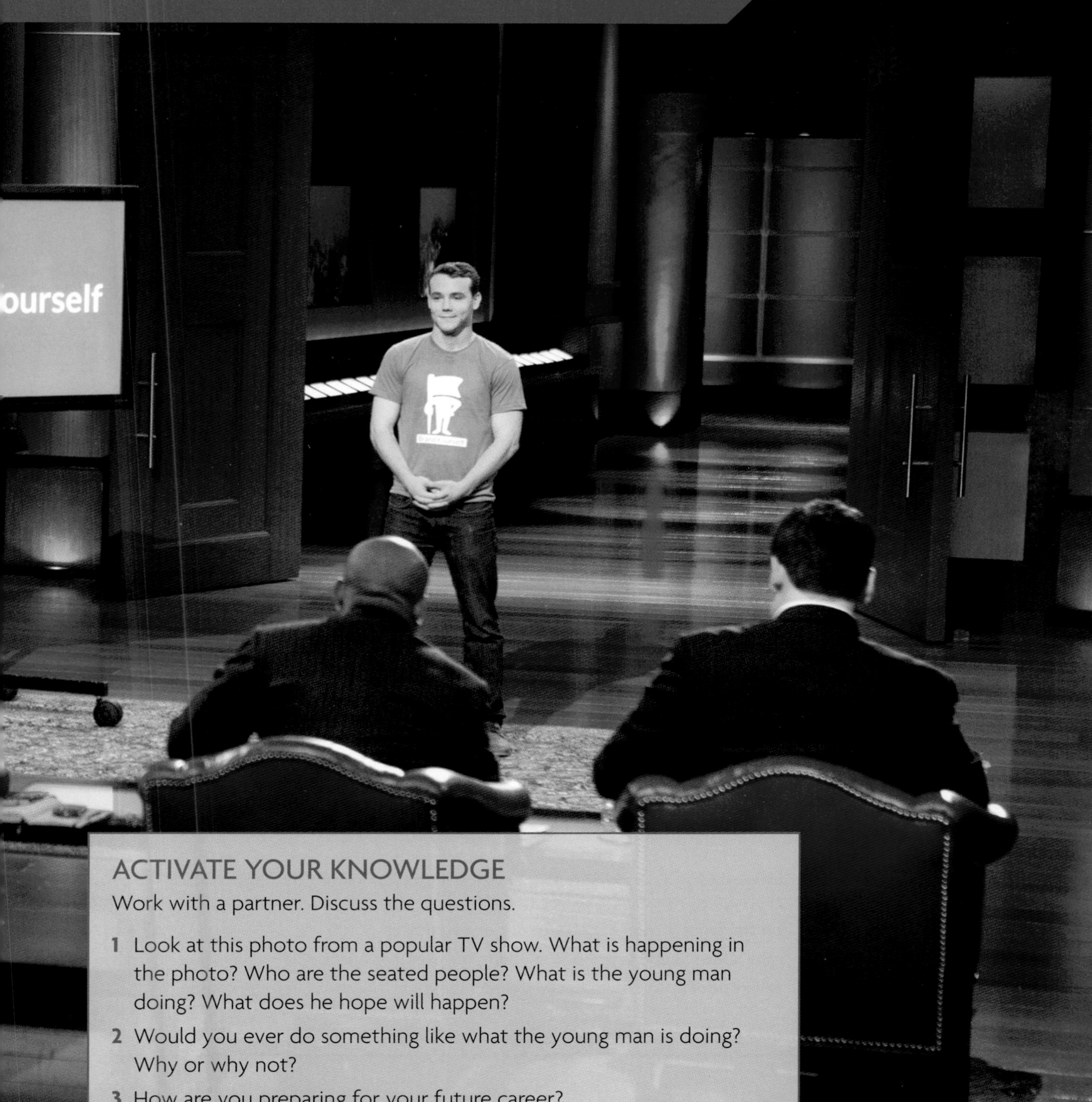

ACTIVATE YOUR KNOWLEDGE

Work with a partner. Discuss the questions.

1 Look at this photo from a popular TV show. What is happening in the photo? Who are the seated people? What is the young man doing? What does he hope will happen?

2 Would you ever do something like what the young man is doing? Why or why not?

3 How are you preparing for your future career?

WATCH AND LISTEN

PREPARING TO WATCH

ACTIVATING YOUR KNOWLEDGE

1 Work with a partner. Discuss the questions.

1 Should both parents in a family have jobs, or is it better for one parent to stay home with the children? Why?
2 What are the difficulties of returning to work or school after a long absence?
3 Why might some parents want to return to the workplace after raising a family?
4 What benefits do you think these parents could bring to the workplace?

PREDICTING CONTENT USING VISUALS

2 Look at the pictures from the video. Discuss the questions with your partner.

1 What do you think the woman in the first picture is doing?
2 What kind of job do you think the woman has?
3 Who do you think takes care of the children when the woman is working?
4 What do you think the statistic in the fourth picture refers to?

GLOSSARY

resolution (n) a promise to yourself to do something, often made at the start of a new year

internship (n) a period of time spent receiving or completing training at a job as a part of becoming qualified to do it

on the fence (idiom) not able to decide something

take a leap (v phr) to go for something; to take one's chances

talent pool (n phr) the suitable, skilled people who are available to be chosen to do a particular type of job

untapped (adj) not yet used or taken advantage of

WHILE WATCHING

UNDERSTANDING MAIN IDEAS

3 ▶ Watch the video. Circle the correct answer.

1 Which statement best summarizes the main idea of the video?
   a The financial and insurance industry needed Julie.
   b There are programs that are helping women return to the workforce and redevelop their skills.
   c While many women don't want to return to the workforce, it is a benefit for them and the companies that employ them.

2 Which statement best describes how Julie felt when the opportunity came up at Credit Suisse?
   a She was interested but unsure.
   b She definitely wanted to take advantage of the opportunity.
   c She couldn't imagine leaving her family.

3 Which statement best describes how Julie felt after getting back into the workforce?
   a She was happy but exhausted.
   b She regretted leaving her family.
   c She felt revitalized.

UNDERSTANDING DETAILS

4 ▶ Watch again. Complete the paragraph with the missing details.

Julie Haim has returned to the workplace after (1)____________________ years. She is taking part in an internship program in (2)____________________, 900 miles away from her home. The (3)____________________ at Credit Suisse and other banks helps women return to the workforce. Julie's (4)____________________ encouraged her to take the leap. Women are leaving the (5)____________________ and insurance industries. Only (6)____________________ of CEOs in Fortune 1000 companies are women.

MAKING INFERENCES

5 Work with a partner. Discuss the questions.

1 Why do you think Julie was unsure about taking the position in New York?
2 What responsibilities do you think have changed at home as a result of Julie working in New York?
3 Why do you think so many women left jobs in the financial and insurance industries between 2002 and 2012?
4 Why do you think there are so few female CEOs?

DISCUSSION

6 Work with a partner. Discuss the questions.

1 How far would you travel from your family for an opportunity like Julie's?
2 What are the benefits of an internship?
3 In what other ways can you prepare for your career?
4 Who do you consult or have you consulted for advice about your career?

LISTENING

LISTENING 1

PREPARING TO LISTEN

USING YOUR KNOWLEDGE

1 You are going to listen to a presentation from a career counselor about different ways to enter the work world. Before you listen, work in small groups. Would you rather work for a large business or work for yourself? What are the pros and cons of each? Compare your chart with other groups' charts.

	pros	cons
work for a large business		
be your own boss		

2 With your group, study this pie chart. Then answer the questions.

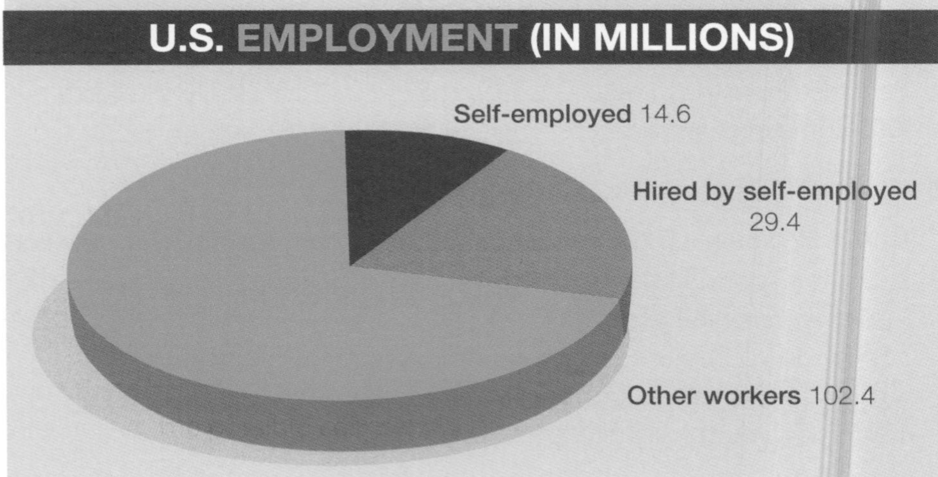

Source: Pew Research, 2015

1 What does the chart show?
2 What kinds of jobs do you think the self-employed workers have?
3 Do you think most of the self-employed people are *entrepreneurs*, that is, people who start an often risky business based on a new idea?
4 What kind of work do you think has the largest percentage of self-employed workers? (Listen for the answer in the presentation.)

UNDERSTANDING KEY VOCABULARY

3 Read the sentences and write the words in bold next to the definitions.

1 These are two **distinct** ideas and should not be confused.
2 I hope Sandra is available to help. I don't want to **get stuck with** doing all the work for this party.
3 Working as a volunteer can be a very **rewarding** experience. You really feel as if you are making a difference.
4 When I moved to Chicago, I had to buy a whole new winter **wardrobe**. My clothes were all wrong for this cold, windy weather.
5 We want a leader who can provide a **vision** for our future as a nation.
6 I would like to start my own catering company, but it is pretty **daunting**. I hear that the failure rate is more than 50%.
7 If you feel you have been a victim of harassment or **discrimination**, you should report it to our office at once.
8 When I first opened my business, I really had to **hustle** to get customers. Now I have a good following and lots of repeat business.

a __________ (v) to work in an energetic way
b __________ (adj) making you feel less confident; frightening
c __________ (n) unfair treatment, especially based on sex, ethnic origin, age, or religion
d __________ (adj) giving a feeling of satisfaction
e __________ (n) a clear idea about what should happen or be done in the future
f __________ (adj) clearly separate and different
g __________ (n) all the clothes that a person owns, or a set of those clothes specific to one time or purpose
h __________ (phr v) to be forced to take responsibility for something or someone unpleasant

WHILE LISTENING

LISTENING FOR MAIN IDEAS

4 ▶ 6.1 Listen to the presentation and take notes. Then use your notes to answer these questions.

1 What is the purpose of the presentation?

____

2 Who is the audience for the presentation?

____

3 What are the three options that the career counselor discusses?

____
____
____

TAKING NOTES ON DETAILS

PRISM Digital Workbook

5 ▶ 6.1 Listen again. Complete the table.

	pros	cons
work for a company		
work as a freelancer		
establish your own start-up		

POST-LISTENING

6 Work with a partner. Compare your tables from Exercise 5. Then compare those tables to the ones you made before you listened. Did any of the new pros or cons in the presentation surprise you? Why or why not?

SKILLS

Making inferences

Sometimes speakers do not say everything they mean. Use logic as well as your own knowledge to infer the speaker's intended meaning.

7 ▶ 6.2 Listen to the excerpts from the presentation. Use logic and your own knowledge to infer the speaker's meaning.

1 a Other graduates don't need this kind of assistance.
  b There is a lot of demand for computer science graduates.
  c Computer scientists need more guidance than other graduates.

2 a Undergraduates are unlikely to choose this option.
  b Start-up companies are the best career option for those with advanced degrees.
  c This option has the most problems.

3 a You will not experience these problems.
  b If you do experiences these problems, you have protection.
  c You may experience these problems anyway.

4 a This is a problem.
  b This is an advantage.
  c This is legally required.

5 a The speaker thinks the answer is obvious – the second.
b The speaker wants to know what the students in the audience think.
c The speaker is testing the students' knowledge of the job market.

6 a Be sure that you and your friends agree about everything before you begin.
b It's probably a bad idea to go into business with friends.
c Don't let your start-up destroy your friendship.

PRONUNCIATION FOR LISTENING

Reduction of auxiliary verbs

Reductions are unstressed words that are spoken quickly and linked to surrounding words. The vowel is often pronounced as a schwa, /ə/. Common reductions include auxiliary verbs such as *do, have, can, could, should, will,* and *would*. Other reduced forms include *going to*, which sounds like "gonna," and *want to,* which sounds like "wanna."

You can immediately start using the skills and knowledge you have gained in your studies.

Reduced words are not always essential to understanding the meaning of a sentence, but it is important to pay attention to them to understand the finer points of meaning, especially with modal verbs.

8 6.3 Listen to the sentences. Write the missing reductions.

PRISM Digital Workbook

1 Keep in mind that some of the legal issues and government regulations that we're ___________ discuss may not apply to you.
2 You can immediately start using the skills and knowledge you ___________ gained in your studies. However, you ___________ also consider the option of using those skills without joining a company.
3 This is what I meant earlier when I said our topic ___________ be the U.S. market.
4 I don't ______________________ scare you, but, as in the case of consultants, you are your own boss.
5 You ___________ engage in some self-reflection.
6 You ___________ take credit for all aspects of that success, and that ___________ be incredibly rewarding.
7 I ___________ emphasize how stressful starting a new company can be.

9 Work with a partner. Take turns saying the sentences in Exercise 8 aloud. Use reductions of auxiliary verbs.

DISCUSSION

SUMMARIZING

10 Work in small groups. Study the graphs about start-ups and freelancers. Then discuss the questions below.

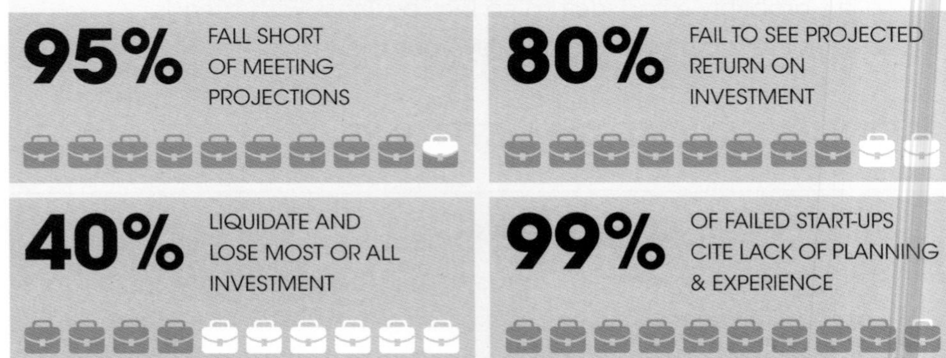

Sources: Harvard Business School, University of Tennessee Research, StatisticBrain.com, and others

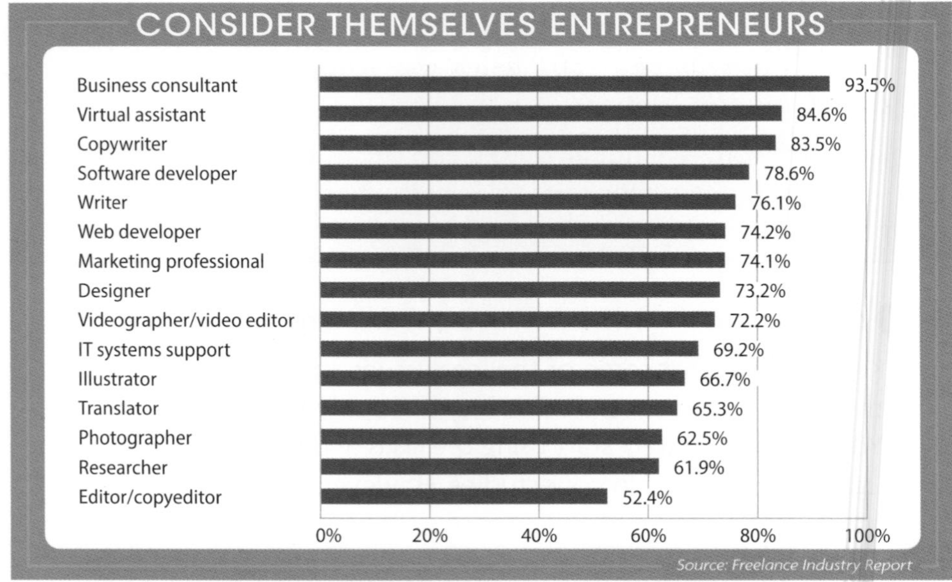

Source: Freelance Industry Report

1 What do the two graphs show? Summarize each of them.
2 Considering the high rate of failure for start-ups, what do you think drives people to keep opening them?
3 Why do you think that entrepreneurs are so optimistic when the odds are clearly against them?
4 How does the information in the second graph relate to the information in the first graph?

11 With your group, discuss these questions. Give reasons for your answers.

1 What career advice would you give a recent undergraduate in computer science?
2 What career advice would you give someone graduating with an advanced degree in computer science?

LANGUAGE DEVELOPMENT

LANGUAGE

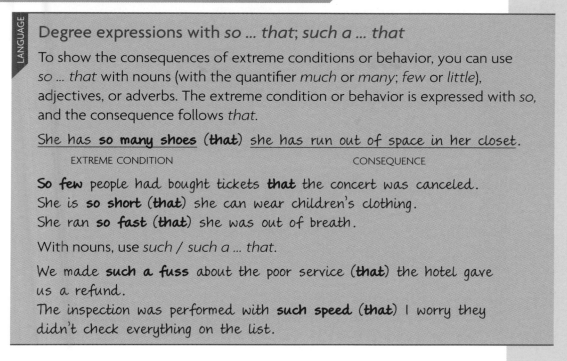

Degree expressions with *so … that; such a … that*

To show the consequences of extreme conditions or behavior, you can use *so … that* with nouns (with the quantifier *much* or *many*; *few* or *little*), adjectives, or adverbs. The extreme condition or behavior is expressed with *so*, and the consequence follows *that*.

She has **so many shoes** (**that**) she has run out of space in her closet.

EXTREME CONDITION — CONSEQUENCE

So few people had bought tickets **that** the concert was canceled.
She is **so short** (**that**) she can wear children's clothing.
She ran **so fast** (**that**) she was out of breath.

With nouns, use *such / such a … that*.

We made **such a fuss** about the poor service (**that**) the hotel gave us a refund.
The inspection was performed with **such speed** (**that**) I worry they didn't check everything on the list.

1 Combine the information in the two sentences to create a new sentence with the degree expression *so … that* or *such (a) … that*.

PRISM Digital Workbook

1 The ocean current can break large rocks. The current is very strong.

____

2 She cannot get out of bed. She doesn't have very much energy.

____

3 Everyone asks for her advice about flowers. She has a very beautiful garden.

____

4 He had to buy another suitcase. He bought a lot of stuff on vacation.

____

5 No one can hear the sound. The volume is very low.

____

6 I made a quick decision. I didn't have much time.

____

2 Write four new sentences, two with *so … that* and two with *such (a) … that*.

1 ______________________________
2 ______________________________
3 ______________________________
4 ______________________________

LANGUAGE

Emphatic expressions

These are common expressions to show emphasis, especially in spoken English:

by all means	*make no mistake*	*it goes without saying*
believe me	*to be sure*	*without a doubt*

These expressions usually precede the statement that the speaker wishes to emphasize; however, they may stand alone after the speaker has already made an argument.

Make no mistake, not every computer science graduate is going to become a millionaire.
Technology skills are highly valued in today's labor market. That goes without saying.

These expressions are also commonly used to give strong advice.

By all means, you should weigh all of your options before making a decision.

PRISM Digital Workbook

3 Work with a partner. Make three strong statements or offers of advice about the job market using emphatic expressions. Did you use the expressions correctly?

1 ______________________________
2 ______________________________
3 ______________________________

LISTENING 2

PREPARING TO LISTEN

UNDERSTANDING KEY VOCABULARY

PRISM Digital Workbook

1 Read the sentences and choose the best definition for the words in bold.

1 Of course, my most **dreaded** exam is on the last day of finals. I'll be a nervous wreck by then!
   a unwelcome because of being unpleasant
   b difficult because of being confusing
   c scary because of being mysterious
2 We're getting too emotional about this. We need to take a more **analytical** approach to the problem.
   a creative and expressive
   b critical and negative
   c careful and systematic
3 The teacher requires a specific **format** for the list of references at the end of the paper.
   a font
   b level of detail
   c layout and organization

4 After she carefully explained the lab experiment twice, our teacher **reiterated** the importance of going slowly, for safety reasons.
   a insisted on
   b repeated
   c listed
5 One of the mayor's most important **accomplishments** has been increasing the number of green spaces in the city.
   a something done successfully
   b something that has been promised but not achieved
   c something cited as a goal for a project
6 The speaker **rambled** for half an hour and never got to the point.
   a spoke in a confused way
   b spoke in a boring manner
   c spoke in a loud and angry manner
7 The new park is the result of a **collaboration**. The city, the state, and private businesses all helped to build it.
   a donation
   b a long time and a lot of work
   c cooperative effort
8 The teacher didn't believe his story about missing the test because of a car accident. It all sounded too **rehearsed** and insincere.
   a practiced and unnatural
   b emotional and dramatic
   c suspicious and intriguing

USING YOUR KNOWLEDGE

2 You are going to listen to a workshop about job interview skills. Before you listen, work in small groups. Discuss the questions.

1 Have you had a job interview? If so, what was it like? If not, what do you imagine it would be like?
2 How would you prepare for an interview?
3 How can you make a good first impression at a job interview?

3 Write five questions that you think are likely to be asked at a job interview.

1 ______________________________ ☐
2 ______________________________ ☐
3 ______________________________ ☐
4 ______________________________ ☐
5 ______________________________ ☐

WHILE LISTENING

4 ▶ 6.4 Listen to the workshop and take notes. Then check (✔) which of your ideas in Exercise 3 are mentioned.

LISTENING FOR MAIN IDEAS

5 Answer the questions.

1 What is the main theme of the presentation?

____

2 What is the counselor's most important advice?

____

LISTENING FOR DETAILS

6 ▶ 6.4 Review your notes and answer the questions. Listen again to check your answers or find missing information.

1 What three things should you do to prepare for a job interview?

____

____

____

2 What topics should you expect questions about?

______________ ______________

______________ ______________

3 How should you respond to a question about weaknesses?

____

4 What kind of advice does the counselor give about answering questions in general?

____

____

____

5 What should you do after the interview?

____

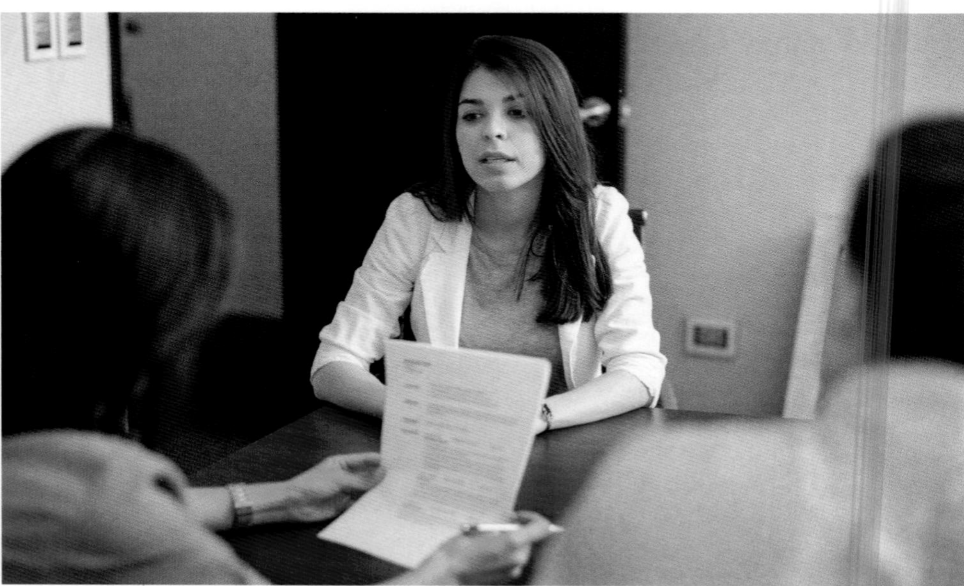

POST-LISTENING

MAKING INFERENCES

7 6.5 Listen to the excerpts from the workshop. What information can you infer from each of the speaker's statements? Circle your answer.

1 a There is no need to do research on anyone in human resources.
  b You should find out as much as you can about anyone you are interviewing with.
  c Interviewers from human resources are more likely to ask you difficult questions.

2 a Don't memorize your answers.
  b Just write out a few answers.
  c Rehearse your answers.

3 a You should have each step of your career planned.
  b Your interviewer will want to hear that you expect to stay with the company for five or ten years.
  c You need to think about your whole career, not just this position.

4 a They will think that you are lying.
  b You may think it is an original idea, but it's not.
  c It's OK not to say anything at all.

5 a The person interviewing you won't have a lot of time.
  b Most interviewers prefer quiet candidates.
  c Inexperienced job candidates sometimes talk too much.

8 Look at this cartoon. What advice from the workshop does it relate to? Discuss your ideas with a partner.

"So, where do you see yourself in ten minutes?"

DISCUSSION

SYNTHESIZING

9 Work with a partner. Discuss the questions.

1 Do you think the counselor in Listening 2 is offering good advice? Why or why not?
2 Would you add anything else?
3 Would you prepare differently for an interview with a big company versus a small start-up? If so, how? If not, why not?

SPEAKING

CRITICAL THINKING

At the end of this unit, you are going to do the Speaking Task below.

Participate in a mock job interview as an interviewer and/or as a job candidate.

SKILLS

Understanding job descriptions

A job description on a job search site usually starts with an introduction that gives information about the company, followed by two main sections:

Duties/Responsibilities: information about the available position

Skills required: information about the skills, experience, and traits that a successful candidate would need

1 Work in small groups. What kinds of information would you expect the different sections of a job description to include? Brainstorm ideas.

2 With your group, look at the two job ads shown here. Answer the questions.

1 What elements are common to both job advertisements?
2 What kind of language is used to describe duties and responsibilities (e.g., verbs, nouns)? To describe the skills required?
3 What information about a candidate is *not* included in the job ads?

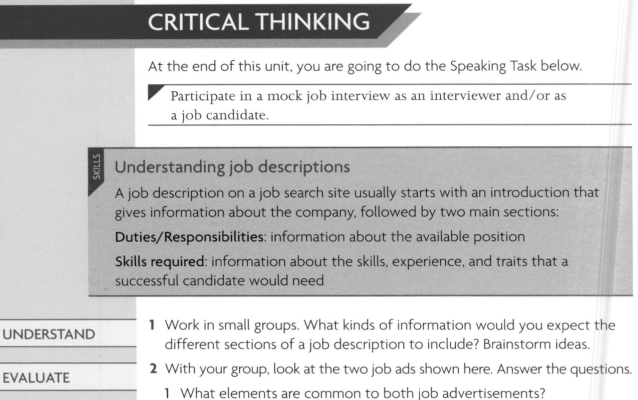

DATABASE MANAGER

JOB RESPONSIBILITIES:

Provides database applications by developing architecture, programming, troubleshooting, and security.

DUTIES:

- Maintains database results by setting and enforcing standards and controls.
- Prepares for database expansion by studying plans and requirements.
- Upgrades hardware and software by assessing processing and database options.
- Maintains database performance by troubleshooting problems.
- Makes upgrades and improvements by supervising system programming.
- Keeps database secure by developing appropriate policies, procedures, and controls.

SKILLS AND QUALIFICATIONS:

Minimum qualifications: BA and five years of experience in related area

MARKETING MANAGER

JOB DESCRIPTION:
Markets products by developing and carrying out marketing and advertising campaigns, tracking sales data, maintaining promotional materials inventory, planning meetings and trade shows, maintaining databases, preparing reports.

JOB RESPONSIBILITIES:
- Carries out marketing and advertising campaigns by assembling and analyzing sales forecasts; preparing marketing and advertising strategies, plans, and objectives; planning and organizing promotional presentations.
- Prepares marketing reports by collecting, analyzing, and summarizing sales data.
- Keeps promotional materials ready by coordinating requirements with graphics department; tracking inventory; placing orders; verifying delivery.
- Supports sales staff by providing sales data, market trends, forecasts, account analyses, new product information; relaying customer services requests.
- Researches competitive products by identifying and evaluating product characteristics, market share, pricing, and advertising; maintaining research databases.
- Monitors budgets by comparing and analyzing actual results with plans and forecasts.

SKILLS REQUIRED:
- Excellent understanding of traditional and emerging marketing methods
- Superior communication skills
- Ability to think creatively and innovatively
- Budget-management skills
- Professional judgment and discretion
- Analytical skills to forecast and identify trends, opportunities, and challenges
- Familiarity with the most recent technology in graphic design, web design, production, etc.

EDUCATION AND EXPERIENCE:
Minimum qualification: BA in business administration or related field; MBA preferred. Five years of management experience.

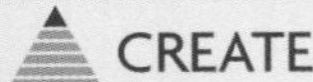 CREATE

3 What kind of job do you have or would you like to have? Work with a group of classmates who have similar interests to write a complete job advertisement.

Job title: ____________________

Job description:

____

____

____

Duties/responsibilities:

- ____________________
- ____________________
- ____________________
- ____________________
- ____________________
- ____________________

Required skills:

- ____________________
- ____________________
- ____________________
- ____________________
- ____________________
- ____________________

Education/experience:

____

____

____

4 Exchange your job advertisement from Exercise 3 with another group. Is there anything in their ad that you would like to include in yours? If so, make revisions to your ad.

5 Imagine you are interviewing candidates for the position in your job ad. What questions would you definitely ask?

1 ____________________
2 ____________________
3 ____________________
4 ____________________
5 ____________________

PREPARATION FOR SPEAKING

BODY LANGUAGE

Body language is an important aspect of communication. It refers to how we position and move our bodies, as well as facial expressions and how and where our eyes focus. Having positive body language is important in a job interview.

Do ...

✔ sit or stand with your back straight and your shoulders back, to show confidence.
✔ shake hands firmly, to show confidence and maturity.
✔ lean forward slightly, to show interest and enthusiasm.
✔ make eye contact, to indicate you are engaged. It also conveys openness and honesty.
✔ smile! It suggests that you feel at ease and are happy to be there.

Don't ...

✘ cross your arms, as this signals resistance or defensiveness.
✘ hold your arms behind your back, as this indicates nervousness.
✘ fidget or touch your face, as this conveys nervousness and anxiety.

1 Work with a partner. Decide whether each photo shows positive or negative body language. Discuss your reasoning.

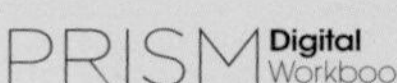

positive ☐ negative ☐

b

positive ☐ negative ☐

positive ☐ negative ☐

positive ☐ negative ☐

PREPARING FOR A JOB INTERVIEW

2 Each person will interview a candidate from another group and/or be interviewed by a person from another group. Complete the tasks for both groups: interviewers and interviewees.

Student A: As the interviewer

1 Finalize your questions from Critical Thinking, Exercise 5.
2 Think about how you will begin the interview: introductions, etc.
3 Think about how you will end the interview.

Student B: As the interviewee

1 Exchange job advertisements with another group.
2 Prepare the talking points you want to be sure to mention in your interview.
3 Brainstorm the kinds of questions you think you will be asked.
4 Prepare responses to possible questions. (You can make notes, but remember that you will not be able to look at them during the interview.)
   - How would you answer the accomplishments question?
   - How would you answer the weakness question?
5 Prepare a few questions to ask the interviewer.

SPEAKING TASK

PRISM Digital Workbook

Participate in a mock job interview as an interviewer and/or as a job candidate.

PREPARE

1 Review your notes regarding the questions you will ask as the interviewer (see Critical Thinking, Exercise 5) and also the questions you anticipate as a candidate and the answers you have prepared (see Preparation for Speaking, Exercise 2).

2 Each person will act as an interviewer and/or an interviewee. Decide on roles for your mock interview. (If you are not an interviewer or candidate, you will observe the interview process. Be prepared to take notes and give feedback.)

PRACTICE

3 Review the information on body language in Preparation for Speaking. Practice your initial greeting with someone in your group and then sit down. Give each other feedback.

- How was your handshake?
- Did you make eye contact?
- Does your posture indicate interest and enthusiasm?

4 Refer to the Task Checklist as you prepare for your interview(s).

TASK CHECKLIST	✔
Read the job advertisement carefully to plan and/or anticipate questions.	
Make a good impression with your initial greeting and body language.	
Ask and answer questions appropriately.	
Maintain positive body language throughout the interview.	
If needed, take a moment to think about the question and formulate an answer before you start speaking.	
End the interview on a positive note.	

DISCUSS

5 Conduct your interviews.

REFLECT

6 In small groups or as a class, discuss these questions.

1. Which interview was the most successful? Why do you think so?
2. How well did you think you did as an interviewer? How did you do as a job candidate?
3. What could you do better next time?

ON CAMPUS

PREPARING FOR TESTS

PREPARING TO LISTEN

1 Work with a partner. Discuss the questions.

1 What is the most important test that you have taken?
2 Are you usually well prepared for tests? Why or why not?
3 What advice would you give a student to help him or her prepare for a test?

WHILE LISTENING

2 ▶ 6.6 You are going to listen to Chiyu, Javier, and Sarah describing their strategies for test preparation. Listen and match the speakers with their main ideas.

1 Chiyu
2 Javier
3 Sarah

a Studying for the test
b Taking the test
c Predicting the content of the test

3 ▶ 6.6 Listen again and complete the summaries. Use your own words.

1 Chiyu uses summarizing, idea maps, and flashcards as a way to ______________________

2 Javier always pays attention to ______________________

3 Sarah has learned that ______________________

4 Work with a partner and compare your answers. Have you ever used any of these strategies? Describe your experiences.

PRACTICE

Ways to prepare for tests:

- Know as much as possible about the test: how it is organized and what it will cover.
- Review the material thoroughly.
- Use strategies during the test to maximize your performance.

5 Read the test preparation strategies. What is the purpose of each one? Write *A*, *B*, or *C*.

A knowing about the test
B reviewing material for the test
C maximizing performance during the test

1 If possible, look at previous tests. _____
2 Get a good night's sleep before the test. _____
3 Make a study plan a few weeks in advance. _____
4 Study with other students. _____
5 Find out what materials are allowed during the test. _____
6 Review your notes regularly throughout the semester. _____
7 Read and listen carefully to the directions before you start. _____
8 Check your answers before you hand in the paper. _____
9 Teach the material to someone else. _____
10 Make sure you understand key words like *define, analyze, evaluate, illustrate*. _____
11 Don't spend too long on any one section of the test. _____
12 Make flashcards to review key terms. _____

REAL-WORLD APPLICATION

6 Work in small groups of four or six. Divide the strategies in Exercise 5 among the group members (three each for a group of four, two each for a group of six). For each of your strategies, make notes to answer the questions.

1 Why is this a good strategy? How does it help?

____

2 Have you ever used this strategy? What was the result?

____

3 If you haven't used the strategy, when could you use it?

____

4 What can happen if you do not use the strategy?

____

7 Present your strategies to your group. Then decide as a group which three strategies are the most useful. Present your ideas to the class. If there is disagreement, make a case for each of your choices.

LEARNING OBJECTIVES

Listening skills	Take unstructured notes as you listen; identify persuasive appeals
Pronunciation	Contrastive stress; emphasis for emotional appeal
Speaking skill	Inclusive language
Speaking Task	Participate in a community meeting about a local environmental health crisis
On Campus	Seeking medical treatment

HEALTH SCIENCES

UNIT 7

ACTIVATE YOUR KNOWLEDGE

Work with a partner. Discuss the questions.

1 Look at the picture. How does this image relate to the topic of health?

2 What other environmental factors can cause health problems? Give examples.

3 How are environmental health conditions different from other health issues or conditions?

WATCH AND LISTEN

PREPARING TO WATCH

ACTIVATING YOUR KNOWLEDGE

1 Work with a partner. Discuss the questions.

1 Where does your city's drinking water come from?
2 In what kinds of communities are people most likely to be concerned about the safety of their food and drinking water?
3 How can food or water become contaminated?
4 What should governments do to protect the food and water their citizens consume?

PREDICTING CONTENT USING VISUALS

2 Look at the pictures from the video. Answer the questions.

1 What do you think the problem is?
2 How do you think this problem began?
3 Where do you think people get their drinking water from in this area?

GLOSSARY

contaminate (v) to make something less pure or make it poisonous

pose (v) to cause something, especially a problem or difficulty

reignite (v) to make something such as a disagreement or worry that was disappearing grow stronger

trump (v) to be better than; to have more importance or power than another thing

peril (n) danger; something that is dangerous

WHILE WATCHING

UNDERSTANDING MAIN IDEAS

3 Watch the video. Write *T* (true) or *F* (false) next to the statements. Correct the false statements.

_____ 1 After a chemical leak, the state of West Virginia tried to convince people that the water was safe to drink.
_____ 2 The effects of the chemical MCHM are known.
_____ 3 The former governor does not support legislation that requires regular inspections of chemical facilities.
_____ 4 Matilda has serious concerns about allowing her children to drink the water.

SUMMARIZING

4 Watch again. Fill in the blanks to complete the summary.

There was a chemical (1)__________ in West Virginia. It (2)__________ the water supply that supports 300,000 residents. State officials tried to convince the residents that the water was (3)__________ to drink; however, residents, like Matilda Murray, were uncertain of the water's safety. Many feel that the state is putting the interests of (4)__________ above their residents' health. The former governor (5)__________ legislation that would require regular (6)__________ of chemical storage facilities, preventing tragedies like this from happening again.

MAKING INFERENCES

5 Check (✔) the statements that can be inferred from the video. Explain your answers to a partner.

1 People became sick after drinking the contaminated water. ☐
2 The business responsible for the leak had to pay the costs of the environmental cleanup. ☐
3 Matilda Murray supports the new legislation. ☐
4 Regular inspections had not occurred prior to the chemical leak. ☐
5 If the law does not pass, similar accidents will likely occur in other states. ☐

DISCUSSION

6 Work with a partner. Discuss the questions.

1 Do you think that the business interests of the coal companies outweigh the environmental concerns in West Virginia? Why or why not?
2 What could Matilda Murray and other residents do to voice their concerns?
3 Are you familiar with cases similar to this one? Describe the situation.
4 What other environmental disasters have posed serious risks to human health?

LISTENING

LISTENING 1

PREPARING TO LISTEN

USING YOUR KNOWLEDGE

1 You are going to listen to a talk about environmental health, specifically asthma. Before you listen, work with a partner to answer the questions. Look up any words you don't know.

1 Do you or anyone you know have *allergies* to something in the environment, such as dust, pets, certain kinds of plants? Describe the symptoms.
2 Do you or anyone you know have *asthma*? Describe the symptoms.

PREDICTING CONTENT USING VISUALS

2 Asthma symptoms are responses by the *immune system* to triggers in the environment. Which of these photos do you think show asthma triggers?

a ☐

b ☐

c ☐

d ☐

e ☐

f ☐

g ☐

h ☐

UNDERSTANDING KEY VOCABULARY

3 Read the definitions. Complete the sentences with the correct form of the words in bold.

correlation (n) a connection between two or more things **deprive** (v) to take away something important **disparity** (n) a lack of equality **disproportionately** (adv) unequally **hygiene** (n) cleanliness; keeping yourself and your environment clean **incidence** (n) the rate at which something happens **ironically** (adv) in a way that is the opposite of what is expected **proximity** (n) nearness

1 The __________ of infection by the Zika virus in South America has been rising since 2015.
2 It is illegal to __________ prisoners of war of food or sleep.
3 One advantage to this apartment is its __________ to public transportation.
4 There is a growing __________ between the life expectancies of the rich and the poor in this country.
5 __________, errors often lead to important scientific discoveries.
6 The prison population in the United States is __________ made up of people of color.
7 There is a significant __________ between educational achievement and health, but this does not mean that one is the cause of the other.
8 Poor __________ is a contributing factor to the spread of disease.

WHILE LISTENING

Taking unstructured notes as you listen

Taking notes in ordered lists, outlines, and tables can be effective, but it is not always possible to know in advance how a lecture or presentation will be organized. Even if speakers provide an outline or summary, they may not follow it exactly or may include other information in the moment.

For the listener taking notes, sometimes a looser organization is necessary and even preferable. Going back to these unstructured notes later allows you to see connections and relationships that you might not have recognized otherwise. Once you understand these connections, you can organize your notes into charts, tables, or mind maps.

LISTENING FOR MAIN IDEAS AND DETAILS

4 ▶ 7.1 Listen and take unstructured notes. Do not try to organize your notes in the moment. Leave space so that you can add details later.

5 7.1 Review your notes. Underline parts that you think may be main ideas. Circle parts that you are not sure of and want to listen to again. Then listen to the presentation again and add to your notes. Write down new things and add details to ideas that you wrote down the first time.

POST-LISTENING

6 Using your notes, fill in the mind map.

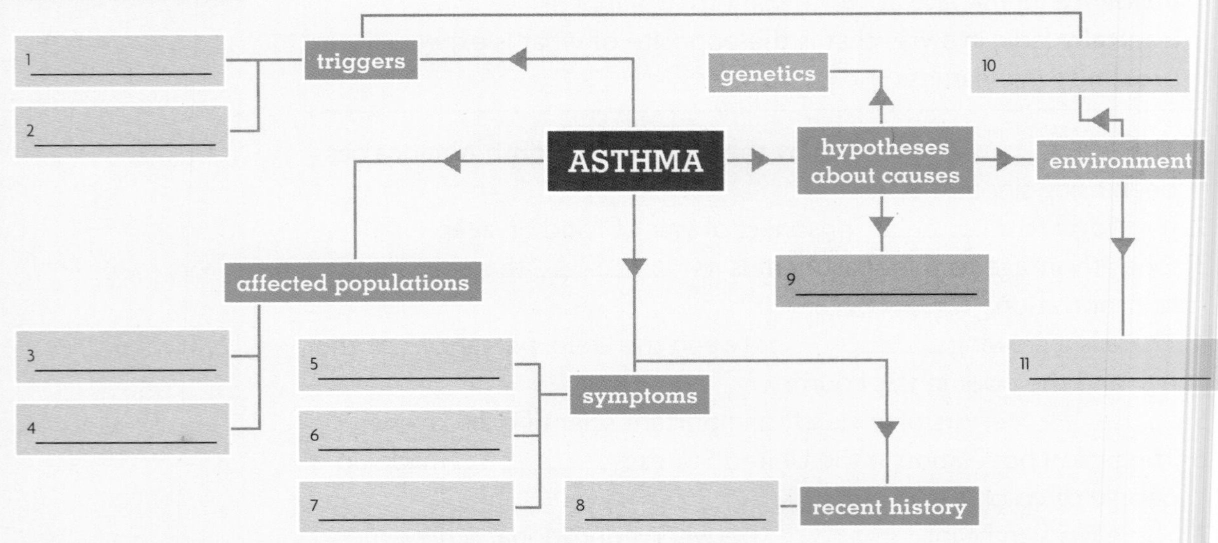

7 With a partner, discuss what the blue line means. What kind of connection does it describe? Mark other connections like this on the mind map.

8 7.2 Use your notes to create a separate mind map about the two main competing *environmental* hypotheses (on the right side of the mind map above). Add boxes for supporting details, examples, and counterexamples for each hypothesis. Then listen to that part of the presentation again to check your ideas.

ENVIRONMENTAL HYPOTHESES

SUMMARIZING

9 Work with a partner. Using your mind maps from Exercise 8, take turns summarizing one of the two hypotheses about the environmental causes of asthma. Give each other feedback.

PRONUNCIATION FOR LISTENING

Contrastive stress

Contrastive stress is the extra stress or emphasis that is placed on words to show contrast or difference. Listening for contrastive stress can help you understand when a speaker is comparing or contrasting ideas.

Indoor pollution includes dust, mold, tobacco smoke, pet hair, and various chemicals used for cleaning. Outdoor pollution includes particulate matter and ground-level ozone.

PRISM Digital Workbook

10 7.3 Listen to the sentences and write the contrasting information.

1 situation for some asthmatics: ______
situation for other asthmatics: ______
2 more common: ______
less common: ______
3 don't know: ______
do have: ______

11 7.4 Listen to the sentences and make note of what is being contrasted and the contrasting information.

1 ______
______
2 ______
______
3 ______
______

DISCUSSION

12 Work in small groups. Discuss the questions.

1 After having heard all of the evidence, what do you think is the most likely explanation for the recent increase in the incidence of asthma?
2 How does this pattern fit in with other health trends that seem to accompany "modern life," especially in the developed, industrialized world?
3 What steps should the government, health officials, and/or individuals take in order to arrest or reverse this trend?

LANGUAGE DEVELOPMENT

ESTABLISHING COHESION WITH *SO* AND *SUCH*

Cohesion refers to the use of grammatical structures and words to tie a text together, especially across sentences. There are many ways to establish cohesion. One way is to use the words *so* and *such* to link new information with ideas that came earlier in a text or conversation.

So

So is often used to avoid repeating a phrase. It is used with *be* or a modal or auxiliary verb, often *do*.

Smoke often triggers asthma attacks, and **so do** some foods.

(Some foods also trigger asthma attacks.)

The city has improved its air quality, and by **doing so**, it may have helped to reduce asthma rates.

(By improving its air quality, the city may have helped to reduce asthma rates.)

Such

Such can also be used to refer to previous information. It usually has the meaning "like the one(s) just mentioned."

Researchers are planning a study of asthma in three different cities. **Such a study** may provide the answers we are looking for.

(A study like the one just mentioned may provide answers.)

Initially, researchers thought that symptoms were related to hygiene in the home, but the study found **no such connection**.

(Researchers found no connection like the one just mentioned.)

1 In your notebook, combine the information given here to create new sentences using *so* or *such* for cohesion.

1 Asthma rates have risen dramatically. Allergy rates have risen dramatically.
2 Early remedies for asthma included warm milk and cool baths. Unfortunately, treatments like warm milk and cool baths do little to relieve the symptoms.
3 My aunt recently quit smoking. Quitting smoking may have reduced her chances of getting asthma, cancer, and other diseases.
4 Vigorous exercise contributes to asthma attacks. Ironically, a sedentary lifestyle also contributes to asthma attacks.
5 Some cities require monthly reports on water and air pollution. Unfortunately, my city does not have any requirement for monthly reports on water and air pollution.

2 Write three new sentences with *so* or *such* to show cohesion.

1 ____

____

2 ____

____

3 ____

____

ADJECTIVES OF STRONG DISAPPROVAL

The English language is rich with synonyms, especially when it comes to emotions.

Adjectives expressing how a person feels

Many of these adjectives are past participle forms of verbs. They often appear as passives with a *by* phrase.

aghast *appalled* *dismayed* *horrified* *outraged* *shocked*

We were **horrified** by the conditions in which the children were living.

Adjectives describing a situation or activity

These adjectives are sometimes related forms of the adjectives above.

appalling *atrocious* *deplorable* *dreadful* *outrageous* *shocking*

The conditions in which the children were living were **appalling**.

The words in each list overlap in meaning, but they are not exactly the same. Use a dictionary to help you understand some of the subtle differences between them.

3 Circle the correct adjective for each sentence.

PRISM Digital Workbook

1 We were *shocked / shocking* at the lead levels in the school's drinking water.

2 The food was bad but the service was *aghast / atrocious*. I'll never go to that restaurant again!

3 The inspectors were *appalled / appalling* at the filthy kitchen.

4 It was *outraged / outrageous* that the situation had been going on for so long.

5 The doctors were *dismayed / dreadful* that the medicine suddenly stopped working.

6 After all day in the hot sun, she has a *dreadful / horrified* headache.

7 When the full story was made public, I was *aghast / deplorable*. How could such a thing happen in our little town?

4 Write three statements that express strong disapproval of something in your own life or experience. Read them with a partner. Did you both use the correct adjectives and the correct form?

LISTENING 2

PREPARING TO LISTEN

PREDICTING CONTENT USING VISUALS

1 You are going to listen to a moderated community meeting about water quality. Work with a partner. Answer the questions.

1 What do these images show?
2 What do you know about the safety of your drinking water? Who ensures its safety?
3 What problems can unsafe drinking water cause?

UNDERSTANDING KEY VOCABULARY

PRISM Digital Workbook

2 Read the sentences and choose the best definition for the words in bold.

1 Exposure to some drugs can **compromise** your immune system and lead to chronic illness.
a harm b decrease c elevate

2 Doctors found a high **concentration** of dangerous chemicals in the patient's blood.
a damage b amount c increase

3 Clearly, the students who failed the test had made **minimal** effort to prepare for it.
a very small b no c initial, in the beginning

4 Lead has some useful **properties** – it doesn't rust and has a low melting point – but it can also be poisonous.
a functions b qualities c ingredients

5 Toxic chemicals from the nearby gold mine have **contaminated** the town's drinking water.
a poisoned b filtered c improved

6 The school has a **protocol** for what should be done if a child becomes ill in class.
a a report b an answer c an established procedure

7 **Federal** laws apply to international trade and foreign policy.
a historical
b related to the national government
c covered by international agreements

8 The two boys were clearly about to start fighting, so their teacher **intervened** and settled the dispute for them.
a asked for assistance
b shouted or spoke in a loud voice.
c entered a situation to stop it from getting worse

3 ▶ 7.5 Listen to the moderator's introduction. Check (✔) the people you expect to hear speak. After you listen to the full discussion, come back and check your predictions.

a a doctor in Iron City ☐
b the mayor of Iron City ☐
c an environmentalist ☐
d a public relations person from city government ☐
e one or more residents of Iron City ☐
f a teacher from one of Iron City's public schools ☐

WHILE LISTENING

SKILLS

Cause-and-effect relationships can be complex. Sometimes it is useful to represent them visually.

LISTENING FOR MAIN IDEAS

4 ▶ 7.6 Listen to the community meeting. Fill in the cause-and-effect chain with the items in the box.

behavioral and cognitive problems	damaged pipes
contaminated water	lead poisoning

Iron City changed water source

↓

a → b → c → d

↑

New water source was acidic

LISTENING FOR DETAILS

5 ▶ 7.6 Listen again. What evidence is presented during the panel discussion for each of the items in the cause-and-effect chain in Exercise 4?

a ______
b ______
c ______
d ______

SKILLS

Identify persuasive appeals

When speakers are trying to persuade listeners, they may use different kinds of appeals to make their case. They consider the people in their audience and think about what is important to them.

Appeal for trust

Speakers may try to show that they are trustworthy. They – or someone else – may cite their credentials (e.g., their education or their job history); they may talk about their experience and expertise or give other reasons why the audience should trust their judgment and accept their point of view.

I have been a federal environmental inspector for 25 years ...

Appeal to emotion

Emotions are powerful motivators. Speakers may try to shock, frighten, or worry their listeners. They may try to make them feel guilty, happy, angry, or sad. They may flatter their audience. They may illustrate their point with stories in order to evoke emotions. Or they may use strong words and expressions to demonstrate how important the issue is.

It is unacceptable that ...
We cannot allow such shocking conditions to continue.

Appeal to logic

To prove that what the speaker is saying is logical and reasonable, speakers may cite statistics, research, and established facts. They may use assertive language to convince their listeners.

It makes sense that ...
It's obvious that ...

6 7.6 Listen again, this time for appeals. Take notes in the chart on the facing page. Try to capture the following information in your notes:

- What appeals are used?
- What type of appeals are they?
- Who made each appeal (city administrator, private citizen, etc.)?

Use the script on pages 216–217 to help you.

appeal for trust	
appeal to emotion	
appeal to logic	

POST-LISTENING

7 Review your notes and discuss these questions with a partner.

1 Which kinds of appeals were typical for the different speakers?
2 Why do you think they chose that type of appeal?
3 What were some strong emotional words that were used?
4 Which types of appeals do you think were most effective?

DISCUSSION

SYNTHESIZING

8 Work in small groups. Discuss the questions.

1 What kind of place do you think Iron City is? Urban or rural? Modern or old-fashioned? Industrial or agricultural?
2 Do you think a situation like this could happen in your city? Why or why not? What would you do if it did?
3 Lead contamination in water and asthma rates have both been increasing. Do the two trends have anything in common?

SPEAKING

CRITICAL THINKING

At the end of this unit, you are going to do the Speaking Task below.

Participate in a community meeting about a local environmental health crisis. You will each take on the role of someone involved with and/or affected by the crisis.

SKILLS

Understanding motivation

Controversial issues can often provoke emotional responses because the stakes are high. If you want to persuade others to adopt your position, it is useful to understand the motivation of the people you are speaking to – what they want and what makes them behave as they do. Understanding the motivation of all parties in a situation can help you anticipate and challenge other points of view.

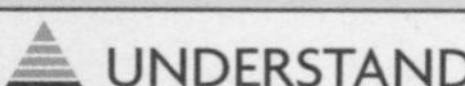

1 7.7 Read the article and then listen to part of a radio show. With a partner, discuss the motivation of the parties in the situation.

TOXIC SPILL IN GOLDEN VALLEY

The residents of Golden Valley are angry. They are angry at Four Star Mining, and they are even angrier at the federal government.

Four Star has been conducting mining operations in and around Golden Valley for many years, operations that produce highly acidic wastewater filled with toxic chemicals. Residents had tolerated these conditions and resisted attempts by the federal government to intervene because they feared that news of the situation would negatively affect the outdoor tourism trade, the community's chief source of jobs after mining.

Then the wastewater began leaking into the water supply.

Public complaints brought the federal government in to inspect the mine and its wastewater. It found that the facility containing the wastewater was not up to federal standards, a fact that the mining company was aware of. To make matters worse, during the inspection, the cap on the container cracked, sending a huge volume of contaminated water into the river, which crosses several states as well as the Navajo Indian reservation.

The consequences were immediate and dramatic. Livestock that drank from the river died or became ill. Thousands of fish died, further contaminating the river and fouling the air for miles around. Tests show that toxic chemicals still line the river bottom. Experts estimate that it will cost millions to clean up the river and repair the damage. Although government inspectors triggered the spill, they blame the accident on the mining company. They are calling for massive and expensive changes to the mine's operations.

The mining company says that the federal inspectors are to blame for the spill. They claim the facility was operating safely before the government intervened. If forced to make the changes called for, Four Star officials threaten to close the mine instead, citing poor profits in recent years that make such changes impossible to implement. Closing the mine would mean the loss of at least half of the jobs in the community.

It's no wonder the residents of Golden Valley are angry.

CREATE

2 With your partner, read through these additional facts. Fill out the relevant portions of the table for each party in the situation, using these facts as well as the information in the news article and radio show.

- Three million gallons of contaminated water spilled into the river.
- 800,000 pounds of metal spilled into the river, resulting in levels up to 300 times the federal limit for copper, lead, and iron.
- The river turned bright orange. Tests revealed that bacteria are the only things that can live in the river water right now.
- Business in town is down 60%.
- The government has ruled that the river is off-limits for recreation for the next six weeks.
- The federal government has begun to treat the water. Acidity has already dropped to normal levels, but toxic metal levels remain high.
- The Navajo nation suffered losses of up to $300 million. Most Navajos depend on farming and fishing, both of which have suffered greatly.
- Scientists are unsure of the long-term impact of the spill.

	Who might they say is to blame?	What effect might this have on them?	What do they probably want?
residents			
business owners			
the Navajo people			
city government			
federal environmental inspectors and scientists			
Four Star Mining executives			
miners			

3 Choose a role to play in the discussion. Officials and experts will sit on a panel at the front; private citizens will be the audience.

officials

- [ ] a representative of Four Star Mining
- [ ] a member of Golden Valley government administration
- [ ] a representative of the federal government's environmental agency
- [ ] an environmental scientist

private citizens

- [ ] a representative of the Navajo nation
- [ ] a local rancher
- [ ] a local hotel owner
- [ ] a miner who works for Four Star

4 Work in small groups of officials or private citizens. Based on the information you have heard and read, prepare a position statement for the person you are representing.

- Private citizen: your position statement should say who you are and how you have been affected. Consider using adjectives of strong disapproval.

  ____
  ____
  ____
  ____
  ____
  ____
  ____
  ____

- Official or expert: your statement should express how you view the situation. Consider citing your expertise or education.

  ____
  ____
  ____
  ____
  ____
  ____
  ____
  ____

PREPARATION FOR SPEAKING

SKILLS

Inclusive language

When speakers want to persuade others, they often try to include listeners in the perspective they are taking. They may use the pronouns *we*, *us*, *our*, and *everyone*.

And wouldn't we all like to have clean water?

They may suggest that they are just like their listeners.

Like every American, I expect the government to protect my health and safety.

They may address their listeners directly.

I want answers. Don't you?

1 Review the statement that you prepared in Critical Thinking, Exercise 4. Write one more sentence that contains inclusive language and add it to your statement.

PRISM Digital Workbook

____

2 Prepare your talking points for the community meeting.

- Review the position statement you have been working on. Make notes so you do not have to read it.
- Gather facts or information that can support your position.
- Consider the motivation of other participants. Which of them do you think might challenge or object to your position? How would you reply to them?
- Consider what kinds of appeals will be the most effective forms of persuasion. Will you appeal for trust, to emotion, or to logic?
  If you are an official, make notes on what you think will happen or what you can promise to do. Consider how you will respond to demands by private citizens.
  If you are a private citizen, make notes on what you want officials to do to improve the situation. Consider how you will respond to offers and explanations made by officials and experts.

____

____

____

____

____

____

____

____

PRONUNCIATION FOR SPEAKING

SKILLS

Emphasis for emotional appeal

Speakers often emphasize words that carry strong emotions or words that they hope will resonate with their audience and generate sympathy for the argument that they are attempting to make.

PRISM Digital Workbook

3 7.8 Listen to the excerpts from Listening 2. Write the missing words you hear. Why do you think these words are emphasized?

1 Lead is __________ toxic – to the nervous system, to the reproductive system, but most of all, it affects __________ development.
2 And the most __________ part is that the damage is __________ .
3 My kids developed rashes and __________ stomach pains.
4 The city is __________ sorry for the problems this has caused your family.
5 You need to understand that __________ level of lead in the blood is considered safe.
6 What I found was __________ , I would say, even __________ .

4 With your partner, take turns reading the sentences aloud. Emphasize the words that show emotion. Did you both emphasize the same words?

1 This situation is unacceptable.
2 I've never seen such appalling conditions.
3 We simply cannot stand by and watch this happen any longer.
4 It's obvious that the city has done nothing to address these problems.
5 Every resident of this community has been affected.
6 I want you to know that the city is taking this problem very seriously.

SPEAKING TASK

PRISM Digital Workbook

Participate in a community meeting about a local environmental health crisis. You will each take on the role of someone involved with and/or affected by the crisis.

PREPARE

1 Assign roles.

- Choose one person from the class to be the moderator. He or she will call on people to make contributions and ask questions.
- You have all prepared a speaker's position. Decide who will make the presentation.

2 Decide on the order of presentation for the members of the panel.
3 Review your talking points and the challenges that you anticipate.
4 Refer to the Task Checklist as you prepare for your presentation.

TASK CHECKLIST	✔
Prepare a position statement.	
Use adjectives of strong emotion where appropriate.	
Use contrastive stress where appropriate.	
Understand and anticipate the motivation and objections of other parties.	
Use inclusive language to gain support for your points.	
Make or respond to demands as appropriate for your role.	

PRACTICE

5 Practice delivering position statements within your group. Give the presenter feedback. Consider the feedback your group gives you. Revise your notes as needed. As you practice your part, think about these things:

- Identify yourself. Say your name and what role you have in the situation.
- Don't speak too quickly. Speak clearly and with emotion.
- Refer to your talking points and notes, but keep your head up and speak directly to the audience or to the members of the panel.

DISCUSS

6 Have the community meeting.

REFLECT

7 As a class, discuss these questions.

1 Which presenter was the most persuasive? Give reasons for your answer.
2 Was your presentation effective? Why or why not?
3 What could you do better next time?

ON CAMPUS

SEEKING MEDICAL TREATMENT

PREPARING TO LISTEN

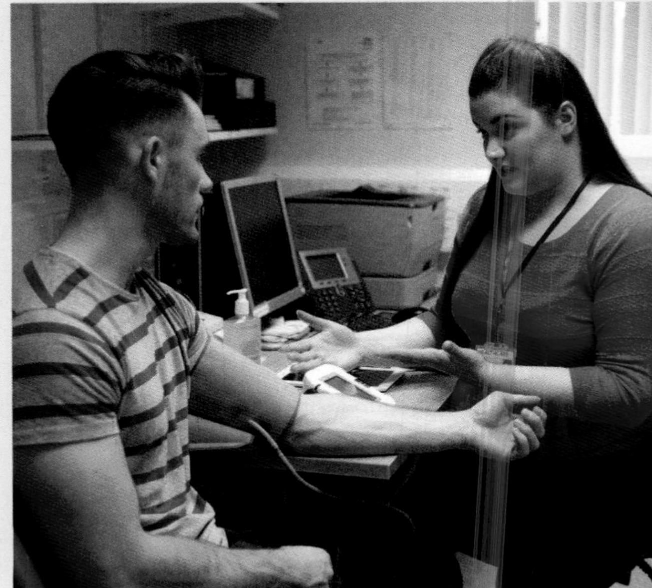

1 You are going to listen to an interview with the director of a health center at a major university. Before you listen, look at the list of services. What do you think is involved in each one? Discuss your ideas with a partner.

a counseling ☐
b emergency care ☐
c health education ☐
d preventive care ☐
e sports medicine ☐
f urgent care ☐

WHILE LISTENING

2 ▶ 7.9 Listen to the interview. Which of the services in Exercise 1 are not available at the University Health Center?

3 ▶ 7.9 Listen again. Choose the correct answer.

1 The University Health Center treats …
   a physical health.
   b mental health.
   c both physical and mental health.
2 In a life-threatening emergency, a student should go to …
   a the University Health Center.
   b the hospital.
   c an urgent care facility.
3 Students should go to urgent care if they need …
   a a checkup.
   b to see a doctor immediately.
   c to see a doctor the same day.
4 Health education is important because …
   a students can begin good habits at this age.
   b many students play sports.
   c many students want to become teachers.

5 One sign of depression is ...
   a feeling sick.
   b feeling tired.
   c feeling stressed.
6 Students should ask for help if they are feeling stressed or depressed because ...
   a a counselor can help them.
   b they need to take responsibility for their health.
   c both *a* and *b*.

PRACTICE

4 Match each problem with an appropriate service.

1 I have a fever. I think I might have the flu. ______
2 I always get very stressed at the end of the semester, and I can't sleep. ______
3 I'm feeling unhappy and homesick. It's affecting my grades. ______
4 I need a flu shot. ______
5 I need to refill a prescription. ______
6 The food here is so strange to me. I'm losing a lot of weight. ______
7 I'm getting headaches when I study. I may need new glasses. ______
8 I hurt my back when I was playing basketball. ______

a counseling
b nutrition counseling
c vision services
d pharmacy
e physical therapy
f stress management
g urgent care
h vaccinations

REAL-WORLD APPLICATION

5 Work in small groups. Go to the website of the health center at your school or visit the health center in person. Find the answers to these questions.

1 Where is the health center located? When is it open?
2 Where should you go in an emergency?
3 How do you make an appointment at the health center?
4 How much does it cost to see a doctor? Do you need insurance?
5 Are vision or dental services available?
6 What kind of counseling or psychological services are available?

LEARNING OBJECTIVES

Listening skill	Use anecdotes and proverbs to illustrate larger ideas
Pronunciation	Contracted forms of *will*
Speaking skill	Collaborative language: suggestion and concession
Speaking task	Participate in a consensus-building decision-making task
On Campus	Handle audience questions

COLLABORATION

UNIT 8

ACTIVATE YOUR KNOWLEDGE

Work with a partner. Discuss the questions.

1 Describe a personal experience you had in making an important decision as a group. How long did it take? What kind of experience was it – productive, pleasant, frustrating?
2 How do formal groups, such government bodies and businesses, make decisions?
3 How do you think collaboration can be a part of decision making? Give an example if you can.

WATCH AND LISTEN

PREPARING TO WATCH

ACTIVATING YOUR KNOWLEDGE

1 Check (✔) the statements that are true for you. Discuss your ideas with a partner.

a I prefer to work alone. ☐
b I prefer to work with one other person and hear their ideas. ☐
c I prefer to work in a small group to hear many ideas. ☐
d I prefer to work alone for some tasks and in a small group for others. Not every task needs input from everyone. ☐

PREDICTING CONTENT USING VISUALS

2 Look at the pictures from the video. Discuss the questions.

1 Which work situation do you think is most valuable? Why?
2 What are the advantages and disadvantages of working alone? Of collaborating with others?
3 Have you attended a meeting recently for school or work? Was it productive? Why or why not?

GLOSSARY

segment (n) any of the parts into which something can be divided
piñata (n) a paper animal filled with candy that people break open as a game
bash (v) to attack someone or something with an object
composition (n) the mixture of things or people that are combined to form something

WHILE WATCHING

UNDERSTANDING MAIN IDEAS

3 ▶ Read the questions. Watch the video and take notes. Then discuss the questions with a partner.

1 Although meetings are intended to help people collaborate, how do most people generally feel about them?
2 What are the main problems with business meetings mentioned in the video?

UNDERSTANDING DETAILS

4 Watch the interviews at the beginning of the video again. Check (✔) the adjectives used to describe the effect of meetings on people.

a brain-dead ☐
b competitive ☐
c dumb ☐
d silly ☐
e productive ☐
f smart ☐

5 Watch the discussion with Bob Rosner again. Complete the table. Then come back to add details of your own to expand on his ideas.

the four P's	meaning/example

MAKING INFERENCES

6 Work with a partner. Discuss the questions.

1 Why do you think so many of those interviewed feel meetings are not making us more productive?
2 At one point, Bob Rosner says that "women need connection and trust ... [but] guys like a competitive environment." How does the female reporter feel about his statement? How do you know?
3 Why do you think managers and bosses assume that meetings help solve problems?
4 Why might stand-up and topless (short for *laptop-less*) meetings be more effective?

DISCUSSION

7 Work with a partner. Discuss the questions.

1 Were you surprised that the people who were interviewed assigned so little value to meetings? Why or why not?
2 Do you think their feelings might change if they participated in a stand-up meeting? How about a topless meeting? Why or why not?
3 Why do you think so many supervisors and bosses want employees to collaborate?
4 In what other ways can companies encourage collaboration among their employees?

LISTENING

LISTENING 1

PREPARING TO LISTEN

USING YOUR KNOWLEDGE

1 You are going to listen to a training session on group dynamics. Before you listen, work with a partner and discuss the questions.

1 What can individuals do to make sure a group in which they are a member works well and that it accomplishes its tasks? In other words, what kind of behavior facilitates group work?
2 What can an individual do to disrupt the work of a group and prevent it from accomplishing its tasks? In other words, what kind of behavior impairs group work?
3 Have you ever had an experience in which one member of a group behaved inappropriately and prevented the group from working well together? Describe what happened.
4 If you have had or know about a negative experience like this, what did you or anyone else in the group try to do to respond to this individual?

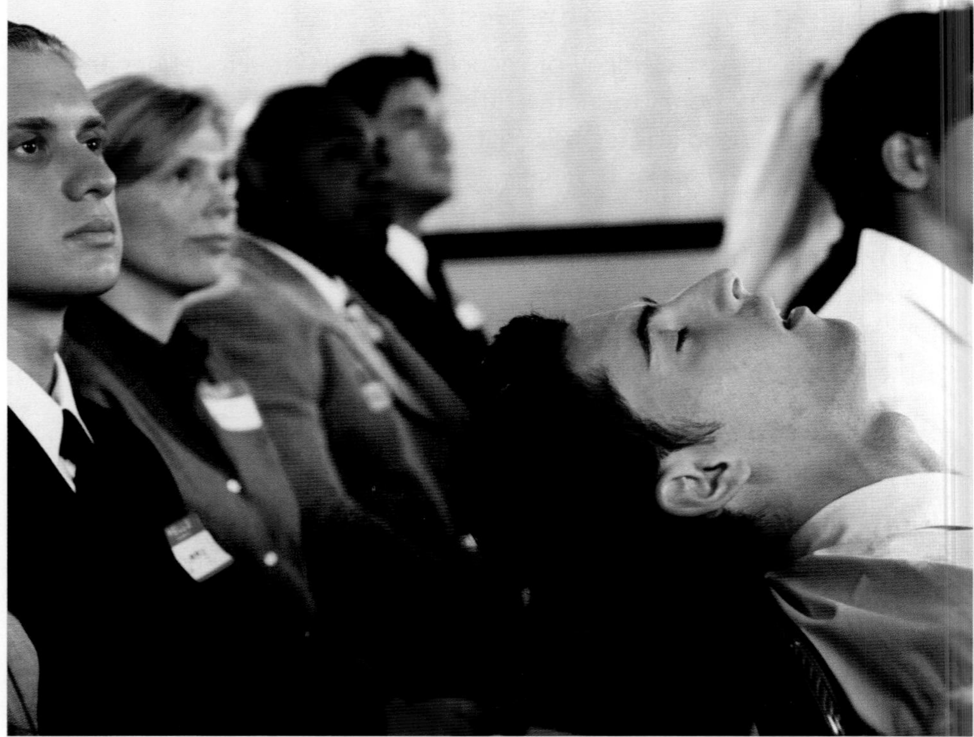

2 Take the quiz and then compare scores with your classmates. What is your style, according to your score? How accurate do you think your score is?

WHAT IS YOUR WORK STYLE?

Do you work well in collaborative settings? Write *T* (true) or *F* (false) for each statement to find out your style.

_____ 1 I tend to give in to group pressure easily.

_____ 2 I produce my best results when I work on my own.

_____ 3 My job would be so much easier if I didn't have to depend on others to do it.

_____ 4 Other people will almost always let you down.

_____ 5 I don't care about my job that much; I just do what they tell me to do.

_____ 6 If too many people are working on the same thing, it usually doesn't turn out so well.

_____ 7 I usually know what's best and get impatient when I have to listen to a lot of other opinions.

_____ 8 Some of the people I work with really annoy me.

_____ 9 When someone talks, I think about how to respond while they're speaking.

_____ 10 You have to protect your own interests because no one else will.

_____ 11 When you disagree with someone, the best course of action is to stay silent.

_____ 12 Meetings are usually a total waste of time.

_____ 13 Creativity is something that applies to individuals, not groups.

_____ 14 I always seem to end up doing the most work on a group project.

_____ 15 I do my best to avoid conflict.

_____ 16 I hate(d) working on group projects in school.

_____ 17 When someone challenges my ideas, I just stay quiet.

_____ 18 If I want the job done right, I have to do it myself.

_____ 19 We spend too much time discussing and not enough time doing.

_____ 20 I'd rather just go with what the rest of the group wants than fight for my idea.

Now calculate your score. Give yourself five (5) points for each *F*.

YOUR SCORE

95–100: You are a collaboration superstar. You generally trust others and enjoy working in collaborative situations.

80–90: You are a team player. You will probably function well in a group. But some of your beliefs and attitudes could interfere with your ability to get the most out of collaboration.

65–75: You are a doubter. You don't always see the value in collaborative work. Perhaps you've had a bad experience in the past.

60 and below: You are a loner. You find collaborative work difficult, and you don't see the value in it. You prefer tasks that allow you to work independently and be rewarded for your own work. When you have to work in groups, you respond negatively.

UNDERSTANDING KEY VOCABULARY

3 Read the definitions. Complete the sentences with the correct form of the words in bold.

constructive (adj) helpful, positive
counteract (v) to reduce the negative effect of something
defuse (v) to make a situation calmer or less dangerous
dynamics (n pl) forces that produce change in a system or group
insight (n) deep understanding
perception (n) belief or opinion based on observation
prevail (v) to become dominant; to win in the end
resentment (n) anger at being forced to accept something you don't like

1 It's important to understand a group's __________ before you add or remove team members.
2 The newspaper reports have created the __________ in the public eye that the police are treating minorities unfairly.
3 __________ feedback on your writing can lead to real improvement in your essays.
4 He made a joke to try to __________ the tension in the room.
5 I know that this is a difficult time, but we hope that good sense will __________ in the end.
6 The latest tax increase has created a great deal of __________ among voters.
7 Spending a week with her in-laws gave her some __________ into her husband's personality.
8 He drank three cups of coffee to __________ the effects of two sleepless nights.

WHILE LISTENING

SUMMARIZING

4 ▶ 8.1 Listen to the presentation and take notes. Summarize the main idea of the presentation in one or two sentences. Compare summary statements with a partner.

____

____

LISTENING FOR DETAILS

5 ▶ 8.1 Listen again. To support her claim, the speaker reports on a research study. Explain the study and its results.

Participants: ____

Methods (How was the study organized and carried out?):

____

Results: ____

____

Conclusion: ____

____

POST-LISTENING

SKILLS

Using anecdotes and proverbs to illustrate larger ideas

Speakers will sometimes use shortcuts to express their ideas. They may use stories, anecdotes, or proverbs to illustrate broader ideas or principles.

6 8.2 Read the items and then listen to the excerpt from the presentation to complete the tasks.

PRISM Digital Workbook

1 Consider the proverb, "One bad apple can spoil the barrel." Explain the literal meaning and then explain how it applies to the content of the presentation.

____

____

____

2 The presenter names three types of "bad apples" and gives examples of their behavior. Fill in the table with information from the presentation.

	type of bad apple	examples of behavior
a		exhibits lack of interest in task
b	naysayer	
c		

3 What larger principles or ideas do you think the presenter is trying to illustrate with the story of bad apples?

____

____

7 Work in small groups. Discuss the meaning of each proverb. What larger principles or ideas do they illustrate?

1 You can lead a horse to water, but you can't make it drink.
2 The squeaky wheel gets the grease.
3 There is no such thing as a free lunch.
4 Too many cooks spoil the soup.
5 The grass is always greener on the other side of the fence.

PRONUNCIATION FOR LISTENING

SKILLS

Contracted forms of *will*

Both speakers and writers use the contracted form of *will* with personal pronouns. In spoken English, however, this contraction is used much more often and with many different types of nouns, proper nouns, and pronouns.

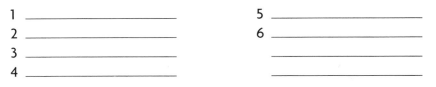

John'll do that tomorrow.
It'll be done tomorrow.
There'll be time to do that tomorrow.
What'll we do tomorrow?

PRISM Digital Workbook

8 8.3 Listen to the sentences. Write out the words that the speaker contracts. Compare answers with a partner.

1 ______________
2 ______________
3 ______________
4 ______________
5 ______________
6 ______________
____
____

9 8.4 With a partner, underline the instances in these sentences where a speaker could and probably would contract *will*. Circle the instances where *will* wouldn't be contracted. Then listen and check.

1 My car will be in the repair shop for at least a week, but it's OK. I will just ride my bike to work.
2 There will be times in your life when you will want to give up. But things will get better if you just stay strong.
3 There is no doubt that the Internet has had and will continue to have a profound effect on the way we communicate.
4 Most experts agree that it will be a long time before we see any major change in transportation technology.
5 We formed four groups. Each group researched and will report on a different phase of the project.
6 I don't know if my mom and dad will join us, but my sister and her husband definitely will.
7 The products that company invented will go down in history.

DISCUSSION

10 With your partner, discuss the questions.

1 What is the best way to deal with each type of bad apple?
2 Why do you think negative behavior and attitudes spread so easily? Do you think positive behavior spreads as easily? Why or why not?
3 Does the bad apple principle change your perspective on difficult group dynamics you have experienced? Will you behave differently in the future if you are in a group with a bad apple?

LANGUAGE DEVELOPMENT

WH- CLEFTS

LANGUAGE

Wh- clefts are constructions that allow speakers to focus the listener's attention on one part of a sentence – the part that contains new information. A *wh-* cleft consists of a clause that begins with a *wh-* word (most often *what*), followed by a form of the verb *be*. *Wh-* clefts are more common in spoken than written language.

What the researchers found was (that) one bad apple can spread to the group.

CLEFT — NEW INFORMATION

Wh- clefts are also used to express a speaker's perspective on new information or to clarify new information:

What surprised me was that the results were so consistent.
What I didn't agree with were the study's conclusions.
So, **what you're saying is** one person can spoil the whole group's dynamics?
So, **is what you're saying** that one person can spoil the whole group's dynamics?

1 Write sentences using *wh-* clefts to focus on the phrases given. Use the words in parentheses in the clefts.

PRISM Digital Workbook

1 bad apples destroy group dynamics (the report / reveal)
What the report revealed was that bad apples destroy group dynamics.
2 their group didn't have a good leader (the participants / say)
____
3 an increase in negative behavior (the researchers / see)
____
4 one member can have a disproportionate effect (the study / show)
____

2 In your notebook, write questions or statements using *wh-* clefts to clarify the sentences. Use the words in parentheses in the clefts.

1 This was a poorly designed study. (I / tell you)
What I'm telling you is that this was a poorly designed study.
2 No one noticed the effect his behavior had on them. (you / mean?)
3 The results were the same for children, teens, and adults. (you / say?)
4 Studies like this are hard to replicate because every group of people is different. (I / mean)

3 Now write four sentences containing *wh-* cleft clauses to express your opinion about something.

What I hate about the mall is the awful smell from the food court.

COLLOCATIONS: PREPOSITIONS

LANGUAGE

Many familiar verbs and verb phrases collocate with particular prepositions.

collocations with *on*	**collocations with *in***	**collocations with *with***
be based on	*believe in*	*be consistent with*
concentrate on	*engage in*	*be familiar with*
count on	*participate in*	*come up with*
insist on	*result in*	*deal with*
plan on	*succeed in*	*fit in with*

PRISM Digital Workbook

4 Complete the sentences with a verb + preposition collocation. Make sure the verbs are in the correct form.

1 The psychologist recruited about 50 students to ____________________ the study as research subjects.
2 I don't think we can ____________________ a new proposal to present to the committee by tomorrow. There just isn't enough time.
3 There are many different directions we could go with this in the future, but I think we really need to ____________________ the fundamental issues for now.
4 I expect that most of you ____________________ the famous study that showed people often obey authority figures even when they are told to do terrible things.
5 Although I believed it was unnecessary, the head researcher ____________________ repeating the study, just to make sure that the initial findings were correct.
6 Though most skydivers prefer to pack their own parachutes, they ____________________ each other to check their straps and safety equipment before jumping.

5 Write three original sentences about working in groups using the collocations in the explanation box.

1 ____
____
____

2 ____
____
____

3 ____
____
____

LISTENING 2

PREPARING TO LISTEN

USING YOUR KNOWLEDGE

1 You are going to listen to a class discussion comparing two systems for decision making. Before you listen, read the definition and answer the questions with a partner.

> *Majority rule is a political principle that states that a majority, usually constituted by 50% plus one of an organized group, have both the right and the power to make decisions that apply to and govern the entire group.*

1 What institutions operate by majority rule?
2 Have you ever participated in a group that operates by majority rule? Describe the group and why it operates this way.
3 Do you think majority rule is a fair system? Is it an efficient one?
4 Are there any downsides to majority rule?

2 With your partner, read the quote and answer the questions.

> *"I do not believe in the doctrine of the greatest good for the greatest number. It means … that in order to achieve the supposed good of fifty-one percent, the interest of forty-nine may be, or rather should be, sacrificed. It is a heartless doctrine and has done harm to humanity."*
>
> Mahatma Gandhi (1909)

1 What does Gandhi mean? Why is the doctrine "heartless"?
2 What kind of harm is he referring to? Can you think of any decisions or laws that were supported by a majority in the past but we now consider unjust?
3 What are the alternatives? If every vote or every voice has equal weight, won't the majority always prevail? Should it always prevail?

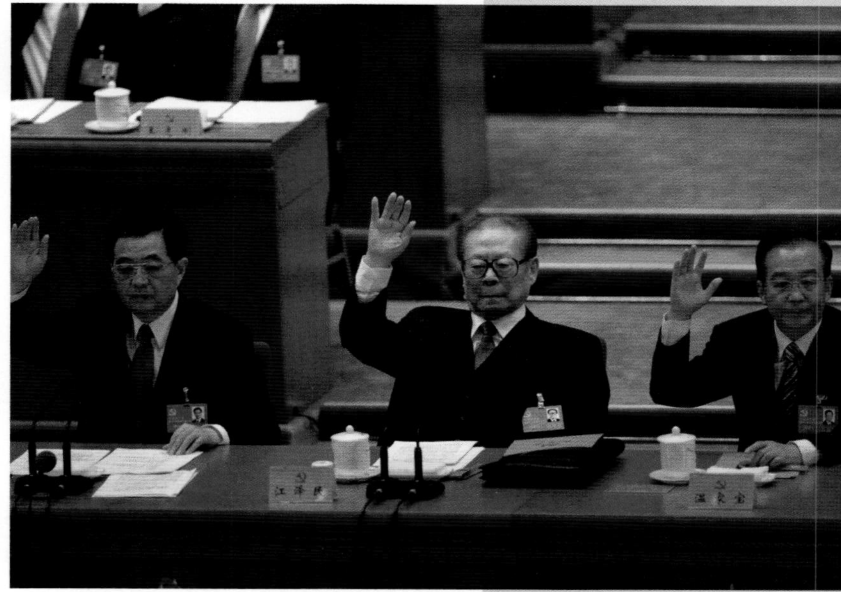

UNDERSTANDING KEY VOCABULARY

PRISM Digital Workbook

3 Read the sentences and write the words in bold next to their definitions.

1 We won't know the **outcome** of these decisions for at least a year.
2 Many of us still have very serious **reservations** about this plan.
3 A lot of different people have a **stake** in this project, so it will not be easy to please all of them.
4 I've been **tinkering** with my presentation, but it isn't quite right yet.
5 This proposal is kind of a **hybrid** of several earlier proposals.
6 After discussing the matter for several hours, we reached a **consensus** on how to move forward.
7 My Internet connection is not working. The company says it is trying to **resolve** the problem.
8 The people in this community feel a **sense of ownership** for the new park. As a result, they take very good care of it.

a ___________ (n) result
b ___________ (n) a generally accepted opinion or decision
c ___________ (v) to solve a problem or end a difficulty
d ___________ (n phr) a feeling of personal responsibility for something connected to you but not yours
e ___________ (v) to make small changes in order to improve something
f ___________ (n) something that is a combination of two or more things
g ___________ (n) a personal interest or investment
h ___________ (n pl) doubts

WHILE LISTENING

LISTENING FOR MAIN IDEAS

4 ▶ 8.5 Listen to the discussion. Use the table to take notes on what the students say about the two approaches to decision making.

voting	consensus building

5 Work with a partner. Use your notes to review the discussion.

1 Describe the issue that the class was trying to resolve.
2 Report the outcome of the first decision-making process, voting.
3 Briefly report the outcome of the second decision-making process, consensus building.

6 ▶ 8.5 Listen again and add to your notes. Focus on the processes in the two different approaches. Think about these questions as you listen.

- In what ways are they similar? In what ways are they different?
- Who participated? Can you describe their participation?
- How did the participants feel about the two processes at the end?

LISTENING FOR DETAILS

7 Work with a partner. Using your notes, give an oral summary of one process to your partner. Listen as your partner gives an oral summary of the other process. Did you both include the most important details?

SUMMARIZING

POST-LISTENING

8 Work in small groups. Discuss the questions.

1 What was the students' response to the two different approaches after they finished?
2 Why do you think they responded differently to the two processes?
3 Why do you think the teacher wanted his students to participate in this activity? What was his goal?

9 Work in groups of three. Complete the tasks.

1 The following groups make decisions by consensus. What do you know about them? If needed, go online and do some research.
   - The Six Nations (also called the Iroquois): a group of Native American tribes
   - The Quakers (the Society of Friends): a religious group
   - The World Trade Organization (it also uses voting)
2 What do you know about the American jury system? Go online to find out more.
   - Is a jury's verdict decided by majority rule or by unanimous vote?
   - Do you think a jury should operate more like the first approach the class used or the second?

DISCUSSION

10 Work with a small group. Discuss the questions.

SYNTHESIZING

1 How do you think a bad apple would affect the consensus-building process?
2 How do you think group dynamics could affect the decision-making process of a jury?
3 Which form of decision making would you prefer to use in groups or organizations where you are a member?

SPEAKING

CRITICAL THINKING

At the end of this unit, you are going to do the Speaking Task below.

Participate in a consensus-building decision-making task. Your goal is to choose one of three options for future food service operations at your school.

SKILLS

A cost-benefit analysis

Important decisions require a careful analysis of the pros (benefits) and cons (costs) of every option.

The benefits of biking to work, for example, might include a savings in transportation expenses and some good exercise; costs might include longer commute times and the discomfort of riding in bad weather.

In considering options, also consider the "winners and losers." Which stakeholders will get the greatest benefit from each of the options? Who will suffer the greatest costs?

UNDERSTAND

1 Work in small groups. Talk about your dining experiences.

1 What are the dining options on your campus or near your school?
2 Do you ever eat at fast-food restaurants? If so, what do you like about them? If not, why not?
3 Describe your experience eating in "institutional" dining facilities, for example, in a hospital, school, or government building.

2 Listen as a university administrator describes each of the possible dining options at the campus student center. Take notes as you listen.

EVALUATE

1 ▶ 8.6 DINESCO (a commercial food services provider)

____

____

____

____

2 ▶ 8.7 Dilly's (a fast-food restaurant)

____

____

____

____

3 ▶ 8.8 Unihub (a café run by students from the Hospitality program)

____

____

____

____

3 Work with a partner. Using your notes, fill in the chart. What are the costs and benefits of each dining option? Who would be the winners and who would be the losers in each option? Give reasons for your decisions.

CREATE

	DINESCO	Dilly's	Unihub
costs			
benefits			
winners			
losers			

4 Which option would be best for you? For the community? Are the two answers the same? Decide on your position. Write a position statement in which you explain the option you support and why.

____

____

PREPARATION FOR SPEAKING

STEPS FOR CONSENSUS BUILDING

SKILLS

The consensus-building process has a sequence of formal steps. Depending on the goal of the particular project, some steps might be given more attention than others, and some might be combined or even skipped.

step 1: Describe the situation in objective terms. Generate key questions that must be answered in the process.

step 2: State the needs and concerns of all participants.

step 3: Generate ideas. Accept everything at this point in the process. Avoid criticizing others' ideas.

step 4: Discuss the costs and benefits of each idea. Discuss consequences of each option for all of the stakeholders.

step 5: Summarize what has been discussed so far. Look for points of agreement and try to synthesize them to create a preliminary proposal.

step 6: Check for concerns and reservations from members of the group.

step 7: Amend your proposal(s) to accommodate concerns or objections.

step 8: Summarize the proposal that is on the table. Test for agreement among the group members (see extra information below).

step 9: Finalize your agreement or return to step 3 and repeat the consensus-building process.

1 Work with a partner or in small groups. Review each of the steps for consensus building. Discuss any questions you have. Then read about the ways to test for agreement below.

TESTING FOR AGREEMENT

- **block**: "I have a problem with the proposal that cannot be resolved. I propose that we reconsider one crucial aspect of the proposal ..."
- **stand aside**: "I can't support this proposal. However, I don't want to stand in the way, so I will stand aside and let the process continue."
- **reservation/concession**: "Although I have some reservations, I am willing to let the proposal go forward. I can live with it."
- **agreement**: "I fully support the proposal."

2 ▶ **8.5** The students in Listening 2 followed the consensus-building process outlined in the explanation box. Listen to the discussion again and identify some of the steps in their description. Identify instances of testing for agreement as well.

SKILLS

Collaborative language: suggestion and concession

When collaborating on a decision, the original proposal is often changed or amended to satisfy all parties. Participants should offer suggestions for changes in a respectful, nonaggressive way.

How about / What about ... ?
Let's try/think about/consider ...
I suggest/propose that ...
Why don't we try/think about/consider ... ?
What do you suggest/propose?

Participants also need to be open to changes in their own positions for the good of the group or project. They can do this graciously by acknowledging objections, conceding points, or offering conditions that would make the idea acceptable.

I understand that this proposal includes things that you don't like, but would you be willing to support it anyway?
Though I don't think this is an ideal solution, I admit that it does have some attractive features.
I would be willing to support this proposal if we add something for vegetarians.

3 Work with a partner. Imagine you are part of a consensus-building process. Read the two scenarios. Choose one and use collaborative language to express each of the possible responses to the proposals:

PRISM Digital Workbook

- block
- stand aside
- reservation/concession
- agreement

Scenario 1

Your group is trying to decide where to place a facility for former prisoners who were convicted of nonviolent crimes (e.g., burglary, drug use, etc.). The former prisoners will live in the facility for six months under supervision before they are released. At the testing-for-agreement stage, the proposal is to place the facility at the edge of town in an old school that has not been used for six years.

1 block: ______________________________
2 stand aside: ______________________________
3 reservation/concession: ______________________________
4 agreement: ______________________________

Scenario 2

Currently, your school has a very harsh policy regarding plagiarism. Any student found guilty of plagiarism is expelled from the school (kicked out forever). Administrators want to adopt a new policy that gives students a chance to learn and change. The first offense would result in a failing grade for that assignment, plus the student would have to attend a seminar on how to avoid plagiarism. The second offense would result in a failing grade in the class. The third offense would result in expulsion from the school.

1 block: ________________
2 stand aside: ________________
3 reservation/concession: ________________
4 agreement: ________________

4 With your partner, discuss the scenarios in Exercise 3. Which position would you actually take for each scenario? Why?

SPEAKING TASK

PRISM Digital Workbook

Participate in a consensus-building decision-making task. Your goal is to choose one of three options for future food service operations at your school.

PREPARE

1 Review the chart in Critical Thinking, Exercise 3, about the costs and benefits of each proposal and the winners and losers for each proposal.

2 Review the position you chose in Critical Thinking, Exercise 4:

- What are the main arguments for the proposal that you support?
- What concessions would you be willing to make?
- What arguments do you think others will make for the other two proposals?
- What will you say in response to them?
- What could make the other two proposals more attractive to you?

PRACTICE

3 With a partner, practice presenting the reasons that favor your proposal, responses to the arguments that you anticipate from others, and suggestions or concessions that you would be willing to make. Be sure to include collaborative language. Give each other feedback on your presentations.

4 Refer to the Task Checklist as you prepare for your discussion.

TASK CHECKLIST	✔
Start with a position statement.	
Offer a cost-benefit analysis of the proposal that you support.	
Use collaborative language as you discuss others' ideas.	
Anticipate and respond to competing proposals.	
Participate appropriately in the consensus-building process.	

DISCUSS

5 In small groups or as a class, follow the steps for consensus building (Preparation for Speaking, page 184) to carry out the Speaking Task. The facilitator (your teacher or another student) will begin the discussion by describing the general situation.

REFLECT

6 In small groups or as a class, discuss these questions.

1 Was the consensus-building decision-making task effective? Did you arrive at a decision that everyone could support or at least live with?
2 Would you use this process again? Why or why not?
3 How well did the class or your group complete each step in the process?
4 What could you do better next time?

ON CAMPUS

HANDLING AUDIENCE QUESTIONS

PREPARING TO LISTEN

1 In your opinion, what is the best way to handle audience questions about a presentation? Compare ideas with a partner.

1 When is the best time to take questions from the audience?
a any time **b** at specific times **c** at the end

2 What should you do if you don't know the answer to a question?
a admit it **b** look it up on your phone
c refer the person to a website

3 How should you react to an awkward (e.g., off topic) question?
a offer to speak to the person individually after the presentation
b point out that the question is outside of your area of expertise
c try to answer it

WHILE LISTENING

2 ▶ 8.9 Listen to the student presentation about jury service in the United States. Number the topics in the order you hear them.

_____ **a** the deliberation stage
_____ **b** the jury selection process
_____ **c** payment for jury service
_____ **d** the reason for jury service

3 8.9 Listen again. Use the chart to take notes.

	Question	Response
1		
2		
3		
4		
5		

PRACTICE

4 Read the functions list for taking audience questions (a–e). Then, assign a function to each of the presenter statements below (1–7).

a Say when you will take questions.
b Welcome the question.
c Check that you have answered the question.
d Admit that you don't know the answer.
e Politely deflect awkward questions.

1 Could you please hold your question until the end? _____
2 Does that answer your question? _____
3 I don't know offhand, but I can try to find out. _____
4 OK, we have enough time for a few questions. _____
5 I'm glad you asked that. _____
6 Maybe somebody else can answer that? _____
7 We don't really have time to go into that here. _____

REAL-WORLD APPLICATION

5 Prepare a short presentation (about one minute) on something you know well. You can use one of the topics given here or an idea of your own.

your hometown
a great place to visit
a hobby, game, or sport

6 Give your presentation to a small group or the class. Invite your classmates to ask questions. Respond to the questions appropriately.

GLOSSARY OF KEY VOCABULARY

Words that are part of the Academic Word List are noted with Ⓐ in this glossary.

UNIT 1 CONSERVATION

LISTENING 1

abundant (n) more than enough; plentiful
conversion Ⓐ (n) the process of changing from one thing to another
intensive Ⓐ (adj) using a lot of effort or energy
nutrients (n) healthful substances that plants and animals get from food
revenue Ⓐ (n) money that a business receives regularly
viable (adj) able to succeed
vulnerable (adj) easy to hurt or attack
yield (n) the amount of something, such as a crop, that is produced

LISTENING 2

accelerate (v) to happen more quickly
accumulate Ⓐ (v) to collect or increase over time
allocate Ⓐ (v) to give something as part of a total amount
combat (v) to try to stop
dispose of Ⓐ (phr v) to throw away
divert (v) to make something go in a different direction
shameful (adj) morally wrong
unprecedented Ⓐ (adj) having never happened in the past

UNIT 2 DESIGN

LISTENING 1

assembly Ⓐ (n) the process of putting parts together to create one thing
customize (v) to make or change something to fit a user's needs
downside (n) disadvantage
drastically (adv) severely; with very noticeable effect
foundation Ⓐ (n) the thing on which other things are based
mass production (n) the process of producing large numbers of one thing in a factory
scenario Ⓐ (n) a description of possible events
shift Ⓐ (v) to change position or focus

LISTENING 2

backlash (n) a strong negative reaction
circumvent (v) to avoid something by going around it
devise (v) to create a plan or system using intelligence and creativity
finite Ⓐ (adj) limited; set and fixed
obstacle (n) something that blocks forward movement
phenomenon Ⓐ (n) something happening that is noticeable because it is new or unusual
resent (v) to feel angry or hurt at being treated unfairly
subsequent Ⓐ (adj) next; happening after something else

UNIT 3 PRIVACY

LISTENING 1

arsenal (n) a collection of weapons
catch up with (phr v) to reach the same level or get in sync
counter (v) to defend against or respond to
creepy (adj) causing discomfort because of being strange or unnatural
informed (adj) having a lot of knowledge about something
target Ⓐ (v) to direct something at someone
trace Ⓐ (v) to find the origin of something
track (v) to follow and collect data on a person's activity

LISTENING 2

compel (v) to force or pressure someone
convincing Ⓐ (adj) able to make you believe that something is true or right
encryption (n) the process of protecting data by changing it into code
expertise Ⓐ (n) advanced knowledge
in the interest of (adv phr) intended for the purpose of
legitimate (adj) true and reasonable
precedent Ⓐ (n) an action or decision that justifies later actions or decisions
tradeoff (n) a balance between two opposing but desirable things

UNIT 4 BUSINESS

LISTENING 1

aggregator Ⓐ (n) a tool that collects and organizes information
buzzword (n) popular word and expression that is sometimes overused in a field
dump (v) to drop without caring where
effectively (adv) in reality but not officially
elaborate (adj) richly detailed
facilitate Ⓐ (v) to make easier
overload (n) too much of something
transaction (n) an activity that involves the movement of money

LISTENING 2

concisely (adv) clearly and using few words
fabulous (adj) great; wonderful
funding Ⓐ (n) money for a particular purpose
mission (n) goal or purpose, especially of an organization
oversight (n) supervision over; management of
overview (n) a short description or general idea of something
scope Ⓐ (n) the range that is covered by something
status Ⓐ (n) official position

UNIT 5 PSYCHOLOGY

LISTENING 1

application (n) a way in which something can be used
approachable Ⓐ (adj) friendly and easy to talk to
competent (adj) skilled; able to do things well
cue (n) a signal; something that causes a response
dominance Ⓐ (n) behavior that aims to control others
exposure Ⓐ (n) experiencing something by being in a particular place or situation
intriguing (adj) very interesting because of being unusual or mysterious
speculate (v) to guess when there is not enough information to be certain

LISTENING 2

definitively Ⓐ (adv) completely; without doubt
deteriorate (v) to worsen
differentiated Ⓐ (adj) specialized
impair (v) to damage
landmark (n) a place or structure that is easy to recognize
navigate (v) to find one's way
orient Ⓐ (v) to establish one's location
reconstruct Ⓐ (v) to recreate

UNIT 6 CAREERS

LISTENING 1

daunting (adj) making you feel less confident; frightening
discrimination Ⓐ (n) unfair treatment, especially based on sex, ethnic origin, age, or religion
distinct Ⓐ (adj) clearly separate and different
get stuck with (phr v) to be forced to take responsibility for something or someone unpleasant
hustle (v) to work in an energetic way
rewarding (adj) giving a feeling of satisfaction
vision Ⓐ (n) a clear idea about what should happen or be done in the future
wardrobe (n) all the clothes that a person owns, or a set of those clothes specific to one time or purpose

LISTENING 2

accomplishment (n) something done successfully
analytical Ⓐ (adj) careful and systematic
collaboration (n) cooperative effort
dreaded (adj) unwelcome because of being unpleasant
format Ⓐ (n) layout and organization
ramble (v) to speak in a confused way
rehearsed (adj) practiced and unnatural
reiterate (v) to repeat, usually using different words or phrasing

UNIT 7 HEALTH SCIENCES

LISTENING 1

correlation (n) a connection between two or more things
deprive (v) to take away something important
disparity (n) a lack of equality
disproportionately (adv) unequally
hygiene (n) cleanliness; keeping yourself and your environment clean
incidence Ⓐ (n) the rate at which something happens
ironically (adv) in a way that is the opposite of what is expected
proximity (n) nearness

LISTENING 2

compromise (v) to risk having a harmful effect
concentration Ⓐ (n) the amount of a substance within another substance
contaminate (v) to make poisonous
federal Ⓐ (adj) related to the national government
intervene Ⓐ (v) to enter a situation to improve it or stop it from getting worse
minimal Ⓐ (adj) very small in amount
properties (n pl) qualities that make something useful in a particular way
protocol Ⓐ (n) an established procedure

UNIT 8 COLLABORATION

LISTENING 1

constructive Ⓐ (adj) helpful, positive
counteract (v) to reduce the negative effect of something
defuse (v) to make a situation calmer or less dangerous
dynamics Ⓐ (n pl) forces that produce change in a system or group
insight Ⓐ (n) deep understanding
perception Ⓐ (n) belief or opinion based on observation
prevail (v) to become dominant; to win in the end
resentment (n) anger at being forced to accept something you don't like

LISTENING 2

consensus Ⓐ (n) a generally accepted opinion or decision
hybrid (n) something that is a combination of two or more things
outcome Ⓐ (n) result
reservations (n pl) doubts
resolve Ⓐ (v) to solve a problem or end a difficulty
sense of ownership (n phr) a feeling of responsibility for something connected to you but not yours
stake (n) a personal interest or investment
tinker (v) to make small changes in order to improve something

UNIT 1

Pelicans Threatened by Oil

Jeff Corwin: Just 10 miles from the nesting grounds of this noisy colony of brown pelicans, more than three million gallons of oil are lurking. That threatens a species already decimated by the disappearance of these marshlands.

How fast are they shrinking?

Woman 1: If we talk for 20 minutes, at the end of that we will have lost a football field or two of land.

Corwin: Coastal Louisiana used to be half land, half water. Now, these areas are more than 61% water, losing about 25 square miles of land each year. The pelicans nest on this coastal island for protection from predators, and so they can dive-bomb waters rich in small fish, like mullet, their main source of food.

Man: The birds are flying out from this island, diving into the water to catch that food.

Corwin: Oil in the water could poison the pelicans' food supply. Oil-saturated feathers also provide no insulation from the cold and would rob them of their ability to float. The pelicans could even drown.

So you're wiping the inside of its mouth.

Woman 2: Right.

Corwin: Why is that?

Woman 2: I'm trying to figure out what it is that he's got in there, make sure it's not oil.

Corwin: At this bird rehabilitation center, they've already nursed one oiled pelican back to health. This one was injured but, thankfully, shows no sign of exposure to oil.

Woman 1: Right now, they don't want to leave their nests. That means they're going to stay, unfortunately, where the oil is.

Presenter: The Green Revolution has been credited with saving several generations of the world's poorest people from starvation. The techniques of high-**yield** agriculture were developed from the 1930s through about 1970. They include the extensive use of chemical fertilizers to improve the quality of the soil and pesticides to kill insects and control diseases. These techniques brought changes that were indeed sufficiently dramatic to earn the title "revolution." These techniques produced **abundant** crops, especially wheat, from relatively small plots of land and with much less labor than previously required. The United States alone produced over two billion bushels of wheat in 2015. That's almost 400 pounds of wheat per capita. There is no doubt that thousands, if not millions, have benefited from the bounty of the Green Revolution.

Today, however, I want to talk to you about the next chapter – about some of the consequences of this type of **intensive** agriculture – and about how we, the next generation, can do a better job of conserving our most basic and most valuable resources.

Presenter: So what is intensive farming, and what happens when we farm intensively? By "intensive" I mean, we grow huge amounts of one crop in the same fields year after year. As I mentioned, the upside is that we get lots of food in return for relatively little labor. Unfortunately, there is also a downside – the effects on the health of the planet and the population. I want to talk about some issues through the lens of sustainability because, let's face it, it won't do much good to produce a lot of food if we are using up all of our natural resources or destroying the planet in the process.

Let's start by talking about natural resources. What are the most important resources in agriculture? Soil and water. I am a professor of agricultural science now, but I grew up on a traditional farm, so I have really seen the situation from different perspectives. On the farm where I grew up, we grew a few different types of crops. On most big farms today, however, farmers grow the same crops every year – they specialize. This kind of farming drains the soil of precious **nutrients**, requiring farmers to replace them with chemical fertilizers.

My colleagues and I are working with a group of farmers to test some more sustainable techniques. Instead of chemical fertilizers, these farmers are using animal waste. They're also rotating crops – that is, planting different crops from year to year – and planting cover crops. This last technique was a really tough sell. A cover crop is planted for the sole purpose of improving the quality of the soil. There is nothing to harvest and sell at the end of the season. So you can imagine how this would not be considered a **viable** option for some farmers – to plant a crop that would result in no **revenue**. Gradually, however, they began to see how much better their cash crops grew in a field that had been filled with a cover crop the year before.

Now, what are some other advantages of practices like crop rotation and the use of cover crops? Diversifying crops can reduce the number of pests, such as insects and small animals, thus decreasing the need for pesticides. Planting cover crops can help farmers with another constant challenge – erosion. Erosion occurs when wind and water lift off the top layer of soil and carry it away. Erosion typically accompanies the **conversion** of wild spaces with natural vegetation to agricultural land. The act of plowing exposes and loosens the soil, making it **vulnerable** to the forces of wind and water. This erosion of the topsoil is a problem for farmers, but it also has an environmental impact. As the topsoil gets carried off into rivers and streams, it can cause serious damage to these waterways, which are important habitats for a wide range of species.

So you can see it's hard to talk about one critical resource – soil – without talking about the other – water. Agriculture uses 80 to 90 percent of the water resources in this country. Some of our most important crops require massive amounts of water. To quench their thirst, we've been drawing from underground reserves, some of which are now drying up. Clearly, this practice is not sustainable. But there is another obvious source of water – rain, right? Unfortunately, many farmers just let rainwater run off into rivers, as I just mentioned, often carrying valuable topsoil with it. The design of conventional farms – wide, flat, open fields – is part of the problem. But it doesn't have to be like this. We can conserve water *and* reduce erosion by altering the design of fields. Another aspect of water conservation is the retention of the soil moisture, and here again, planting cover crops can make a huge difference. They trap surface water and prevent it from evaporating. So you see, everything in nature – the soil, the water, and the food we eat – is all interconnected.

So why doesn't everyone just switch to sustainable practices? Good question. One reason is that some of the costs of sustainable agriculture are higher than those of conventional agriculture, in particular, labor. Sustainable practices require more people to manage them. But from a global perspective, perhaps a more important issue is yield. It has long been believed that crop yields of sustainable farming are no match for those of modern, intensive agricultural practices. And there is some truth to this, but with improved technology and greater knowledge, studies show that it is possible to shrink the gap between the two systems. Nevertheless, farmers aren't going to risk changing their time-tested methods without strong and direct proof that their yields won't suffer because of it.

I'll finish my talk by reporting on a recent study that compares three different forms of farming. It compared conventional methods that use chemical fertilizers and pesticides with two more sustainable approaches – one that relies on animal waste for nutrients and another that relies on crop management – the use of crop rotation and cover crops. The findings support the claim that conventional methods have higher yields than sustainable methods, but the differences were not large. Furthermore, the conventional farmers spent more to achieve that greater yield, so their profits were actually lower. When you combine those results with the environmental damage that conventional farming can cause, you really begin to wonder why we continue with conventional farming practices at all. Well, there are some good reasons for this, and we will explore them next time.

 1.3

See script on page 21.

 1.4

Moderator: Join us tomorrow for *Our Planet*. I'll be hosting a panel discussion with people representing four different organizations and points of view on climate change. Learn which parts of the world have the highest emission rates for CO_2 and other damaging greenhouse gases. Which parts of the world have the highest *per capita* emission rates? Who's to blame for damage to the environment caused by these emissions? And how should we hold these countries responsible? With economic sanctions? With boycotts? We'll get opinions on these issues tomorrow at 2:00 p.m. So join us.

1.5

Moderator: Welcome, everyone, to our session on global responsibility and climate change. Today we have a panel of four speakers who come from a wide range of organizations and points of view. Please welcome Grace Chin from StepUp, Russell Sanchez from Fair Share, Dara Sinee from Citizens for Global Justice, and finally, Vijay Gupta from the Fund for the Environmental Future. Each of our panelists is going to make an opening statement that explains his or her organization's perspective on climate change and related issues. Then we will open up the discussion to our audience.

So, one of the most controversial issues at the United Nations' talks on climate change in Paris was the respective roles and responsibilities of developed and developing countries in **combating** climate change. Panelists, can you address this issue for us? Our first speaker is Grace Chin. Grace?

Grace: Thank you. Climate change is an immediate threat to the entire planet, but it's not a new problem. CO_2 and other greenhouse gases are **accumulating** largely as a result of the human activity in developed countries over the past century. The emissions per capita figures are quite clear. The responsibility for global warming falls squarely on the shoulders of the developed world. The United States has the highest per capita emissions of any major country in the world. So shouldn't the United States and other developed nations be the ones making changes, even if those changes are expensive? The United States is a country with enormous economic resources. It's not fair to put the burden of lowering emissions on countries that are trying to fight their way out of poverty. For many of these countries, economic development, including the extraction of natural resources, must remain a priority, even if the process has a negative impact on the environment. They can't afford to change to more expensive alternative energy sources even if they are less polluting. It is the governments and citizens of the developed world who need to step up and accept responsibility for the health of the environment.

Moderator: Thank you, Grace. And now Russell Sanchez from Fair Share.

Russell: We at Fair Share recognize the difficulties that developing countries face, and we agree that the developed world needs to provide some assistance, for example, by buying carbon credits. However, we should keep in mind that the per capita figures that Grace cited are somewhat misleading. Many developing countries, such as India and especially China, have huge populations. So, although their per capita figure may be lower, the overall emissions rate is very high. The emissions rate for China is almost double that of the United States. But it's not just China. One recent study estimated that 20 to 25 percent of annual CO_2 emissions come from countries where farmers still burn forests and grasslands to prepare their land for farming. So, those forces are **accelerating** climate change.

We are also losing our best hope to *slow* this process. The loss of trees in the Amazon rainforest, often called the "lungs of the world," has reduced by half the ability of the planet to absorb CO_2. Overall, it's the rapid industrialization of the developing world that is bringing **unprecedented** levels of CO_2 emissions. In the 19th century, we didn't know any better, but now we do. Developing countries have what we might call a "late-comer's advantage." They know the consequences of their actions. If they don't use that knowledge wisely, there have to be some repercussions – economic repercussions. Why not organize a global boycott of any products whose manufacture causes significant negative environmental effects? If we refuse to buy wood that comes from a forest that should still be standing, or beef that was raised on land that was once a rainforest, perhaps developing countries will begin to make wiser choices.

Moderator: Thank you, Russell. Now we turn to Dara Sinee from Citizens for Global Justice.

Dara: The position that Russell has described is deeply unfair, but I'm afraid I find the position taken by Grace's organization almost equally troubling. There is simply no way that developing countries can be held to the same standard as countries in the developed world. They don't have adequate economic resources, and punishing them with a boycott or other economic sanctions will push some of them even deeper into poverty. However, I also question the wisdom of encouraging developing countries to continue on a path that could eventually lead to their own destruction. It is as much in their interest to slow climate change as it is in ours. If global warming continues at its current pace, Bangladesh, a country of 150 million people, for example, could be under water in the not-too-distant future. How useful will economic development and resource extraction be to the people of Bangladesh then? Russell talks of buying carbon credits – developing countries get economic support and rich nations get the right to increase their emissions. Buying carbon credits is just another form of exploitation in which the people of the developed world buy the right to cause environmental damage. It's not much better than the current **shameful** practice of **disposing of** their old computers – so-called *e-waste* – in countries that can't afford to refuse the money they are willing to pay to dump them there. Developed nations need to provide real support to poor countries so that their development does not come at the expense of the environment!

Moderator: Thank you very much. And finally, Vijay Gupta, from Fund for the Environmental Future, what is your position?

Vijay: What good is pointing fingers and blaming one another? It's not going to help us solve this problem. The planet is warming up faster than ever. The last two years have been the warmest on record. If we have any chance of slowing climate change, all countries, both developed and developing, need to **allocate** more funding to this effort, even if it means **diverting** money from other worthwhile projects. The bottom line is that global warming is not just continuing; it is accelerating. As several of the panelists have suggested, there is not much point in economic development if it puts the health of our planet in danger. If we allow even a single country to increase its emissions, the problem will only grow worse. This is not an issue we can put off until another international conference or chip away at gradually. We need to take immediate, dramatic, and unified action if we want to preserve our world for the next generation.

Moderator: Many thanks to all of our participants. I am sure our listeners have a lot of questions, so let's open us the phone lines and ... .

1.6

Ranger: We are facing numerous challenges here at Grand Canyon National Park. In 2015, we hosted 5.5 million visitors. It's the second most popular park in the nation. All of those visitors put a lot of pressure on the park, so we've had to spend most of our annual budget on maintaining services for them. But there are many other problems that need attention. Most of the water in the Colorado River, which carved out the canyon over thousands of years, has been diverted to other uses: to cities and nearby farms. The river's level continues to drop, which has seriously affected the habitat of many of the plants and animals that live in and around the river. Outside of the park, there are mining operations that threaten to pollute the groundwater flowing under the park, and nearby power plants produce air pollution that regularly blocks the view of our beautiful canyon. Above the park, we have tourists in helicopters enjoying the view, but at the same time, creating so much noise that it disturbs park animals. Non-native species, mostly brought in by the park's many visitors, are endangering the native species. We need another $6.2 billion to address these and other pressing issues.

1.7

See script on page 32.

1.8

Patrick: I volunteer at a local state park about once a month, on a Saturday morning. We pull up invasive plants and clear the trails so that they're safe for people to walk on. I really enjoy it. It feels good to do something physical and to be out in the open air. Plus it's good exercise! It always makes us hungry too, so they provide a big lunch afterwards for all of the volunteers. It's usually the same people every month, so I've made some new friends.

Bahar: I had an incredible experience last year. During my spring break, I spent two weeks building houses in a low-income area. We built the houses from the bottom up: we mixed concrete, made the walls, installed the plumbing, everything. I'm an architecture major, so it was a great opportunity to see how a building actually gets built. I learned a lot and I'm sure this knowledge will help me in my building designs. But the best part was when we met the people who were going to live in the houses. They were so grateful. It really made me realize how lucky I am. I'm hoping to go back again this summer.

Yolanda: I run a campus organization called Students for Schools. We raise funds for local schools, and every year we hold a big concert on campus. It's a lot of work to organize the event: we have to get a permit, find musicians, get donations of food and drink from local restaurants, and so on. I spend a lot of time talking on the phone. It's given me a lot of management skills though – being organized, meeting deadlines, managing other people. It's taught me a lot about myself and given me a lot of confidence. This will look great on my résumé when I'm looking for a job after I graduate.

UNIT 2

The Appeal of Large Cell Phones

Reporter 1: Molly Wood is a personal tech columnist for the *New York Times*. Welcome.

Wood: Thank you, good to be here.

Reporter 1: Just show us what Galaxy is doing.

Wood: Exactly.

Reporter 1: That's what we want to see.

Wood: I brought the toys. So Samsung really took this opportunity ...

Reporter 1: Samsung.

Wood: ... on the cusp of Apple maybe announcing a bigger phone next week, Samsung took this opportunity to remind everyone that they really pioneered this idea.

Reporter 2: Yeah, "We did it first."

Wood: "We were here first with the big phones," or the phablets, a phone that's as big as a tablet. So this is the fourth version of their Note phone which has been around for a while, and it's a 5.7 inch screen. You can use it to ...

Reporter 1: Yeah.

Wood: Gayle was wondering if you could talk on it.

Reporter 2: Yeah.

Wood: And so they announced the fourth version but they also, you know, Samsung is a design-oriented company and so they kind of, introduced this new model that also has this wrap-around screen. They're actually two touchscreens on here.

Reporter 1: Yeah.

Wood: And you can sort of customize this with other, other kind of elements. You know, I need to try it out and see if it will be interesting or not. But it's, it was a good time for Samsung to make a splash.

Reporter 2: But I like, Charlie, what the guy in Samsung said – Phillip, who's in the green room said, "It's not just pretty, it's functional too."

Wood: Yes.

Reporter 2: Because one feature he pointed out was the alarm, the alarm clock, which I did think was very cool.

Wood: It does, it has a nighttime alarm clock, and so you can see, when it's actually sitting on a table, if there were sort of dim numbers here, an alarm clock, it's actually quite useful.

Reporter 1: So –

Reporter 3: I'm sorry, I just think it's funny that big is more popular now.

Wood: It is a really interesting trend, and it's very popular. In fact in Asian countries in particular, phablets outsell smaller phones. There's a ton of research to suggest that people, you know, browsing on a 4-inch device, which is the size of the iPhone, is down 11% from last year, according to Adobe. People really want these bigger phones because you can do more.

Reporter 1: So they want something bigger so they don't have to have a tablet?

Wood: Exactly. I think that you know we got tired of carrying a laptop, a tablet, and a phone, in a bag or for business travel.

Reporter 2: What about the mini iPad? That was too small, is that what you're saying?

Reporter 1: No, it's too big.

Reporter 2: Is it too big?

Wood: It's a good size, but if I have phone that's this big, I don't need that. And for me, I'd rather have a bigger phone, than a smaller tablet because this is an all-in-one device.

Reporter 1: So everyone wants one device.

Wood: Exactly.

Reporter 2: Got it.

Reporter 1: And so what will this do to the competition with Apple? Because they're coming out with their big announcement in a week or so?

Wood: Yeah, so it was good timing for Samsung to announce something early, to say we have a brand new big phone. And Samsung and Apple are the two big competitors in the smartphone race right now. And so if Apple does come out with bigger phones, as we expect, then I think we'll have a real horse race.

Reporter 1: Do we expect anything else from Apple?

Wood: There's a lot of rumors that we may finally see the smartwatch, the new kind of wearable device from Apple.

Reporter 2: And Samsung said, "We did that too."

2.1

Speaker: No shoes for the wedding? No problem, just print a pair. A part inside your dishwasher has broken? No problem, just print a replacement. Kidney failure? No problem; we can print you a new organ – on demand.

The technology behind 3D printing, the process of creating a solid object from a digital model, has been around since the 1980s, but only recently have the costs fallen far enough and the computer software improved enough to make some of these **scenarios** more than a dream.

I think some of the most dramatic uses of 3D printing have been in biomedical research, where scientists have been working on 3D-printed organs. In these projects, the "ink" that the printers use is actually made of human cells. So in the case of 3D-printed skin, a printer builds up layers of skin cells. You can imagine how this could help a patient with a burn or a wound that hasn't been healing on its own. Other printers are creating bone, muscle, ears, and even brain tissue. Doctors and researchers have been working on recreating human organs for years, but 3D printing is really an advance. For one thing, the computer software that guides the printing process is extremely accurate, right down to the micron, an accomplishment that human hands cannot match. In addition, since the new organs come from human cells, often the patient's own cells, there is a lower risk of rejection. This biological 3D printing function is the one that I am the most excited about; but the research and testing still have a long way to go before we can automatically include this technology among a patient's options.

On a lighter note, 3D printing has also entered the world of high fashion, where designers are actively using it in their collections. What really attracts designers is the idea that they can **customize** their designs. And consumers? Well, they're dreaming of the day when they can download a design from the Internet and print it out at home. That day too, however, is some distance in the future, at least until we can come up with better "ink." Today, the material fed into 3D printers is a type of plastic. It's stiffer than fabric and not very comfortable. The cost of printing is also too high to make this a practical form of production. So you're more likely to find 3D fashions on the runway than in a department store. That said, the possibility that this innovation could **shift** the production of clothing to local centers and away from large facilities, most of which are now in the developing world, could seriously disrupt the apparel industry and global markets.

There is no doubt that this technology has had and will continue to have the greatest impact in the manufacturing sector, where it is referred to as "additive manufacturing," or AM. In the past, the key to keeping costs low was **mass production**. The more units you produce, the lower your cost per unit. 3D printing has the potential to turn this equation on its head. In AM, there are no drawbacks to printing small quantities; quite the opposite, actually. The attraction of this technology is that you can customize each item to your needs. It also completely disrupts two key elements that are part of the **foundation** of manufacturing: **assembly** and the supply chain. Rick Smith, a 3D entrepreneur, cites the case of a man who was able to print an airplane part that had previously consisted of 21 separate pieces, all of which were manufactured in different factories, and then shipped to one factory where they were assembled. The man had no background in manufacturing, yet he was able to print the part as a single piece, on the spot, right where the part was needed. What's more, because it was printed as one piece, the 3D-printed part was five times stronger than the original part and 83 percent lighter, which reduced fuel costs by 15 percent. So even though the raw materials for the part were relatively expensive, the potential cost savings more than made up for them.

Consider the potential impact on manufacturing: no more need to maintain an extensive inventory, no more need for an assembly plant or a global supply chain. Everything could just be created on demand and on location. AM would reduce waste and shorten supply chains, in the process reducing our environmental footprint as well. It could also help us keep our stuff working for longer. If an appliance breaks today, the cost of repairing it is often as high as the cost of replacing it. With all of its efficiencies, AM printing could **drastically** lower repair costs, so we would need to replace equipment, even cars, less frequently.

All of this sounds like a dream come true. So, what's the **downside**, you may ask? There always is one, of course. Although I mentioned the positive impact AM could have on the environment, it could also have the opposite effect. First of all, the plastic that is used in most 3D printers has a long supply chain and most of it, though not all, is petroleum based. Also, printing that is this easy could encourage our already casual attitude toward disposing of possessions. Don't like your shoes? Throw them out and print a new pair. But that old pair will have to end up somewhere. So I worry that along with all its advantages, 3D printing may bring an explosion of junk.

There is also the potential for abuse. The technology might be so easy to use that you could just download instructions and print something dangerous – like a gun. Already, criminals have printed parts for bank machines in order to withdraw money illegally. So yes, there will be problems, but I want to end my talk by stressing that in spite of these concerns, I am optimistic and excited about the possibilities presented by this 3D printing technology. Some have predicted that it will bring the third industrial revolution. Is this an exaggeration? Perhaps, but then again, perhaps not.

2.2

Speaker: It also completely disrupts two key elements that are part of the foundation of manufacturing: assembly and the supply chain. Rick Smith, a 3D entrepreneur, cites the case of a man who was able to print an airplane part that had previously consisted of 21 separate pieces, all of which were manufactured in different factories, and then shipped to one factory where they were assembled. The man had no background in manufacturing, yet he was able to print the part as a single piece, on the spot, right where the part was needed. What's more, because it was printed as one piece, the 3D-printed part was five times stronger than the original part and 83 percent lighter, which reduced fuel costs by 15 percent. So, even though the raw materials for the part were relatively expensive, the potential cost savings more than made up for them.

Consider the potential impact on manufacturing: no more need to maintain an extensive inventory, no more need for an assembly plant or a global supply chain. Everything could just be created on demand and on location.

2.3

1 The technology behind 3D printing, the process of creating a solid object from a digital model, has been around since the 1980s.

2 The computer software has improved enough to make some of these scenarios more than a dream.

3 I think some of the most dramatic uses of 3D printing have been in biomedical research, where scientists have been working on 3D-printed organs.

4 What really attracts designers is the possibility of customizing their designs.

5 The possibility that this innovation could shift the production of clothing to local centers and away from large facilities, most of which are now in the developing world, could seriously disrupt the apparel industry and global markets.

6 It also completely disrupts two key elements that are part of the foundation of manufacturing.

7 Rick Smith, a 3D entrepreneur, cites the case of a man who was able to print an airplane part that had previously consisted of 21 separate pieces, all of which were manufactured in different factories, and then shipped to one factory where they were assembled.

2.4

Teacher: Welcome everyone, and thanks for coming to this special presentation event that marks the end of our semester. The topic that students explored in this project is planned obsolescence. The students formed four groups, and each group investigated and will report on a different aspect of this **phenomenon**. Each group is represented by one of its members. We'll start with group 1 and Robert, who is going to help us understand the concept in general. Robert?

Robert: I want to begin by defining what *planned obsolescence* means. This term was coined in the 1950s and describes a deliberate design policy. It means that a product is designed to become obsolete – to break, fail, become outdated, or go out of fashion – in a set – and usually relatively short — period of time.

As you might imagine, the purpose of planning a product's obsolescence is to make sure that consumers will have to buy new products on a regular basis. So planned obsolescence is a design, marketing, and financial policy all rolled into one. Now it's easy to think of this process as a plot **devised** by large corporations to take advantage of consumers. And there is certainly some evidence to support this point of view. However, it is also important to see the other side of the issue, especially within the tech sector, where things change very rapidly. It wouldn't make sense to build a piece of equipment to last for twenty years when the technology it uses will probably be replaced in one or two. In this way, planned obsolescence may have the positive effect of encouraging innovation.

You could also argue that there is a consumer benefit because making products stronger, more durable, would probably push prices out of reach for many consumers. That said, most consumers **resent** planned obsolescence. Besides the financial burden of constantly having to buy new things, people also point to the enormous amount of waste it generates, waste that has to be put somewhere.

I hope this gives you the general idea of the issues around planned obsolescence. The next two groups will provide us with some specific examples.

Anjali: We are surrounded by products that are designed to become obsolete, especially anything that involves new technology. Some products are actually designed with a **finite** lifespan; others could last much longer, but their design makes it either impossible or impractical to extend their life. Not surprisingly, consumer electronics top this list. Let's start with phones.

Some people run out to get the newest model as soon as it comes on the market because they truly are early adopters, eager to own the newest gadgets. For many of us, however, upgrading isn't a choice, but rather a matter of necessity. Phones are complex devices, and companies have made it difficult for people to repair them on their own. Something as simple as replacing the battery is often the biggest **obstacle** to a longer product life. For some phones, the price of the new battery is very close to the price of a new phone, leading many customers to conclude that they might as well upgrade.

In other devices, software upgrades, issued automatically, and often with no warnings, may actually impair the performance of older models. Or you may find that the software company no longer supports your older version at all. You have to upgrade the hardware, and with a hardware upgrade, a software upgrade may become necessary too. You have no choice but to keep trading up. But, as Celia will explain, technology products are really just the tip of the iceberg when it comes to product obsolescence. Celia?

Celia: Thank you. So, Anjali has given you some examples of obsolescence in the tech sector, but we also encounter this phenomenon in the world of clothing, where it is referred to as "fast fashion."

Fast fashion is a relatively recent trend in which designers and manufacturers try to move fashions from the runway to retail stores as quickly as possible. It also involves responding immediately to consumer preferences. This is how it works. An apparel company spots a trend, say, white lacy blouses are selling quickly at their stores in California. An order is placed for hundreds of white lacy blouses, which appear on shelves two weeks later, encouraging the trend. A few months later, no one is buying white lacy blouses, but many customers have bought ripped black jeans. So another order is placed, and suddenly ripped black jeans are everywhere.

Some companies have gotten so good at this that they can design, manufacture, and have clothing on store shelves in just two or three weeks at a very low cost. The quality standards for the material in this apparel are low, and manufacturing is done in locations where labor costs are also low, resulting in cheap but low-quality products. Yet this has not slowed sales. On the contrary, the low prices and perhaps, ironically, even the low quality, encourage customers to buy more and more. Their attitude seems to be, "This will be out of fashion by next year, but it's so cheap, who cares if it falls apart in a couple of months? I'll just buy the next big thing." Without a doubt, fast-fashion businesses generate enormous profits, but they also generate a lot of waste, so much that some people have begun to refer to their products as "landfill fashion."

Jun: We are going to end this presentation by discussing some of the consumer **backlash** to planned obsolescence. There is an ongoing battle between big tech companies and consumers who want to modify or repair their devices. Manufacturers try to prevent this by limiting access to parts and repair information and by using digital locks. In some cases, there are penalties for even trying to open up the back of a phone or a tablet: the warranty is no longer valid or the company will refuse to make any **subsequent** repairs.

In response, a consumer-led movement has risen to share knowledge that allows people to **circumvent** these restrictions. The organization ifixit.org argues that consumers have the right to repair their own possessions and that manufacturers should give them access to the information that they need to do so. They share information about how to fix products and how to get around the obstacles that manufacturers place in the way of repairs. There are numerous similar websites and blogs that promote the idea of repairing, reusing, and recycling possessions. Other sites, such as buymeonce.com, recommend products that will last and permit repairs, and they also offer tips on maintaining your high-quality products so you can hold on to them for a long time. Their goal is to reduce waste of all kinds.

We've only had a short time today to present you with a lot of material. We have lots of other examples and links to organizations. We would be happy to share more of our research or answer any questions you have about this topic. Thank you.

See scripts on page 52.

Excerpt 1

Our topic is e-waste. First, I'll give a definition of e-waste. Then I'll look at the growth of e-waste globally: the countries that produce the most e-waste and the products that are most often thrown away. David will explain the effects of e-waste on the environment and on human health. Finally, Jia-Lin will look at some steps that are being taken to reduce the amount of e-waste that consumers generate.

Excerpt 2

Globally, consumers are buying and using more and more electronic goods: cell phones, laptops, tablets, televisions, game consoles, and so on. And as you know, most people use these products for only a couple of years before they trade them in for a newer model. Unfortunately, this has created a global problem of e-waste. In one year, the average consumer in Europe or North America produces somewhere between 26 and 33 pounds of consumer electronic waste in one year.

Excerpt 3

The amount of e-waste is growing. In 2012, approximately 37.8 million tons of e-waste were generated worldwide. By 2014, that number had risen to 41.8 million tons. In 2018, it is estimated that we will produce close to 50 million tons of e-waste worldwide.

Excerpt 4

One positive development is that people are starting to recycle more and more. In the United States in the year 2000, nearly two million tons of e-waste were generated, and only 190,000, or ten percent, was recycled. In 2009, there was a lot more e-waste: more than three million tons – but 600,000 units were recycled – that's 18%. And by 2012, nearly three and a half million tons were generated, but 1,000,000 tons, or approximately 29%, was recycled. So this shows that people are becoming aware of the need to recycle.

Excerpt 5

If we look at energy use over the lifespan of a computer, we find that much more energy – 81 percent – is used in the production of that computer. Only 19 percent is used in operation. So the energy is used in making the computers rather than in using them.

UNIT 3

Security Breaches at Big-Box Stores

Reporter 1: Now to what could be one of the biggest data breaches ever to hit a major retailer. This morning, Home Depot is investigating whether its customers' credit and debit cards were exposed. It's not clear how many stores or shoppers could be involved, but experts say it could be larger than the breach that affected 40 million shoppers at Target last year. In a statement, Home Depot says, "Protecting our customers' information is something we take extremely seriously." CBS News contributor and analyst Mellody Hobson is in Chicago. Mellody, good morning.

Hobson: Good morning.

Reporter 1: So why do these security breaches keep happening?

Hobson: It's like that old saying, "Why do you rob a bank? It's where the money is." The cyberthieves know, they're the new organized crime, that there's a lot of money to be made online because 60% of us are banking online. Most of us are shopping online, so when they get these numbers, they can sell them. And just to use the Target example, the estimates are that the thieves made in the neighborhood of $50 million from that one breach.

Reporter 2: So what are these companies going to do? What are potential targets going to do?

Hobson: Well, now what they're saying, ... Target was the wake-up call. They knew that they lost almost $2 billion in market cap, their profits plummeted, the CEO lost his job. So now the retailers are saying, we have to get in front of this and play offense. On top of that, the credit card companies have said that if the new card-reader technology hasn't been adopted by October of 2015, if there's fraud, the retailer is responsible.

So now everyone's trying to get in front of this new card reader, which has dual verification, which makes the transaction much, much safer, for both the retailer and the customer.

Reporter 1: Yeah, so let's talk about that new technology, we keep hearing about it, called chip-and-PIN technology. When's it going to be available? What does it mean for consumers when you're shopping?

Hobson: So I'm told (I talked to one of the major retailers yesterday), the next 18 to 48 months, you're going to see most retailers adopt this. Now interestingly, Walmart adopted it eight years ago, and even Home Depot has a lot of these card readers in their stores right now. But you need the new credit card.

Reporter 2: Yeah.

Hobson: And interestingly, I just got my new AmEx that has chip-and-PIN technology, they sent me a letter saying that it is going to be safer. So this is now rolling out right now, and you'll probably see much, much more of it coming, if you haven't already.

Reporter 2: I assume that the credit card companies and others, who are having to take these extra measures, will simply pass on the cost of that to the customers, to their customers.

Hobson: Again, I talked to this major retailer yesterday, I don't know how they can do that. Now the costs are huge, they're estimated to be about $8 billion to change all these systems around the country. But I don't know how they could pass it on.

3.1

Speaker: Welcome everyone, and thank you for coming to this talk in our series on technology and privacy. Our speaker today is Casey Chan, who is an expert in the field. She is going to explain how some of the technology works and then talk about sensible steps you can take to protect your privacy when you use the Internet. Casey?

Casey Chan: Thank you. So, you've probably all had this experience: you're surfing the Internet; maybe you're looking for some new camera equipment. There is a new lens you really want, but it's kind of expensive, so you decide to put it off for a while. Maybe you'll be able to afford it next month. You move on. Later, you're reading an online newspaper or blog and then, bam! An ad for that lens you want flashes onto your screen. Kind of **creepy**, right? I mean, how did they do that? How do they know what you were looking at on a completely different website? Well, that's what I want to talk about today.

What you experienced is called "behavioral targeting." With every click, you create and expand an online profile of your desires, preferences, and behavior. Companies **track** your browsing activity and use it to send you advertisements that **target** you specifically. Their hope is that by understanding what you like and want, they can send you ads, which you are more likely to click, for products and services that you are more likely to buy.

How did this all begin? Well, it actually started with you, the web user, in mind. Let's be honest, when a website tracks and remembers where you've been, it can be pretty useful, right? You start typing the name of a website you've visited before in the search bar, and it automatically fills the rest of it in for you. Or, if you can't remember the name of the site, you can check your browsing history, and there it is. You don't want to fill in your information every time you visit a site? No problem. It's all saved for you when you come back. The primary tool that companies use to track and remember you is the *cookie*.

A cookie is a small text file, which is downloaded onto your browser when you visit a site. It saves information about what you do while you're on the site. Cookies were first developed when online retailers were looking for a way to make shopping easier for customers. You've probably all used an online shopping cart, right? Well, cookies are what make that cart possible. Without cookies, the cart could not collect the items you select. The site would forget them as soon as you left to go to a new page. But with cookies, you can even think it over and come back the next day. The items are still in your cart. So cookies are clearly useful. In general, cookies have made it possible to personalize the user experience in a way that makes searching and using the Internet more efficient and satisfying.

That's how cookies work within a single website. The creepy part starts when they cross over to *other* websites. Advertising companies that have hundreds of clients can connect cookies all across the Web. For example, if you click on an ad when you visit a website, then another cookie is sent to your browser by the advertiser. This is sometimes called *a third-party cookie*. Now, every time you visit another site that has ads from the same company, the cookies can be **traced back** to you. As you surf and shop your way around the Internet, these cookies eventually build a profile of your preferences and interests. It shows when and where you clicked and how long you spent on each page, all of which is very valuable information for companies that want to sell you services and products, like that camera lens.

One final cookie issue that you should be aware of is that some cookies are transmitted over a secure network; that is, they are sent in a type of code. These are usually called *secure cookies*, and many retail sites use these. *Nonsecure cookies*, in contrast, are vulnerable to theft. If someone grabs one of these during transmission, it can be used for the purpose of identity theft. Lots of sites you probably use, including social media sites, use nonsecure cookies. I think more sites will probably move to secure cookies in the future, but for now, only about half of all websites use secure cookies.

So now you know a little bit about how it all works. Maybe you're thinking you should stop using the Internet altogether! Don't despair! I'm going to give you some advice about a few easy ways to manage and protect your privacy without going offline!

Many of the tools you need are right there on your browser, or are offered by individual websites. You just need to actively choose to use them. For example, you may be asked for your permission to let the browser know where you are and where you're going. You may be asked to turn on or enable your cookies. We get so many long and often complicated messages that we often just click "yes" or "I agree" because it's too much trouble to do anything else. If that describes you, then you need to become a more educated Internet user and make more **informed** decisions. You should say "no" if you don't want that company to store information about you.

Most browsers have a setting that allows you to disable cookies, preventing sites from collecting information on your web activities. But you may not want to disable this feature all the time; in which case, you can simply delete your browsing history – for the past week, month, year – or from the beginning of time, giving you some level of control over what information can be collected and stored. Most browsers also have an option that allows you to surf *incognito*, which means no information is collected on your activity. But remember, this means you will also get none of the benefits of that stored information. Finally, there are alternative browsers, ones which do not collect or store any data about users and their activities. If you take some of these steps, you will probably be OK – or at least less vulnerable.

However, these cookies are just the first weapon in an online retailer's **arsenal**. There are other, more sophisticated methods for recording user activity, including ones that are more difficult for users to manage and control. Some tools, such as so-called flash cookies, also store information about you, but they are stored *outside* of your browser. And *web beacons*, tiny invisible graphics on web pages, can tell the server you're on a specific page, and these are not removed when you clear your cookies or browsing history. No doubt, tech privacy experts will soon **catch up with** these developments and find ways to **counter** them as well.

To sum up, you can't control everything, but you can take charge of some aspects of your privacy and online identity. I hope that this talk has given you some useful information and tools. And remember, think before you click!

See script on page 66.

Host: In recent months, the news has been filled with a debate that sets individual privacy against national security. We've heard the views of the government, as well as those of technology companies and experts in the fields of national security and technology. But what about the views of ordinary people, the people who are affected when either their privacy or national security is threatened? To find out, we've invited six people from different walks of life to come to the studio and share their thoughts. We will take questions and comments from listeners at the end of the program.

Before we bring in our guests, however, let's talk about the two questions that we are going to ask them. Our first question is: should technology and communication companies be **compelled** to hand over information about the activities of private individuals to law enforcement agencies (for example, the police, the FBI, etc.) **in the interest of** national security or to combat crime?

This question addresses the millions of records that these companies have – names, contacts, IP addresses, etc. – so called metadata, but also actual content, for example, what people said in phone conversations or in text messages, and information they have stored on their devices, such as lists of contacts.

Our second question addresses a different but related issue: should technology companies be compelled to help law enforcement agencies break into the electronic devices of private individuals, again, in the interest of national security or to combat crime?

So, in this question, we're asking whether tech companies should have to write computer code to create a "back door," that is, a way to circumvent the **encryption** of information on devices that they make.

Host: Let's start with Joel, who works in the insurance industry. Joel, should companies have to hand over information about their customers?

Joel: Absolutely. Law enforcement's got to have as much information as possible in order to keep us safe. We've learned that lesson the hard way. The good guys need to know more than the bad guys.

Host: And should they be required to help law enforcement break into private devices?

Joel: Well, I am not so sure about that one. That may be crossing the line.

Host: Lauren, a high school teacher here in town, is next. What do you think, Lauren?

Lauren: Hey, if I contract with a private company for phone service or web access or whatever, that's between me and the company. They shouldn't give out information about me to anyone. That's what I think, but I'm not sure it matters. You know tech companies are *already* doing it. A recent report showed they've actually been doing it for years, usually without even getting a court order.

Host: Then I guess your answer to the second question would be ...

Lauren: Don't get me started. If we're worried about national security, the *last* thing we should do is make these companies write code to circumvent the encryption. If there's a back door for the government, then you can be sure that all kinds of bad guys – terrorists, criminals – well, they'll find a way to use it too. Think of all the information you have on your digital devices – health records, financial information, passwords. A back door is an invitation to criminals to steal your identity. Encryption is the only thing that is protecting us.

Host: OK, we'll see whether our next guest agrees with you. This is Drake and he's a police office. Drake, as someone in law enforcement, what are your thoughts?

Drake: People just don't understand. Law enforcement is very difficult without access to this kind of information. I've had cases when I couldn't arrest a criminal because of some law about *his* privacy. If the criminals know more than we do, how can we protect good, law-abiding people? Isn't safety more important than privacy?

Host: Is it important enough to make tech companies break into our devices?

Drake: No doubt in my mind. If we have to give up a little bit of freedom and privacy for the sake of national security, so be it. Information is power these days, and law enforcement doesn't have enough of it.

Host: Let's hear from someone with some legal **expertise**. Karina is a lawyer. Karina?

Karina: To my mind, if the government wants my data, it should have to ask me for it or get a court order. The law requires this. So, if there is a **convincing** need for the information, and if a judge gives the government permission, then yes, I think this is perfectly **legitimate**.

Host: And do you think we should ask tech companies for help in cracking private devices?

Karina: Absolutely not. This is a free speech issue. The courts have ruled in the past that writing computer code is a form of speech. And in a democratic country, the government cannot compel you to say something if you don't want to. It's a fundamental principle of our society.

What everyone needs to understand is that in your *first* question, you're asking about information that the tech company actually *has*. But in the *second* question, you're asking if the company should be forced to write new software to break into an encrypted phone and *get* information. That is an entirely different story. The information on that phone does *not* belong to the tech company; it belongs to a *private individual*.

Another thing: if the government really wanted to get information off a particular device, you know it could find a way to do it. I think the government just wants to set a legal **precedent**, so the next time it needs something, it can point to this case as an example. But precedents like this are dangerous. What about foreign governments? Right now, tech companies can say it's their policy not to help anyone break into encrypted devices. But if they change their policy for *our* government, it will be a lot harder to refuse *other* governments. We certainly don't want that.

Host: OK, Tony, your turn to weigh in. Tony is a small business owner.

Tony: I think we need to do everything we can to help the government and law enforcement agencies put a stop to terrorism, so my answer is yes, tech companies should turn over any information the government asks for.

But breaking into people's phones? Well, I think that's kind of odd – not just odd – it's disturbing that the government can't already do this. Why does the government have to ask tech companies for help? Doesn't it have its own experts? Karina there, she said she thinks the government does have the expertise to do it on its own. But I guess if it doesn't, then maybe the tech companies do have an obligation to help the government – if it's really a matter of national security.

Host: Finally we come to Sunjoo, a data analyst, who might be able to give us some insight from the tech side.

Sunjoo: I think if the information is limited to metadata – you know – phone numbers, dates, times – that kind of thing, it's fine, but I would not want them to hand over the actual content of text messages or stuff like that. And I definitely don't think we should be asking tech companies to break into people's devices. Look, the government is trying to make it look as if this is a **tradeoff** between privacy and security. That might be true if we were talking about the physical world – like unlocking the door to your apartment. But the digital world isn't like that. Any technology expert can tell you that if a company gives the government the key to the back door of one phone, it's the same thing as giving up the key to thousands of other phones. Doing that would actually make all of us much *less* secure, not *more* secure.

Host: OK, we've heard views from six residents of our city. Now let's hear from you. Call the station to tell us what you think. OK, I see we have our first caller. Yes, caller, go ahead ... .

3.5

1 How can we protect good, law-abiding people?
2 Isn't safety more important than privacy?
3 Is it important enough to make tech companies break into our devices?
4 Do you think we should ask tech companies for help in cracking private devices?
5 What about foreign governments?
6 Why does the government have to ask the tech companies for help?
7 Doesn't it have its own experts?

3.6

Host: This morning we're talking to Dr. Gareth Huang. Doctor Huang is an educational consultant who specializes in student learning preferences. Welcome to the show, Dr. Huang.

Huang: Thank you.

Host: Let's start by defining some terms. What do we mean when we talk about "learning preferences"?

Huang: Well, it's really just the idea that students have different ways they prefer to learn. Some students, for example, are more dependent on the teacher. They want clear direction, and they want feedback. Other students are more independent.

Host: OK ...

Huang: Another typical difference that we see is in attitudes to participation – classroom discussion and group work, that sort of thing.

Host: Oh, yes! Some students love it, some students hate it.

Huang: Broadly speaking, yes. Some of us learn better when we discuss things, but others prefer to listen to lectures or read a book and think about the concepts on their own.

Host: Right.

Huang: And then finally there's the issue of structure. Some students really need teachers to provide a lot of structure. They want to know what's expected of them – how many words to write, in how many pages, and so on. Others are more, kind of, global – they don't care so much about the details.

Host: Which can get them into trouble, I imagine?

Huang: Yes, indeed. If a teacher has a very specific set of standards, and a student disregards that, then that can be a problem. In fact, often when there is conflict between a student and a teacher, it's because of different expectations. Sometimes students don't realize that instructors in college can be quite different from each other. What works in one class might not work in another.

Host: So they have to be able to adapt.

Huang: Yes, and sometimes that means they have to work in a different way from what they like, or what they're used to.

Host: What advice do you give students in that case?

Huang: First, get to know what is important to that particular teacher.

Also, read the syllabus. That can help you understand what the teacher values.

Another good idea is to read the directions for assignments carefully, to make sure you're doing the assignment as the teacher intends it to be done.

Finally, if the expectations are not clear, ask. Don't be shy. Ask for clarification whenever you're even a little unsure. You can also ask other students if they seem to understand something you don't.

In college, you have to take responsibility for your own learning, even if the teacher's style is not what you would like.

Host: Well, thank you, Dr. Huang. This has been very interesting. Join us next week when my guest will be ...

UNIT 4

A New Chapter for Independent Bookstores

Ann Patchett: Two huge profitable bookstores have closed, this is a no-brainer, somebody can open a small bookstore.

At the time I just thought, it's fun, it's my gift to the city, I don't care if we don't sell books, you know. I just have to live in a city that has a bookstore, but we're doing really well.

People in communities woke up and said, hey, I really miss having a little bookstore that I can take my kids to, and I can see things, I can shop, I can browse.

Customer 1: Even if I'm not going to buy anything I like to browse. And I just, I like to be able to, I'm like, I like to get my hands on things and look at stuff.

Employee: He writes about the year 1968 and, believe it or not, it's a page-turner.

Ann Patchett: We have a brilliant staff of people who read. So you can come into this store, tell me the last book you read, and I can tell you three more books that you're going to love. Now Amazon has an algorithm that says, you bought this book, other people bought this book, and that is not the same thing as dealing with a human being.

Customer 2: Our youngest son, we could take him to a bookstore, and when he found one and said, "Mom, I like this one," it was a done deal.

Ann Patchett: With the advent of ebooks and sort of just the book not as an object but as a collection of information, I think that what we're attracted to more and more are beautiful books.

Customer 3: I really value the physical product too.

Customer 4: Mm-hmm.

Customer 3: So I mean, I have a Kindle and I enjoy it, but it's also really nice to have an actual physical book.

Author giving talk: For a French person, it's a kind of ghost, but it's a ghost that comes back for a certain purpose.

Ann Patchett: I can't imagine starting out now as an author because the landscape is so different than it was when I was coming along. All my adult life I have been going to independent bookstores. And these are the people that sell my books. These are the people who took a chance on me when I had a first novel, a second novel, no one knew who I was.

Myra McEntire: Those are the places where authors get to go and sit down and build relationships with readers. We can know them online, Twitter, Facebook, whatever, but these are the places where we get to talk to them.

Ann Patchett: What I care about is that people read. Just because ebooks are becoming popular doesn't mean that we should scoop all the other books into a pile and burn them. And there is a sort of attitude of like, well, books are dead, it's over, forget it. And it's not over.

4.1

Professor: You may have heard the **buzzword** "disruptive innovation," which is when a new technology or business model fundamentally changes a market. The classic example is the personal computer, which was pioneered by IBM, a company that had previously dominated the market for large mainframe computers. The company's primary customers had been businesses. With IBM's new smaller model, however, computers became accessible to an entirely new group of customers – individuals, which changed the market forever.

Professor: You may have heard the buzzword "disruptive innovation," which is when a new technology or business model fundamentally changes a market. The classic example is the personal computer, which was pioneered by IBM, a company that had previously dominated the market for large mainframe computers. The company's primary customers had been businesses. With IBM's new smaller model, however, computers became accessible to an entirely new group of customers – individuals, which changed the market forever.

The Internet has become the engine of disruptive innovation in dozens of markets, from travel to publishing to insurance. By creating a system of universal access, the Internet **effectively** redefined many business **transactions**. By universal access, I mean two things: first, suddenly, anyone with a computer and a network connection could access all kinds of information that had previously only been available to professionals, who acted as "middlemen" in transactions between businesses and their customers. Massive amounts of information were **dumped** onto the Web for individual consumers to see and use. And second, networks among individuals were now possible. Buyers and sellers no longer needed intermediaries. They could connect directly to one other.

As a result, most people no longer bothered with these intermediaries – the middlemen. Why use a travel agent? Airfares and hotel rates could now all be found on the Internet. The public also began to abandon insurance agents and even bankers, instead going directly to the Internet to find products and services. Sellers also changed the way they did business. Musicians could sell their songs directly to the public. Authors didn't need publishers. Small manufacturers no longer needed big stores to carry their products. They could sell directly to customers from their own websites.

This revolution introduced two new business models. First, we have **aggregators**; these are businesses, such as Amazon, which bring together every product imaginable and make them available with one click. Customers no longer have to visit different websites, let alone different stores, to get everything they need. Travel sites, such as Expedia and Kayak, aggregate information on dozens of airlines and car rentals, and hundreds of hotels, allowing customers to compare and make their choices from a single site.

This model is perhaps just a larger, more **elaborate** online version of the supermarket or department store, but in the second business model, referred to as peer-to-peer (or P2P) retail, there is more of a departure from the past. In peer-to-peer businesses, all traces of the middleman are truly gone. Customers don't even bother with a hotel at all. Instead, they rent a room from another private individual. They don't rent a car from a car rental company; they rent it from another person. These peer-to-peer transactions are **facilitated** by a new breed of start-up companies. To find a room to rent, there are companies like Airbnb. To get a ride, you can go through Uber. To buy a pair of jeans, a toaster, or even a car from another individual, the public can turn to online market sites like eBay.

The key element shared by these two models is new technology. The Internet has allowed universal access, but in addition, it has allowed the automation of transactions, reducing what Bill Gates referred to as "friction" in the market. In online transactions, there is no need for people, no need for interaction, which could slow things down. Just a series of clicks. In 1995, Gates predicted that online markets might allow for "frictionless capitalism"; in other words, the smooth and easy exchange of goods and labor, with no middleman and no transaction costs.

So, has his prediction come true? Well, yes and no. The elimination of the middleman has indeed reduced costs generally. And it is true that the number of these intermediaries has dropped significantly. There are far fewer travel agencies today than there were 25 years ago. But some problems emerged with the disappearance of the middleman – starting with a lack of trust. How do consumers know if an individual seller on eBay is honest, for example? It's not like the old days when they ordered products from a familiar and reliable store. Furthermore, the massive amount of information a consumer encounters online may lead to indecision, in some cases, even paralysis. There is so much information available that consumers just don't know what to do with it. Part of the problem is sheer volume, and part of it is that all this raw information can be difficult for end users to interpret. How are ordinary consumers to make sense of this information **overload**?

In fact, what they need is a middleman to sift through it all – all the news, all the data, all the songs, all the prices, all the products. The buzzword for this sifting activity is "curation." Customers want someone to help make intelligent choices in this sea of information, and curation can help them do this. This need has created an entirely new set of businesses. Paul English, who founded and later sold the online travel aggregator Kayak, is still in the travel business. His latest venture is a travel app that provides all of the information available on other sites, but with one difference. It also offers the services of travel agents – humans who will help customers make decisions.

These new "curators" have become experts at harnessing the power of the Internet. And as far as reestablishing trust is concerned, wary eBay customers can now turn to what are often referred to as "power sellers," participants who act as intermediaries on the site, buying and selling large volumes of items. In the process, these power sellers build a reputation so that other participants generally trust them more than they trust individual small-scale sellers.

A final casualty of the elimination of the middleman has been luxury. Some customers want more than curation, more than just a little guidance. They want a middleman who will actually do everything for them. The buzzword for what these customers want is a "concierge," and yes, the Internet can provide this too. Concierge apps like AnyWysh will make your travel arrangements, do your errands, and arrange deliveries.

And so disruptive innovation has brought us full circle. The Internet and accompanying technology have successfully eliminated the middleman in a wide range of markets, only to have the public realize that middlemen actually add value to the transaction, value that they miss.

See script on page 88.

Presenter: Welcome everyone. Please grab something to drink and a seat, and we'll get started.

Your professor has told me that you are all interested in becoming entrepreneurs for social good, and so she thought it might be a good idea for you to learn something about the nonprofit sector. I'll start by talking a little bit about the basics of a nonprofit organization, then offer a few tips for those of you who are seriously thinking of going in that direction. After that, I will take you over to the offices to meet some of the staff, many of whom have been with our organization since it began. I hope this will give you a good **overview**.

There are many different kinds of nonprofits established for many different purposes, but we usually think of them as providing some sort of social good. This may seem obvious, but the most important aspect of a nonprofit is its **mission**. You really need to be able to express clearly and **concisely** the purpose of your organization. With for-profit businesses, the mission is easy to describe. They are in the business of making money. Unlike a for-profit organization, however, all of the revenue, that is, all the donations, grants, etc., in a nonprofit organization, must be returned to the organization. Most of the money should be used for the organization's programs, although some of it, obviously, must be used to actually run the organization. I'll return to that point a little later, but I want to stop and talk about what we mean by "programs" because this is where, unfortunately, some organizations have abused their nonprofit **status**.

An organization's programs are the activities that provide direct benefits to the people whom the organization is trying to help, for example, teenagers receiving job training, disaster victims who need medical assistance, etc. However, organizations can, and sometimes do, include other activities in their programs, but this is where you need to be very careful. One well-known example is the Central Asia Institute, a charity with the mission of building schools in Afghanistan. It was getting lots of donations until it was revealed that included among its "programs" were activities to promote the director's books and lectures. That caused a very damaging backlash against the organization.

Although we call these organizations *nonprofits*, this term is somewhat misleading. It's absolutely essential that the money coming into a nonprofit is greater than its expenses; otherwise, it won't be able to help anyone. In other words, the organization needs to make money. What a nonprofit cannot do, however, is create and distribute equity. A company's equity basically means its value, for shareholders, or owners. But a nonprofit has no shareholders and no owner. Perhaps the biggest organizational difference between a nonprofit and a for-profit enterprise is that no single person controls it. Boards of directors, generally composed of at least five members, have **oversight** responsibility for the operation of the organization.

So that tells you about some of the nuts and bolts of running a nonprofit, but I know that all of you are more interested in how you can get started on turning your dreams into reality. Well, you may think that the starting point is your **fabulous** idea, but the real starting point is money. Money is what makes the wheels of commerce turn, and the same can be said of nonprofits. But you're not going to be selling anything – not technically – so where will the money come from? The answer can vary, depending on the organization, but nonprofits rely heavily on fundraising, so you need to accept this as a fact of life, right from the start. A lot of money comes from individual donors. Some nonprofits also receive **funding** from corporations and private foundations; others receive funding from the local, state, or federal government. Whatever the source, I cannot stress enough that fundraising is the lifeblood of a nonprofit. The more money you raise, the closer you will come to reaching your goals. So, if you hate going around and asking for money, you may need to reconsider your options because running a nonprofit is like having a child that is always hungry!

Now I'm hoping I haven't discouraged any of you, but I do want you to have a realistic perspective. And I want you to be able to take advantage of some of the lessons that others in this sector have already learned. So let me offer a few words of advice.

Protect your mission. You are here because you believe in a cause. Sometime in the future, you may be offered funding by a donor or by a foundation for something that falls outside the **scope** of your mission. You will be tempted to take it, especially if it is a lot of money, but don't do it. You will end up trying to do too many things and doing none of them well. More important, you will not be doing what you set out to do.

Invest in administration and development. This may sound like strange advice, but nonprofits, like for-profit companies, need to innovate, and they need to lead. They can't do those things on a starvation budget. This doesn't mean you should pay everyone on your staff a fat salary, but you do need to invest in the operational side of your organization if you want to be effective and you want to succeed in the long term.

I mentioned the need for innovation. Today's most successful new nonprofits are changing the way this sector works. Instead of relying exclusively on the goodwill of donors, they are learning from the for-profit sector about how to harness market forces, but for social good. Authors and nonprofit experts Crutchfield and Grant express it this way, "[G]reat nonprofits find ways to work with markets and help business 'do well while doing good.'"

And that is exactly what we are doing here. We are trying to reduce global poverty by connecting workers in the developing world with job opportunities worldwide. We are training the world's poorest workers for the digital workforce. But we also have a foot in the for-profit world. We sell our services to some of the world's biggest companies. We also have training centers in the countries where our workers live, which helps the local economy. By hiring workers where they live, much of the revenue from the company will remain in those countries, where it is desperately needed. By tying our nonprofit mission to our for-profit success, we can indeed do well while we are doing good.

4.5

Olivia: OK, so we've decided to focus our nonprofit on educational opportunity. Did everybody read those articles that the professor sent us?

Matt: Yes. I read the one about the effects of poverty on education. There are a lot of people who don't get a good education – even in this country. I think our nonprofit could help children right here, in this city.

Megan: I agree. This is the place we know best. We understand how the system works here.

Olivia: I'd like to help high school students who want to go to college.

Matt: That's definitely something we know about.

Eric: What about doing something to help low-income students get into college? There are a lot of students who want to go to college, but they feel they can't. Maybe they think their grades are too low, or they can't afford it. But there are lots of different ways to get financial aid. What if we did something to help students find financial aid, or scholarships?

Matt: That sounds like a great idea. But how would we do that? How do you identify the students?

Olivia: You'd have to get access to the high schools. Through the teachers, or something.

Megan: Don't they already have college counselors?

Eric: They don't have enough. In my school, we had, like, three counselors for six hundred students!

Olivia: Yeah. Mine was the same. If you were lucky, you might see the counselor one time. I remember when I was applying to college, I had to do everything by myself.

Matt: OK, but let's get back to the project. Our mission would be to help high school students get into college. But how would we go about it? What kind of programs would we offer?

Olivia: What about a mentoring program?

Eric: Mentors? What do you mean?

Olivia: We could match high school students with volunteers who are already in college. The volunteers would act like mentors. They could help students figure out how to apply, how to get financial aid ...

Eric: Oh yeah! That sounds interesting. There would be a personal connection. They could visit campus, or spend a day with their mentor ...

Matt: That's a nice idea. What do you think, Megan?

Megan: Yeah, I like it. There was something like that at my high school, actually.

Matt: Really? Tell us about it.

Megan: Well, ...

UNIT 5

Modern Shock Therapy

Reporter 1: By applying an electrical current to the outside of the skull, they say it has the potential to treat brain injury or Alzheimer's disease without drugs or surgery. CBS News medical correspondent Dr. David Agus joins us now. David, it's always good to see you. I'm telling you, this little device here is so intimidating, and I just don't think of the words "electrical current" and "brain" going together. So why are you so excited about this?

Dr. David Agus: Don't push the button, Gayle, we'd all be in trouble here.

You know, the year 200 A.D., the Greek physician Galen said, if you have a bad headache, put an electrical eel on your head. And ever since then we've been using electricity for the brain. At the turn of the century, they used it for psychiatric disorders. Well, that device on your table, transcranial stimulation using a magnet, was actually FDA approved for bad depression several years ago. And a group at Northwestern mapped the brain, and they showed that an area of the brain, the hippocampus, which is the orchestra, connected to near the surface of the brain, and so they stimulated that area with that device, and they improved memory 30% in young people aged 20 to 40.

Reporter 2: So David, when you actually apply this device, which Gayle has got right next to her, to the brain, and forgive me –

Reporter 1: I'm trying to figure what do you do. These two little red dots, do I put them on the top of my head or the side of my head?

Reporter 2: This looks like a 1960s sitcom device to me.

Reporter 1: Yes, it does.

Reporter 2: But how does – how does it feel when you apply that to the head? Do you know?

Dr. David Agus: Well, there's not a lot of feeling to it. You hear a popping, so it's some – a little popping in the background, but you don't feel that electrical stimulation. It's not like you see in the movies where you're doing major zaps to the brain. This is a small stimulation to an area that connects to that hippocampus that improves memory by improving the orchestration of the brain.

Reporter 3: So is it instantaneous, or are you meant to do a treatment and then you have results later on?

Dr. David Agus: Well, in the study, it was 20 minutes a day for five days, and after three days they started to see a benefit, and the benefit lasted the 24 hours they looked in the study. The key question going forward is how long it'll last, and what happens if you give it to people who are older with memory disorders.

Reporter 2: This is a pretty significant improvement, David, but I mean, how close to being available is this? How – I mean, are we months away, years away?

Dr. David Agus: Well, the device exists, but the studies to show what happens in people with Alzheimer's, after stroke or other brain injury, that's going to take several years to get to fruition. You know, with any of these, the data are dramatic, I bet you it happens a lot quicker.

5.1

Eva: OK, so has everyone read all the material?

Leo: Yep. So how do you think we should organize it? There is so much information.

Alexa: Yeah, the assignment is to present research findings, but I think we should present what we think will be the most interesting to the rest of the class – something they can relate to.

Eva: I like that idea. Let's talk about what we found in our readings and then plan the presentation.

Leo: Sounds good. OK, if I had to draw one generalization from all the readings, it would be that humans are sensitive to a variety of different **cues**, and we respond to them really, really fast.

Eva: I got the same sense from what I read. So what about some of the cues?

Leo: For first impressions, in a nutshell, it's physical appearance. It's the most important cue, especially the face. In the study I read, the participants had just a tenth of a second to decide how likeable, **competent**, trustworthy, and aggressive they thought a person in a photograph was. It was pretty incredible; in just a few milliseconds, they were able to make these decisions, and even more amazing, their judgments were pretty consistent with the judgments of people who had unlimited time to make them. Of the four characteristics, the one that was the most consistent was trustworthiness. The scientists who conducted the study **speculate** that, in general, being able to decide if you can trust someone quickly was really important during early human evolution.

Eva: It probably still is! That's really interesting. I read another study on a similar topic, but it was a little more specific. It was just about attractiveness. Based on a few milliseconds of **exposure**, participants had to decide if they would want to date the person in the picture, on a scale of one to four. The researchers looked at images of the participants' brains as they made these judgments and saw that a specific area of the brain was very active. Then, a few days later, the participants actually met the people in the photos. Overall, it turns out the judgments they made were pretty accurate. Most participants ended up liking the people they rated as fours and not really liking those they had rated as ones.

Alexa: Yeah, I reviewed that study, too. There was another part that I thought was really **intriguing**. Some of the photos were of really attractive people, and all the participants pretty much agreed they were fours. But there were some photos that only a few people found attractive. When the researchers examined the participants' brain activity as they were rating those photos, the activity was in a different area from the rating of the really attractive photos.

Leo: So what does that mean? What can we conclude from that?

Alexa: Well, the authors of the study had an interesting explanation, similar to the one you mentioned about an evolutionary advantage. They conclude that our first response is to go for someone who is generally attractive, what they call "a good catch." In evolutionary terms, that would be a good mate, and everyone seemed to agree on who that would be. But the different preferences suggest we also make judgments about who would be "a good catch for me." And judgments about that are made in a different part of the brain.

Leo: Wow, I guess that means that speed dating is effective after all.

Eva: There were a lot of other cues, too – like voice, how people walk, if they look into your eyes when you talk. But I think maybe we should keep a narrow focus and just talk about faces. We only have fifteen minutes for our presentation. What do you think?

Leo: I think you're right. There's no way we can present everything we read about. But there was another really interesting study about faces that we could include.

Alexa: The one with the computer-designed faces?

Leo: Yeah! It's really interesting, right?

Alexa: Totally.

Eva: Wait! I didn't read that one. What was it about?

Leo: OK. So this one psychologist had probably read all of the studies that we have, and he wanted to take the idea a step further.

Eva: What do you mean? Can you just summarize it?

Leo: All the other studies had used actual human faces, which made it really hard to tell exactly what the participants were reacting to when they made their judgments. So he took a set of 1,000 photos and showed them to a group of people. They had to make judgments on a range of traits. Then, he took 65 different measurements of the faces. Bottom line – he was able to get consistent judgments, in relation to particular features of the faces, on three traits – **dominance**, attractiveness, and approachability – which I think basically means friendliness.

Eva: Sixty-five? Wow! What features did he measure?

Leo: Oh, the tilt of the head, the width and shape of the eyebrows, the gap between the lips, the shape of lips – stuff like that. Then, using artificial intelligence, his team created a set of computer-generated drawings of faces that demonstrated the range of difference in these traits – so, from very **approachable** to not at all approachable, etc. Then they had human participants judge the computer-generated faces. The researchers think they're pretty close to identifying the specific facial features that result in these first impressions.

Alexa: I think this one would be a good one to present to the class because of the cool visuals. Some of the features are obvious, like the smile, but I was surprised how important other features were – like eyebrow shape.

Eva: Yeah, I never thought much about eyebrows. I guess we aren't really aware of some of the things we respond to, even in less than a second.

Leo: We should probably include some practical **applications** in our presentation. The authors of the study discussed how useful this will be in computer-generated graphics in games and movies. It will give artists a good rule of thumb for how to create the faces of different kinds of characters.

Alexa: Well, OK, so it's not exactly solving world hunger, but I guess that *is* a useful application. OK, this is a great start. I think we are in good shape. Should we think of a title?

Eva: How about this: "How to Judge a Book by Its Cover."

See the script on page 110.

Professor: Perhaps you have had the experience of getting step-by-step directions from someone or using your smartphone to find a place, and later, when trying to find your way a second time, you discover that you have no memory of the route you took, even if you had followed the route repeatedly with assistance in the past.

Today, I want to discuss some research that has been carried out over the past ten years that sheds light on this phenomenon – research about some interesting findings about the connection between our increasing reliance on aids to help us **navigate** (such as GPS) and our cognitive health.

Psychologists have known for some time that we create mental maps to make sense of our world. In the 1970s, scientists discovered that the site of this map-making ability is the hippocampus, an area deep inside the brain, in the temporal lobe. Within the hippocampus, **differentiated** cells allow us to **orient** ourselves in relation to **landmarks** and to adjust our position as we move through space – sort of our own internal GPS. The hippocampus plays a key role in spatial memory and navigation. These are among the first abilities to **deteriorate** as we age, sometimes ending in dementia. So, you can see why understanding how it works is a top priority for researchers today. Spatial memory is involved in more than just remembering where things are, however. It plays a crucial role in memory overall because it allows us to **reconstruct** experiences and events that are connected in our minds to physical spaces.

Humans navigate in one of two ways. The first is the spatial or landmark strategy. This strategy relies on the hippocampus and involves building a mental map that uses landmarks, such as buildings, parks, trees, etc. The second method is the response strategy, which is more or less memorization. Using this strategy, knowledge emerges as the result of repeated trips along the same route. Most of you will have had the experience in which you take a familiar route and arrive at your destination with little memory of the journey. This strategy does not require the construction of a mental map. Scientists have shown that these two strategies use different parts of the brain.

Eleanor Maguire, a psychologist at University College, London, became interested in the role of the hippocampus in navigation. She was particularly interested in the brains of people who use the first strategy intensively. For study participants, she chose a very specific population of landmark strategy users – London taxi drivers. London taxi drivers are famous for knowing the city's 250,000 streets incredibly well. They study for three or four years to prepare for the very demanding test they have to take for a taxi license. As she suspected, the MRI images of the drivers' brains as they planned their routes showed a high level of activity in the hippocampus. She also found that this part of their brain was unusually large and, furthermore, that the more experience a driver had, the larger the hippocampus. These results strongly suggested that the constant creation of mental maps had affected the drivers' brains. However, Maguire could not be sure that the relationship was causal. An alternative explanation was that people with a large hippocampus were more likely to pass the demanding exam and become drivers.

So, Maguire did a longitudinal follow-up study. She took MRI images of applicants for a taxi license before they began their studies for the test. All participants had hippocampi of relatively similar size at the start of the study. Four years later, Maguire studied these participants again. Some of the applicants had failed the test while others had passed and become drivers. The hippocampi of the second group – the ones who had become drivers – were much larger, and these participants also did much better on cognitive tests. So all this points to a causal relationship between the creation of mental maps and the increased size of the hippocampus.

Maguire's studies came at a time when digital devices with GPS were just emerging. As they became more popular, some researchers began to wonder whether the increasing use of these devices might **impair** our ability to create mental maps. In 2005, Gary Burnett at Nottingham University in England conducted a study in which half of the participants were given step-by-step instructions to their destinations, and the other half had to find their way using maps. When they were later asked to draw a map of the route they took, the drivers who had simply followed directions did much worse than those who had navigated on their own. These findings support the idea that the choice of navigation strategy impacts this type of memory.

McGill University Professor Veronique Bohbot also pursued this line of inquiry. In her study, she compared a group of participants who were accustomed to navigating with spatial landmark strategy with another group who relied on GPS for navigation. The participants in the first group had more gray matter in their hippocampi and exhibited a higher level of activity in this part of the brain. Perhaps more important, this group also performed better on a cognitive test that often reveals the first sign of dementia as a person ages.

As with Maguire's first study, it isn't possible to say **definitively** that this connection between GPS use and lower test performance is a causal one. Similarly, we cannot yet say whether engaging in spatial navigation and the creation of mental maps can delay the effects of aging on cognition. More research is needed. Nevertheless, Professor Bohbot says that these results are strong enough to suggest that if we limit our reliance on GPS, we will strengthen our brain's navigational skills.

5.5

Professor: Today, I'm going to talk about motivation – in particular, as it affects college students. Motivation is crucial in college. It has an impact, not only on how well a student performs, but on whether a student is likely to stay in college or drop out.

Generally, we talk about two types of motivation: intrinsic and extrinsic. I'll discuss each of them in turn.

Intrinsic motivation is like a flame that burns inside you. It's what keeps musicians and artists working even when they don't make a lot of money. They just love doing what they do, and they want to get better at it. People who are intrinsically motivated are driven by the love of the work itself.

Now, research into college students has found that intrinsic motivation is the most important indicator of success. If a student is intrinsically motivated, he will always be willing to work that little bit harder, not because he has to, but because he wants to. And a student who clearly enjoys what he is doing is in a much better position to succeed in college – and in the working world as well.

But, of course, not all students find intrinsic motivation in studying for a math test. Not everybody is intrinsically motivated all the time. But you still need to be motivated to study, even when you'd prefer to be doing just about anything else.

So that's where extrinsic motivation comes in. Extrinsic motivation comes from the anticipation of a reward or a punishment: a good or bad grade, a better salary, the expectations of your parents. The truth is, we all need extrinsic motivation at times, just to get the job done.

So what's important is to identify your motivators – your reasons for doing things – and keep them firmly in focus. What motivates you? Maybe it's the idea of becoming a professional, or getting the job you want. Maybe you want to make your parents proud, or help your family have a better life.

The bottom line is, identify what motivates you, and use it as a light to guide you through the difficult times.

UNIT 6

Returnships: Hiring Moms

Julie Haim: I think I'll make that chicken with the cheese melted on top.

Reporter: Julie Haim's family in Alpharetta, Georgia, does their grocery shopping on Saturdays. Monday through Friday Julie works at Credit Suisse, 900 miles away in New York City.

Haim: Everybody makes New Year's resolutions, and mine for the last few years has been: Hmm, is this the year I'll return to the workforce or not?

Reporter: Julie had a job in corporate bond management when she became pregnant for the second time. She decided to leave finance and concentrate on raising her two daughters.

Haim: I was out of the workforce for just over ten years. I always knew I was going to go back to work, it was just a matter of how I would do it and when the right opportunity would arise.

Reporter: That opportunity came this spring when Julie applied to a new program at Credit Suisse called the Real Returns Program. It's like a ten-week paid internship offered at Credit Suisse and several other banks to help women return to the workforce.

Haim: I was on the fence 50/50 whether or not I would come, and my husband was the one who said, "Julie, if you don't do this, you're going to regret this for the rest of your life."

Reporter: Julie's husband, Ken, encouraged her to take the leap. He stays in Georgia with their daughters during the week while she commutes to New York.

Haim: Ask daddy to pick out some salsa.

Reporter: Janet Kang oversees hiring for the Credit Suisse initiative.

Kang: If you look, at probably across the board, in most of Wall Street, you don't see a lot of female talent sort of remaining at the bank, and I think we recognize the female talent pool as one that's really been untapped.

Reporter: Between 2002 and 2012, 200,000 women left jobs in the financial and insurance industries. No women hold a CEO position in finance today, while only 5% of all Fortune 1000 companies have a woman in the CEO role.

Kang: They have an incredible skill set of, you know, 10-, 15-, 20-year careers that they're able to pick up and bring back to the surface.

Reporter: With Julie's past experience in finance, the fixed-income research team welcomed her. Julie receives wages relative to an employee of her experience.

Reporter: What's been the best part?

Haim: The best part has been reengaging with the markets. I love the energy and the dynamic nature of the financial services industry. I feel like it makes me whole.

Reporter: Julie hopes her daughters, now ages 11 and 13, will one day understand the importance of mom's 10-week "returnship" in New York.

Counselor: Good afternoon, everyone. This is a special session that the Career Service Office is offering for computer science students. We wanted to target this session for all of you in computer science and related programs because, frankly, you will probably have a lot more options when you finish your degree than other graduates. Of course, having options is a good thing, but options are often accompanied by a degree of confusion. Specifically, what we want to address here today are some of the pros and cons of three **distinct** ways that you can enter the job market, focusing on the situation in the United States. If you are considering taking a position abroad, keep in mind that some of the legal issues and government regulations that we're going to discuss may not apply to you.

The most traditional and common route is simply to take a position as an employee with an established company, and for many of you, this may be the most appropriate choice. You can immediately start using the skills and knowledge you have gained in your studies. However, you could also consider the option of using those skills without joining a company – as a consultant, or what is often referred to as an independent contractor, or freelance worker. Finally, especially for those of you graduating with more advanced degrees, there is the option of establishing your own business – a start-up company.

So, now that you know what the three options are, let's talk about some of the pros and cons of each, starting with the employee option. For those of you getting an undergraduate degree and who have not had a lot of work experience, this option may be your best bet. It is certainly the easiest way to start out. Employees at most big companies get benefits and have relatively good job security (though, of course, you can always be fired or laid off!). If you're an employee, you know you will be getting a paycheck and how much it will be. So it's predictable, reliable. And other than the cost of getting to and from work (and maybe a **wardrobe** upgrade), there are no business expenses for employees. Finally – and this is what I meant earlier when I said our topic would be the U.S. market – in this country, the government provides employees with some measure of protection. In theory, at least, you should have a safe workplace and be protected against **discrimination** and harassment.

As an independent contractor, you have no such protection, and your life will be far less predictable. You have to **hustle** to find your own jobs, so how much you make is very much dependent on how much and how hard you work. In general, independent contractors, or consultants, earn more money than employees – up to 40 percent more, but don't let that fool you. The companies who hire you as a consultant are willing to pay you more because they don't have the same costs that they have for an employee, such as health insurance, retirement benefits, and certain taxes. You also don't get any sick leave. If you don't work, you don't get paid. If you want health insurance, you have to buy it yourself. However, these are all business expenses if you own your own company, and, as an independent contractor, *you* are your own company. So these expenses are paid by the business, not by you personally. There are other expenses as well. You have start-up costs, insurance, business taxes, and if a customer won't or cannot pay your bill, you may **get stuck with** those costs too.

So that's a look at the downside. The most important positive aspect of being an independent contractor is that you have much more control over your work and your income. You are your own boss. There is no cap on your salary, no limit to your growth. Some people like this kind of independence, but for others, the responsibility and uncertainty are so **daunting** that they don't even consider it. As an independent contractor, you take the responsibility and the blame. There is no one else above you.

Now, if you already have quite a bit of work experience, and if you already have an idea that you think can be developed into an innovative product or service, you may want to take the last route – the start-up. I'm sure you've heard all sorts of stories about start-ups – probably at both extremes – the entrepreneur who became a billionaire by age 30 or the group of friends who slept under their computer desks for days on end in an unsuccessful effort to launch their company. And both are probably true, but which one do you think is more common?

Make no mistake, a start-up is risky and a lot of work. I don't want to scare you, but, as in the case of consultants, you are your own boss, with full responsibility for the success or failure of your company. In this case, however, you're even more independent in that not only do you decide how much to work, when to work, etc., you're also able to decide *what* that work will be, and that's a crucial difference. When you're a consultant, the companies that hire you tell you what they want you to do. In a start-up, *you* provide the **vision**. So before you go down this road, you should engage in some self-reflection and decide if you have the discipline that this life requires. Just having a great idea will not be enough to carry you through to a successful launch and beyond. But if you are successful, you can take credit for all aspects of that success, and that can be incredibly **rewarding**.

One last note about this option. I have been discussing it as if you're going into it alone, but frequently, several people – often friends who went to school together, just like you – begin start-up companies together. I want to emphasize how stressful starting a new company can be, especially in the early days. So if you decide to do this, be sure to take care of your personal relationships at the same time that you are taking care of business.

There are lots of other details to discuss, and I encourage all of you to make individual appointments with our office if you have questions or you have a specific opportunity you'd like to talk over.

1 We wanted to target this session for all of you in computer science and related programs because, frankly, you will probably have a lot more options when you finish your degree than other graduates.

2 Finally, especially for those of you graduating with more advanced degrees, there's the option of establishing your own business – a start-up company.

3 In theory, at least, you should have a safe workplace and be protected against discrimination and harassment.

4 However, these are all business expenses if you own your own company, and, as an independent contractor, *you* are your own company. So these expenses are paid by the business, not by you personally.

5 I'm sure you've heard all sorts of stories about start-ups – probably at both extremes – the entrepreneur who became a billionaire by age 30 or the group of friends who slept under their computer desks for days on end in an unsuccessful effort to launch their company. And both are probably true, but which one do you think is more common?

6 ... frequently, several people – often friends who went to school together, just like you – begin start-up companies together. I want to emphasize how stressful starting a new company can be, especially in the early days. So if you decide to do this, be sure to take care of your personal relationships at the same time that you are taking care of business.

See script on page 131.

6.4

Counselor: Welcome everyone. This is supposed to be an informal session guided by any questions you have about the whole job interview process. Keep in mind that there are going to be aspects of this process that are specific to different fields and industries, but I'm going to try to give you an overview and some advice that is general enough that it can apply to many different experiences.

So, I'm going to divide our session into before, during, and after the job interview, with an emphasis on the first two stages, which are really the most important. So, let's open the floor to questions about the before stage. Yes?

Student 1: You say it is really important, so what do I need to do before the interview?

Counselor: I can answer that in a single word: *prepare*. There is absolutely no substitute for being prepared. That means doing research on the company or organization that you're hoping might hire you. There is a lot of information available on most public and many private companies, as well as nonprofit organizations, on the Web. We also have a lot of resources here in the office that you can consult. You want to know as much as possible about what the company does, what it sells, and how it works before you set foot in the interview room.

Student 2: Do I need to do research on the person who is going to interview me?

Counselor: If your interview is with someone with whom you might be working, by all means; you should find out what you can about that person. But often you will be interviewed by people in human resources who are just in charge of the hiring process.

Student 1: I've heard that there is a standard set of questions that always get asked. Is that true, and should I prepare answers for them?

Counselor: Yes and no. I think there are some questions that you can anticipate being asked – and I'll mention some of them in just a sec, but you shouldn't count on those being the only ones. And as for preparation, yes, I think you should know how you want to answer the questions you think might be asked, but you shouldn't prepare so much that your answers sound **rehearsed** or mechanical. If, for example, you write out and practice giving specific answers, you probably won't sound natural or sincere. My advice would be to develop what we call "talking points," that is, information that you want to be sure gets out there. You can probably work your talking points into some of your answers, no matter what the question.

Student 3: So what kind of questions should we expect? Will they be really general, like – What are your most important **accomplishments**? – or really specific, like questions about a specific computer language?

Counselor: Good question, and again, both are possible. As part of your research, you should find out the **format** for the interview. Will there be just general questions like the one you mentioned, or will there be a written part, or even a test of your knowledge or **analytical** skills?

Student 3: Well, what if it's just general questions?

Counselor: OK, so the kinds of things you can expect to be asked about are your accomplishments, for sure. You may be asked about your goals – where you see yourself in five years or in ten years. You may be asked about your work style – whether you do well in teams or if you like working on your own, how you deal with conflict, how well you adapt to change – things like that. You may also be asked the **dreaded** "weakness" question.

Student 2: The weakness question?

Counselor: What is your greatest weakness?

Student 2: What should we say?

Counselor: Well, don't say something that makes you look bad, like "I'm always late." But you also shouldn't say something cute, like "My standards are too high." Believe me, they've heard that one before. Your best bet is to think of something you have struggled with but have been working on trying to improve. For example, you can say in the past you had some problems with time management, but now you use an app that helps you stay on top of tasks.

OK, let's switch gears and talk about how to behave during an interview.

Student 2: Yeah, I need some help with that. I get nervous just thinking about it.

Counselor: Well, one thing you can do to help you feel less nervous is a practice interview with one of the counselors in this office. We record the session and then review it with you to make suggestions for improvement. But let me just give you a few tips to get us started. Probably, if I could make only one suggestion, it would be to listen.

Student 1: Why is that? I thought they wanted information from us, not the other way around.

Counselor: It's both, but they want to know about your communication skills, and listening is an important component of communication. You want to make sure that you answer the question that is being asked, not the one you *think* or *hope* is being asked.

Student 1: Makes sense.

Counselor: And try to be concise in your answers. Say just enough to answer the question. Don't **ramble**. Whenever possible, provide concrete examples. So, if you are asked about your work style, don't just say you are collaborative; prove it by giving an example of a successful **collaboration** that you were part of.

Student 2: What if I can't answer the question? That's my biggest nightmare.

Counselor: Just be honest. Don't make things up. If you don't have the skill or haven't done what they are asking about, just say so. Better for them to know now than find out later, right? OK, one final thing. Make sure you have some questions for them, just in case you are given that opportunity at the end of the interview. It shows that you have done your homework and also demonstrates your enthusiasm for the job.

Student 3: I know you said the first two stages were the most important, but what about afterward? Do I need to write a thank-you note?

Counselor: It can be an informal email, but yes, you should always follow up an interview with a brief message, thanking the person for his or her time. Also **reiterate** your interest in the position and remind the interviewer why you would be a good fit for the organization.

Student 3: OK, thanks.

Counselor: That's about all we have time for today. If you already have an interview scheduled, please make an appointment for a practice interview as soon as possible. Thanks for coming everyone.

6.5

1 If your interview is with someone with whom you might be working, by all means; you should find out what you can about that person. But often you will be interviewed by people in human resources who are just in charge of the hiring process.

2 And as for preparation, yes, I think you should know how you want to answer the questions you think might be asked, but you shouldn't prepare so much that your answers sound rehearsed or mechanical. If, for example, you write out and practice giving specific answers, you probably won't sound natural or sincere.

3 You may be asked about your goals – where you see yourself in five years or in ten years.

4 Well, don't say something that makes you look bad, like, "I'm always late." But you also shouldn't say something cute, like "My standards are too high." Believe me, they've heard that one before.

5 And try to be concise in your answers. Say just enough to answer the question. Don't ramble.

6.6

Chiyu: The best way for me to remember stuff is to organize it and put it in my own words. So I usually go through all of my notes and try to summarize the main points. I also reread the chapters in the textbook and add to my notes. I use idea maps sometimes, so that I can have everything all on one page. Sometimes I make flashcards so I can study on the bus.

Javier: I'm a junior in college now, so I'm used to taking tests and quizzes. I've learned to listen carefully to what the teachers say in the weeks before the final exam. Different instructors have different approaches, but one thing is, if a teacher says something like, "... and this is really important" or "You need to remember this," that means, **write it down**, it's going to be on the test! If you just listen carefully, they kind of tell you what to expect.

Sarah: I had a tutor once who gave me some really good advice. He said, when you're looking at multiple choice answers, if there are words like "always," "never," or "all" in the sentence, it's usually false, because it's too strong. Anything that sounds really extreme like that is likely to be false. I've used that advice lots of times and it always helps. Even if I don't know the answer, I can at least eliminate one or two choices that way.

UNIT 7

Water Pollution in West Virginia

Reporter: West Virginia state officials say the water is safe, but Matilda Murray doesn't believe them. What do you say to them?

Murray: No way. You guys can drink it. I'm absolutely not going to let my kids drink it, or me. I won't even let my cat have the water.

Reporter: More than a week after a chemical leak contaminated the water supply of 300,000 West Virginians, the water company and the state's health officials are still trying to convince people that the water no longer poses a threat, even though the effects of the coal-cleaning chemical known as MCHM are unknown. Here in coal country, the chemical leak has reignited a debate about whether the power of industry trumps health and environmental concerns, and whether the politicians have blocked changes. Senator Joe Manchin is the state's former governor.

Reporter: The signs were there. West Virginia did not act. Is that fair?

Sen. Manchin: It depends on what side you're looking if it's fair. Could we have done more? Should we have done more? Must we do more? Absolutely. Is other states in the same peril that we're in? Probably so and don't know it.

Reporter: Manchin is a key supporter of legislation that will require regular inspections of chemical storage facilities nationwide like the Freedom Industries plant responsible for the leak.

Sen. Manchin: This legislation will prevent this from ever happening again. What I can do is, take from the situation that we're dealing with today, and hopefully prevent it from ever happening. And that's what you should do – learn from what has happened.

Reporter: Matilda Murray wants to know why oversight hasn't been there from the beginning.

Murray: Why haven't they been inspecting their equipment? And now it's all leaking in our water.

Reporter: She says it will be months before she even considers letting any of her children near it. For CBS This Morning, Jeff Pegues, Charleston, West Virginia.

7.1

Presenter: Good evening, everyone. In this day and age, everyone knows someone who has asthma. Maybe it's you, your child, a sibling, or a friend, but asthma touches everyone in some way. I want to give you an overview of what this disease is, what we know about it from both scientific and historical research, and the current thinking on how to manage it.

Asthma is a chronic disease of the lungs; specifically, it affects the airways that carry air in and out of your lungs. These airways become irritated and swollen if you have asthma, often causing symptoms such as difficulty breathing as well as coughing, especially when you lie down. As I'll explain a little later, it turns out that asthma is probably not just one disease. So, for some people, the symptoms only appear when they are exposed to some sort of trigger in the environment. Other asthma sufferers experience some level of these symptoms all the time.

So here is the big mystery. Asthma rates are soaring. In the first decade of the 21st century, the number of cases climbed 25 percent. Today, one in twelve people in this country suffers from asthma. The global figure is 300 million. This disease **disproportionately** affects children and people of color. Seventeen percent of all African-American children in the United States suffer from asthma. And here's one more fact for you about the **incidence** of asthma: it is 50 times more common in urban centers like Los Angeles and Chicago than in areas of rural Africa. The big question is why? Why this enormous and relatively sudden increase, and why the huge **disparity** between the developed and developing worlds?

Let me begin by telling you that we don't have definitive answers to these questions. We don't know what causes asthma, nor do we know how to cure it. However, we do have some idea of what triggers symptoms, and we do have effective ways to manage these symptoms.

Now, a lot of what I'm talking about today is "environmental health," and indeed, although genetics is the single most powerful predictor of the development of asthma, it cannot be the whole story. Our genes change far too slowly to explain the rapid increase of this disease. So scientists and medical researchers have turned to the environment for explanations.

Frequently mentioned triggers include indoor and outdoor pollution. Indoor pollution includes dust, mold, tobacco smoke, pet hair, and various chemicals used for cleaning. Outdoor pollution includes particulate matter – very small pieces of dirt, chemicals, and pollutants trapped in the air – and ground-level ozone, formed when pollution from cars and factories combine with heat and sunlight. Studies have found a **correlation** between **proximity** to both of these types of pollution and the development of asthma. These factors are also strongly associated with the severity of its symptoms. Nevertheless, there is conflicting historical data. For example, the rapid increase in air pollution in Chinese cities has been accompanied by a similar rise in asthma in that country – as much as 40 percent in the past 20 years. On the other hand, the reunification of Germany in 1990 provides a counterexample. East Germany suffered from far more serious pollution than West Germany at the time, yet asthma was a much bigger problem in the West than in the East. **Ironically**, as the former East Germany tackled its air pollution, its rate of asthma actually rose.

About this time, another proposal was made, the so-called **Hygiene** Hypothesis, which goes something like this: when children are young, parents make an effort to keep the home and school environments as clean as possible. One might even go so far as to say that many parents try to keep these places free of germs, often with the use of anti-microbial products. In doing so, they may actually be interfering with the natural development of the immune system by **depriving** it of exposure to infectious microbes. Without this exposure early in life, the immune system is unprepared when it encounters these microbes later in life. Environmental triggers can cause the immune system to overreact with an allergic response – or for some people, an asthma attack. This was the hypothesis used to explain the German situation. Germ-conscious West Germany may have prevented children from being exposed to infections – exposure that might have protected them later in life.

The problem with this theory is that, although the explanation works pretty well for allergies, it didn't always hold up as well for asthma, particularly its most chronic forms. Let me explain. Where asthma rates are rising dramatically today is in poor, urban areas, which are not particularly clean or germ-free.

So, what are we to conclude? Both the pollution and hygiene hypotheses may explain some of the increased incidence of asthma, but neither provides a complete explanation. Other factors seem to come into play as well, for example, diet. Specific foods, like eggs, milk, and nuts, trigger asthma attacks in some people. How much you eat is also an issue; there is a high rate of obesity among asthma sufferers. It is interesting to note that all of these factors – increased air pollution, an increased focus on cleanliness, rising rates of obesity resulting from an unhealthy diet and sedentary lifestyle – might all be placed into the category of "modern life." Certainly, none of these factors is present in the rural communities of the developing world that show such low rates of the disease.

So there simply are no clear and simple answers regarding cause – yet. However, we do have a pretty good track record on managing asthma symptoms. Of course, any asthma sufferer should consult a doctor regarding options for medication, but here are just a few guidelines sufferers can follow to keep themselves safe and healthy:

- Check daily air quality reports. On days when pollution levels are high, stay indoors as much as possible and don't engage in vigorous exercise.
- Plan exercise and outdoor activities in the morning or early evening when pollution levels are lower.
- Maintain a healthy diet and a healthy weight.
- Control the amount of dust in your home.
- Avoid the use of cleaning sprays, scented candles, and air fresheners.
- Don't smoke – which is good advice in any case.
- Learn your specific triggers so you can reduce or avoid them.

These are just some general suggestions. Each person is different and to some extent, he or she will have to learn about their triggers and reactions by trial and error.

7.2

Now, a lot of what I'm talking about today is "environmental health," and indeed, although genetics is the single most powerful predictor of the development of asthma, it cannot be the whole story. Our genes change far too slowly to explain the rapid increase of this disease. So scientists and medical researchers have turned to the environment for explanations.

Frequently mentioned triggers include indoor and outdoor pollution. Indoor pollution includes dust, mold, tobacco smoke, pet hair, and various chemicals used for cleaning. Outdoor pollution includes particulate matter – very small pieces of dirt, chemicals, and pollutants trapped in the air – and ground-level ozone, formed when pollution from cars and factories combine with heat and sunlight. Studies have found a **correlation** between **proximity** to both of these types of pollution and the development of asthma. These factors are also strongly associated with the severity of its symptoms. Nevertheless, there is conflicting historical data. For example, the rapid increase in air pollution in Chinese cities has been accompanied by a similar rise in asthma in that country – as much as 40 percent in the past 20 years. On the other hand, the reunification of Germany in 1990 provides a counterexample. East Germany suffered from far more serious pollution than West Germany at the time, yet asthma was a much bigger problem in the West than in the East. **Ironically**, as the former East Germany tackled its air pollution, its rate of asthma actually rose.

About this time, another proposal was made, the so-called **Hygiene** Hypothesis, which goes something like this: when children are young, parents make an effort to keep the home and school environments as clean as possible. One might even go so far as to say that many parents try to keep these places free of germs, often with the use of anti-microbial products. In doing so, they may actually be interfering with the natural development of the immune system by **depriving** it of exposure to infectious microbes. Without this exposure early in life, the immune system is unprepared when it encounters these microbes later in life. Environmental triggers can cause the immune system to overreact with an allergic response – or for some people, an asthma attack. This was the hypothesis used to explain the German situation. Germ-conscious West Germany may have prevented children from being exposed to infections – exposure that might have protected them later in life.

The problem with this theory is that, although the explanation works pretty well for allergies, it didn't always hold up as well for asthma, particularly its most chronic forms. Let me explain. Where asthma rates are rising dramatically today is in poor, urban areas, which are not particularly clean or germ-free.

So, what are we to conclude? Both the pollution and hygiene hypotheses may explain some of the increased incidence of asthma, but neither provides a complete explanation. Other factors seem to come into play as well, for example, diet. Specific foods, like eggs, milk, and nuts, trigger asthma attacks in some people. How much you eat is also an issue; there is a high rate of obesity among asthma sufferers. It is interesting to note that all of these factors – increased air pollution, an increased focus on cleanliness, rising rates of obesity resulting from an unhealthy diet and sedentary lifestyle – might all be placed into the category of "modern life." Certainly, none of these factors is present in the rural communities of the developing world that show such low rates of the disease.

7.3

1 So, for some people, the symptoms only appear when they are exposed to some sort of trigger in the environment. Other asthma sufferers experience some level of these symptoms all the time.

2 It is 50 times more common in urban centers like Los Angeles and Chicago than in areas of rural Africa.

3 We don't know what causes asthma, nor do we know how to cure it. However, we do have some idea of what triggers symptoms, and we do have effective ways to manage these symptoms.

7.4

1 East Germany suffered from far more serious pollution than West Germany at the time, yet asthma was a much bigger problem in the West than in the East.

2 Without this exposure early in life, the immune system is unprepared when it encounters these microbes later in life.

3 Both the pollution and hygiene hypotheses may explain some of the increased incidence of asthma, but neither provides a complete explanation.

 7.5

Moderator: This is the story of how things went wrong and how some people tried to fix the problem, and some people tried to hide it. It's the story of one place, Iron City, but the lessons are relevant for cities and towns all over the country. We've invited some of the people who played a part in this story to discuss Iron City's troubles. Not everyone agreed to participate, but we'll try to give you a balanced perspective, nevertheless. We will also take some questions from the audience.

Let me introduce our panelists.

 7.6

Moderator: Let me introduce our panelists:

Dr. Evan Hardwick, an environmental scientist who works for the **federal** government. He did a lot of the testing of water quality in Iron City.

Dr. Mira Vaswani, a pediatrician, who documented the health of Iron City's children.

Michael Kirk, an assistant to the current mayor of Iron City.

I should point out from the start that none of those responsible for the deplorable condition of Iron City's water during the crisis would agree to participate in our discussion. Mr. Kirk and the current mayor are both new to their jobs. Dr. Hardwick, could you start by explaining how all of this happened, from a scientific perspective?

Hardwick: Of course. In many of our cities, the water and sewer systems were installed more than a hundred years ago, when lead pipes were standard. Lead was cheap and easy to work with, and no one had any idea about its toxic **properties** at that time. Even when we did discover the damage that lead can cause, we weren't thinking that much about lead poisoning because if the pipes are in good condition, it was thought that the amount of lead that escaped into the water would be **minimal**. On top of that, we have federal guidelines that every city must follow. Cities are required to test lead levels regularly using a standard **protocol**. For the most part, this had been working pretty well.

Moderator: So why was the situation in Iron City different? Why were the pipes there a problem?

Hardwick: About a year and a half ago, the city switched its water supply and began using water that was more acidic than the previous supply.

Moderator: That's a problem?

Hardwick: The problem is that the acidity in the water began to eat away at the pipes, allowing the lead to **contaminate** the water. Every city is required to have a plan to test water for acidity and, based on those tests, take measures to counter the damage the acidity can do to water pipes, especially lead pipes. And that's where the city completely dropped the ball. They had no such plan. It was an astounding lapse in judgment. As a result, the **concentration** of lead in the city's water rose well above acceptable levels.

Moderator: So, Dr. Vaswani, what did this mean for the people of Iron City? What happens when people drink water with high levels of lead?

Vaswani: Lead is incredibly toxic – to the nervous system, to the reproductive system, but most of all, it affects brain development. And for that reason, lead poisoning has the most damaging impact on children. Numerous studies have demonstrated that children with high levels of lead in their systems often end up with cognitive impairments, learning disabilities, behavioral problems, and in some cases, these can be quite severe. Even a small increase in lead levels has been shown to have a negative impact on cognitive development. And the most heartbreaking part is that the damage is irreversible. This means people who have been exposed to lead as children may face a lifetime of problems, in school, at work, in everything they do. Their futures are deeply **compromised** because of this lead exposure.

Moderator: Thank you. I see we have a question from someone in the audience.

Johnson: My name is Monica Johnson. I moved to Iron City because I thought it would be a nice place to raise our children, and until about a year and a half ago, it was. But then things changed. The water coming out of the faucets was yellow, sometimes orange. It smelled terrible and tasted worse. After I took a shower or my kids had a bath, our skin turned red. My kids developed rashes and terrible stomach pains. After a few months, our hair started to fall out. I panicked. I knew something was wrong, but I didn't know what to do. I called the city, but they kept claiming that nothing was wrong. I finally found someone I could trust, Dr. Hardwick. He agreed to come test the water in our home.

Moderator: Mr. Kirk? I know you were not in your job at the time, but can you tell us anything about what happened?

Kirk: Well, what I can tell you is that the city was not conducting the tests of water quality correctly. Our protocol was not up to federal standards, which led to results showing the water wasn't as contaminated as it really was. The people Mrs. Johnson spoke to at city hall really believed the water was safe. Since then, we have updated the protocols for testing water quality. With the new tests, the damage to the pipes is very clear. The city is deeply sorry for the problems this has caused your family.

Johnson: Problems? You bet it's caused problems. Both of my children have learning disabilities. My six-year-old son has trouble with his ABCs. My eight-year-old has gotten into so many fights that he has been kicked out of two schools. What kind of life do they have to look forward to?

Moderator: Doctor Vaswani?

Vaswani: In fact, I began to notice some of these problems in a lot of the patients at the clinic. I recognized them as possible symptoms of lead poisoning, so I started doing blood tests, and I was appalled by what I found. You need to understand that no level of lead in the blood is considered safe, and 5 micrograms per deciliter is considered highly toxic, capable of causing serious and permanent damage. And I was finding levels *above* that. So I started researching hospital records and found a dramatic difference between the lead levels in children before and after the water supply was changed. What I found was shocking, I would say, even criminal.

Hardwick: Dr. Vaswani's findings are consistent with the test results on water from the Johnsons' house and many other homes that I tested. I found lead levels seven times higher than the federal action level. The action level is the point at which the local government is supposed to step in to take measures to address the problem. In fact, they did nothing until the federal government finally **intervened**.

Moderator: Mr. Kirk, can you tell us what measures the city is taking now? You said you have gone back to the original water supply.

Kirk: Yes, but the problem is that all those pipes are now damaged and need to be replaced, which is an incredibly expensive undertaking. The federal government has given the city a grant to begin replacing them, but that will be a lengthy process. For now, the city is supplying residents with bottled water. I know these are not permanent solutions, but fixing a problem this big is going to take more time.

7.7

Host: Good morning, welcome to the *Morning Show*. You're on the air. Tell us your name and your problem!

Cam: My name is Cam Stewart, and I own Stewart's Canoe and Kayak in town. Since all of this happened, my business is down 75 percent. Last week, I rented out just two boats. Normally at this time of year, every boat in my shop is out every day. I have a waiting list. Now, days go by without a single customer.

Host: That's terrible. I know a lot of business owners in Golden Valley are suffering.

Cam: Yeah, it's gotten so bad that I may have to close my business. I want to know what Four Star and the government are going to do about this mess!

Host: That's something we would all like to know. Well, thanks for your call. We've got two more callers. Hi, you're on the air.

Tahoma: Hi. My name is Tahoma. I'm a member of the Navajo nation. This disaster has poisoned the river and other areas that are sacred to my people. We have taken fish from this river for hundreds of years, long before Europeans came to North America. It will take years to restore it. It may never be the same. We cannot maintain our traditions without the river.

Host: Thank you, Tahoma. I'm very glad to have the thoughts of someone from the Navajo nation. Your community is suffering from this mess in so many ways. Ah, another call. Yes, you're on the air.

Beverly: My name is Beverly. I'm not Navajo, but my family has also lived in this community for many generations. All of our water comes from the river. I've got two kids and always felt safe giving them tap water. Now, I'm buying bottled water for them to drink. I don't even know if it's safe to take a shower!

Host: That's a good point. It looks as if I have the town manager on the line now. Let's get her on the air and ask her. Ms. Villega, what can you tell Tahoma and Beverly?

City manager: We are working very hard with the federal government and Four Star to clean up the spill as quickly as possible. For now, environmental experts are telling residents to do what Beverly is doing – drink bottled water. The town is providing bottled water, so you don't have to buy your own. But our experts are saying that the water is *safe* to wash with and bathe in.

Host: Well, you heard it, folks. You can decide for yourselves whether to believe it! We'll take more questions from listeners in just a moment.

7.8

See script on page 164.

7.9

Interviewer: Today's interview is with Doctor Juliana Ochoa, Director of the University Health Center here on campus. Welcome Dr. Ochoa.

Ochoa: Thank you.

Interviewer: First, can you give us an overview of the services that you provide at the Health Center?

Ochoa: Yes. We have a full staff of doctors, nurses, nurse practitioners, nutritionists, social workers, psychiatrists, and health educators. We treat all aspects of physical and mental health here in one place.

Interviewer: Would a student come here in an emergency?

Ochoa: Well, if it's a life-threatening situation, we advise students to call 911 or go to the emergency room at the hospital. That's always the fastest way to get help. We have an "urgent care" facility here.

Interviewer: Can you explain what that means? What is urgent care?

Ochoa: If you feel you need to see a doctor today, but your life is not immediately in danger, you would go to urgent care. Maybe you have the flu, or something like that. We treat people according to how serious the situation is, so you usually have to wait. But you will be able to see a doctor and get treated that same day.

Interviewer: What other services do you provide?

Ochoa: Most students come to us for regular doctor visits and checkups. We do preventive care: flu shots and other vaccinations. We have a pharmacy, so we can fill prescriptions. We do sports medicine and physical therapy. We do a lot of health education. That's a priority for us. For many students, it's the first time that they're away from home and in charge of their own health. We really encourage them to establish good health habits now that can last a lifetime.

Interviewer: Is stress a problem?

Ochoa: Oh, yes. Stress management is another big part of what we do. We have a full range of counseling and psychological services here.

Interviewer: What kind of issues do you see?

Ochoa: Well, depression can be a problem. Some students we see come to us because they feel tired all the time. They think that they're sick – that it's a physical problem – but it can, in fact, be a sign of depression.

Interviewer: So if students are feeling stressed or having trouble, they can find help?

Ochoa: Absolutely. We have trained counselors available, and we really encourage students to seek help if they need it. It's not a sign of weakness to ask for help. It means you're taking charge of your own health. Most students benefit tremendously from just a couple of sessions with a counselor.

UNIT 8

Are Office Meetings Useful?

Narrator: Now, a study done by the Virginia Tech Carilion Research Institute tells us that people might actually be more productive working alone and that meetings can make us dumber.

Businessman: I think I feel dumb leaving meetings 50% of the time. I mean, that's the state we're in.

Narrator: Listen to what Read Montague, who led the study, says, "You may joke about how committee meetings make you *feel* brain dead, but our findings suggest they make you *act* brain dead as well."

Businesswoman 1: There's so much information given, so you go into a meeting feeling like you know something or a certain amount, level of things, and then you come out feeling, gee, I really didn't know as much as I thought I did.

Narrator: And apparently, these group settings diminish expressions of intelligence, especially among women.

Businesswoman 2: Often there's a lot of terms thrown at me in a meeting that I have no idea what they mean till I leave and I Google it and I get up to speed, and I at least feel I can contribute next time. But during the meeting, definitely, very silly.

Reporter 1: Leave and Google. That is a good approach.

Reporter 2: Yeah, exactly. I would just Google during the meeting. Anyway, lots and lots of meetings went into the planning of this segment, so stay tuned.

Reporter 1: Yes, indeed. Bob Rosner is a workplace expert. He's author of *The Boss's Survival Guide*. Bob, good morning.

Rosner: Good morning.

Reporter 1: So the big question is, do meetings really make us stupid?

Rosner: Of course they do! When I think of meetings, I think of a piñata because you can't bash meetings enough. Everybody hates them.

Reporter 2: Yeah.

Rosner: And you feel like a piñata when you attend one. So meetings are a huge problem. On paper they make sense – bringing people together, collaboration – but the reality is not that. They're a waste of time to most people.

Reporter 2: I find it interesting in this study that women are more impacted by meetings than men.

Rosner: Well, women need connection and trust. And the problem with meetings is they don't provide that. They damage it. So, to me, if you really want to connect, ... Now guys like a competitive environment. They're like, they're built differently. Women ...

Reporter 2: I would say there are women who like a competitive environment too.

Rosner: On average, let's say, ...

Reporter 2: I don't know anyone like that, but ...

Rosner: On average. But to me, connection and trust are real keys, and we forget that.

Reporter 2: Yeah.

Reporter 1: What can happen to make a meeting more productive, to get more out of a meeting if you have to actually have one?

Rosner: Well, let me start with the bad side. A guy wrote to me a while ago – I get a lot of emails – and he said his boss got up in front of the meeting and said, "We're going to keep having meetings until I figure out why nothing's getting done around here." On average, executives, we attend 62 meetings a month and about half of them are wasted. The key issue with meetings is efficiency versus effectiveness. When we try to be more efficient, we get less effective, and that's the difficult balance of meetings.

Reporter 2: What about the composition of the meeting – who actually attends it, and what their roles are in the meeting?

Rosner: Well, a lot of that isn't defined before the meeting. I'm a – I have client right now and they run the best meetings, so I wanted to figure out what they were doing right. So I came up with the four Ps. First, *preparation* – they prepare before the meetings. It's excellent. Second, *purpose* – you can go around the table and everybody knows the purpose of the meeting. That doesn't usually happen. *Participation* is another key. If people are in the room, they should be participating. If they're not participating, why are they there? So you've got to get everybody involved. And then you need a *plan* moving forward. So you can run an effective meeting using the four Ps. I just made that up for you guys, by the way.

Reporter 2: I appreciate that.

Reporter 1: So meetings may actually be good in some cases?

Rosner: They can work. Some of my trends that I love – there's a trend now of stand-up meetings, and they found that these meetings are 30% shorter and they cover the same amount of ground. And then there's *topless meetings* – it's not what you think. Topless meetings – you don't, you can't bring any electronics into the meeting. No phones. No computers.

Reporter 1: No Googling, that will be a problem.

Reporter 2: Yeah.

Reporter 1: Alright.

Rosner: What they're finding is, they're the most effective meetings.

Reporter 2: Thanks, Bob. We appreciate it.

Reporter 1: Bob Rosner, thanks so much.

Speaker: All of you have worked in groups at one time or another – at school, at work, in your community, or even on a jury – groups that have to make decisions. Knowing how to work effectively in groups is very important in all kinds of settings. And knowing something about group **dynamics** – that's the technical name for this – can be very useful. It'll help you develop **insights** into your own behavior and how that behavior can affect the dynamics of the groups you participate in, especially when there is conflict.

In general, groups have an assigned task to complete – a report, a project, or an assessment – giving the group members a shared goal. Completing the assigned task requires making decisions. Of course, individual members of a group may also have their own goals, which may or may not be consistent with the group goal. And some individuals may not be interested in arriving at a decision or completing the project at all. So then what happens? What'll you do if your group has a "bad apple" – a person who consistently engages in some sort of negative or destructive behavior?

Now, "bad apple" behavior can take several forms. Some bad apples are slackers. Slackers express a lack of interest in the task. They may not actively oppose the actions and ideas of other members of the group; they simply refuse to contribute any effort or deal with the task. Their attitude can be summed up in one word: "whatever." Other bad apples express generally negative feelings about the group, its task, and its chances of success. These "naysayers" reject or criticize the ideas and opinions of others without proposing any **constructive** ideas of their own. Finally, some bad apples are simply bullies. They'll insist on doing things their way and only their way.

Now, you might think that in a group, especially in a large group, one person might not make that much of a difference, no matter how badly he or she behaves. The majority should **prevail**, right? But apparently, this is not how group dynamics works. Research suggests that it only takes one member of a group to act badly – one bad apple – for a group to stop functioning effectively. One bad apple actually does "spoil the barrel." In one study in which the researchers hired actors to play "bad apples" in group decision-making tasks, groups with a bad apple member generally performed 30 to 40 percent worse than groups with no negative members. The researchers concluded that the group's worst member was the best predictor of the whole group's performance. This was true even when a group's other members were all intelligent, well-educated, otherwise effective people.

But it's even worse than that. What these researchers found was that the behavior of one bad apple can spread to the whole group. The other members began to adopt the same negative behavior. If the bad apple was a slacker and, say, pulled out his smartphone and started texting during the discussion, other members began to follow suit. They stopped making any effort and began to withdraw from the group interaction. If the bad apple was overly critical of others or made pessimistic statements like, "This'll never work" or "This is so stupid," other members also became critical or began to express similarly negative views. And if the bad apple bullied the other members, for the most part, they did not try to resist. They just let the bad apple have their own way. And perhaps just as important, everyone had a negative response to the entire experience. Just one bad apple destroyed the group's positive dynamics. Specifically, the bad apple's behavior resulted in **perceptions** of unfairness among members, reduced trust in the group, withdrawal from interaction, and generally negative emotions – anger, **resentment**, even fear.

So what can you do if you are stuck in a group with a participant who displays such negative behavior? A few strategies have been shown to be effective in **counteracting** the "bad apple effect." The most obvious approach is to simply remove the individual from the group, but, as I am sure you know, that's not always possible. A second option is to demand that the individual change his or her behavior – which is probably only possible if someone in the group has sufficient authority to make that happen, and that's a big *if*. But the study also found that sometimes a group just gets lucky. If the group has an exceptional individual who is able to engage all of the group members, including the bad apple, it may be possible to **defuse** conflict. This kind of skilled leader can keep the decision-making process moving forward no matter what. Unfortunately, there's no guarantee that there'll be a skilled leader in a group. In fact, very few of the groups in the study had one. And if results of this study are reflective of group dynamics in more natural situations, it's safe to assume that the bad apple effect is pretty widespread.

But perhaps you already know that. The lead researcher in the study said he had become interested in the topic because of a personal experience, and as he spoke about the idea to colleagues and friends, he found that just about everyone had had a bad apple experience – a situation in which one person made the atmosphere in an office, a class, or other group thoroughly unpleasant.

It can be difficult to prevent bad apples from ruining a group and its dynamics, but recognizing them early and understanding how they operate may help you defuse the conflicts they create so that your group can achieve its goals. I hope that this presentation has helped you gain that understanding.

8.2

In general, groups have an assigned task to complete – a report, a project, or an assessment – giving the group members a shared goal. Completing the assigned task requires making decisions. Of course, individual members of a group may also have their own goals, which may or may not be consistent with the group goal. And some individuals may not be interested in arriving at a decision or completing the project at all. So then what happens? What'll you do if your group has a "bad apple" – a person who consistently engages in some sort of negative or destructive behavior?

Now, "bad apple" behavior can take several forms. Some bad apples are slackers. Slackers express a lack of interest in the task. They may not actively oppose the actions and ideas of other members of the group; they simply refuse to contribute any effort or deal with the task. Their attitude can be summed up in one word: "whatever." Other bad apples express generally negative feelings about the group, its task, and its chances of success. These "naysayers" reject or criticize the ideas and opinions of others without proposing any constructive ideas of their own. Finally, some bad apples are simply bullies. They'll insist on doing things their way and only their way.

Now, you might think that in a group, especially in a large group, one person might not make that much of a difference, no matter how badly he or she behaves. The majority should prevail, right? But apparently, this is not how group dynamics works. Research suggests that it only takes one member of a group to act badly – one bad apple – for a group to stop functioning effectively. One bad apple actually does "spoil the barrel." In one study in which the researchers hired actors to play "bad apples" in group decision-making tasks, groups with a bad apple member generally performed 30 to 40 percent worse than groups with no negative members. The researchers concluded that the group's worst member was the best predictor of the whole group's performance. This was true even when a group's other members were all intelligent, well-educated, otherwise effective people.

But it's even worse than that. What these researchers found was that the behavior of one bad apple can spread to the whole group. The other members began to adopt the same negative behavior. If the bad apple was a slacker and, say, pulled out his smartphone and started texting during the discussion, other members began to follow suit. They stopped making any effort and began to withdraw from the group interaction. If the bad apple was overly critical of others or made pessimistic statements like, "This'll never work" or "This is so stupid," other members also became critical or began to express similarly negative views. And if the bad apple bullied the other members, for the most part, they did not try to resist. They just let the bad apple have their own way. And perhaps just as important, everyone had a negative response to the entire experience. Just one bad apple destroyed the group's positive dynamics. Specifically, the bad apple's behavior resulted in perceptions of unfairness among members, reduced trust in the group, withdrawal from interaction, and generally negative emotions – anger, resentment, even fear.

8.3

1 And knowing something about group dynamics – that's the technical name for this – can be very useful. It'll help you develop insights into your own behavior and how that behavior can affect the dynamics of the groups you participate in.

2 So then what happens? What'll you do if your group has "a bad apple"?

3 If the bad apple was overly critical of others or made pessimistic statements like, "This'll never work" or "This is so stupid," other members also became critical or began to express similarly negative views.

4 Unfortunately, there's no guarantee that there'll be a skilled leader in a group. In fact, very few of the groups in the study had one.

5 He plans to donate his spectacular art collection to the museum and provide a huge amount of money to make sure it'll run for a long time.

6 We decided to let the museum proposal move forward, but with a very different design. The building'll be much shorter, and the design'll be more organic and consistent with the natural setting. Also, the parking lot'll be underground and out of sight.

8.4

See script on page 176.

8.5

Teacher: OK, class, we have come to the end of our unit on decision making, so I would like to take some time today to review what we have learned. We took a difficult, real-life problem and approached it in two ways. So first, let's review the problem. Would someone describe it for us briefly? Yes, go ahead.

Student 1: OK, well, there is a basic disagreement about how to use a piece of waterfront property. An old structure has just been demolished, and a billionaire hi-tech entrepreneur wants to build a museum on the site. He plans to donate his spectacular art collection to the museum and provide a huge amount of money to make sure it'll run for a long time. On the other side, a group of city residents, Citizens for Open Spaces, wants to add the property to the existing waterfront parkland and keep the area open for public use.

Teacher: Thank you. So the class's job was to make a decision about how to use this land. We went through two different decision-making processes. The first one was pretty familiar. Can someone else describe that? Uh-huh.

Student 2: Representatives from the two different sides presented their arguments to us. We discussed the two different options and then we took a vote. Citizens for Open Spaces won, 18 to 8.

Teacher: OK, so one side won, but a lot of people must have been unhappy with the result.

Student 2: True, but the majority won.

Teacher: OK. And then we moved on to a different process, addressing the same issue. How was this process different?

Student 3: It took a lot longer!

Teacher: That's for sure. What else? Can someone describe the steps we went through in this **consensus**-building process?

Student 4: Well, we were all pretty familiar with the issues already, but the facilitator just described the two options again. She was clearly trying to be objective and not take sides.

Student 5: Yeah, that was one big difference. We had a facilitator, a person who sort of kept the process moving and helped us organize our ideas. She stressed the process has to start out with everyone in agreement about one thing.

Teacher: What's that?

Student 5: That they are willing to work together to reach a decision; that they want to solve the problem. Without that, the process cannot work.

Teacher: OK, great, so how did it start out?

Student 5: Everyone had a chance to talk. We all stated what our concerns were, especially things that we didn't like about one or the other of the options.

Student 2: And we also talked about how to **resolve** differences, not just about choosing between the two options. I mean, we came up with lots of different ideas.

Teacher: What do you mean?

Student 2: We kind of broke down both options into components so that we could look at them separately.

Teacher: Can you give an example?

Student 1: I can. So one of the objections to the museum was the design. It'll block the view of the lake, and it doesn't really fit in with the surrounding park area.

Student 4: And it'll have a big ugly parking lot, too.

Teacher: So did this step make a difference?

Student 1: Yes, I think it really did. It helped everyone to clarify what exactly they did and didn't like about the two options, and it allowed alternate and **hybrid** proposals to emerge.

Teacher: So did everyone agree on one of those?

Student 4: Not right away. But it gave us a place to start. We had to go back to the drawing board when some people expressed **reservations**.

Teacher: So then what did you do?

Student 4: We **tinkered** with all of the elements until we came up with a proposal that everyone could live with.

Teacher: That *everyone* could live with? How do you know that?

Student 2: That's one of the steps in the consensus-building process. The facilitator tested for agreement. She asked everyone if they could support the proposal – or at least that they wouldn't oppose it.

Teacher: So there was no vote?

Student 4: No, not really. She just kept checking for agreement with each new version of the proposal until she got consensus from the whole group.

Teacher: So everyone was in favor of the final proposal?

Student 3: Well, that may be a bit of an exaggeration, but I think everyone felt as if they had participated in the decision-making process and that their concerns had been addressed.

Teacher: So what was the final proposal?

Student 3: We decided to let the museum proposal move forward, but with a very different design. The building will be much shorter, and the design will be more organic and consistent with the natural setting. Also, the parking lot will be underground and out of sight.

Teacher: Anything else?

Student 1: Yeah, the museum's founder, the high-tech entrepreneur, agreed to donate some money to improve and expand the park next to the museum.

Teacher: Wow. So a very different **outcome** than with the first process. So how do you feel now about these two different ways of approaching decision making?

Student 2: I think everyone was a lot happier with the second way. Well, let me rephrase that: in the consensus-building process, there were no winners and no losers. I'm sure in the voting process the winners were happy, but the losers were really unhappy. When the decision was made by consensus, everyone still had a **stake** in the project going forward. No one felt like their opinion was ignored or dismissed.

Student 5: Yes, it felt like, even the people who initially opposed the museum might end up visiting it. With the first process, you had the feeling that the losers might resent the museum and never get any enjoyment out of it. The conflict had never really been resolved.

Teacher: So a compromise?

Student 4: Not really. In a compromise, everyone has to give something up. And maybe that happened here, but we all created the new proposal together, so it didn't feel as if anyone was giving something up exactly. Everyone felt some sense of **ownership**. It just felt like a better decision all around.

Teacher: Well, this all sounds pretty positive. Is there a downside to this? Why aren't all decisions made this way?

Student 2: Well, it took forever to arrive at the final decision. In the first process, the decision was made in an hour. In the consensus process, we worked most of the day. I'm not sure everyone has that kind of time.

Student 1: Also we're a pretty small group. I think it could be really challenging if you tried it with a big group of people.

Teacher: All very interesting and insightful comments. Well, I hope that this has been a learning experience for all of you and that you will use some of what you have learned here in the future, when you run the city for real!

Speaker: Our first candidate is DINESCO.

DINESCO has been on the campus for more than 20 years, providing a range of dining services across the campus, including the current dining room in the student center, which is open from 7 a.m. to 11 p.m. It serves hot meals, salads, burgers, snacks, desserts – everything you would expect from a dining service.

DINESCO holds the campus dining service contract, so that means that the university pays an annual fee to DINESCO for their services. Students who live on campus can eat at the student center facility as part of their dining contract. They can eat as much and whatever they want. Other students and members of the public have to pay for individual meals or snacks there. The cost is reasonable for those who use unlimited services, perhaps less so for those who pay for individual meals.

Many students and visitors have complained about the quality and choice of the food that DINESCO provides.

 8.7

Speaker: The next candidate for the campus dining service contract is Dilly's.

Dilly's is a popular fast-food and casual dining chain that started right here in our state. Many of our students grew up eating and enjoying Dilly's food. They serve breakfast, burgers, pizza and pasta, and salad from a salad bar. They also sell snacks such as yogurt, fruit, and chips. Service is fast and the prices are moderate.

Dilly's already operates a 24-hour restaurant in the natural sciences building, which is very popular with students and always crowded. The student center restaurant would also be open 24 hours. It would be included in the student dining contract, but there would be limits on amounts.

Some students and health services staff have complained that a diet of Dilly's food is not healthy and could contribute to obesity and other chronic health issues.

Dilly's would pay the university a significant sum of money to rent the space in the student center. Ten percent of these funds would go to support student activities.

8.8

Speaker: The final candidate for the campus dining service contract is Unihub.

Unihub is the name of a proposed café and casual dining spot that would be managed and operated by students in the tourism and hospitality program. Students would manage the business operations, the kitchen, and the dining room under the supervision of the college faculty. Working at Unihub would serve as the required practical experience component of their degree.

This new facility would serve sandwiches, salads, pasta, and other casual food. It would be open for lunch and dinner. During late night hours, a small section of the restaurant would be open for take-out food.

Though it would be included in the student dining contract, it would only cover lunch and dinner. And the prices of any meals that people would buy are expected to be higher than at the current DINESCO facility.

In addition, the university would have to subsidize the operation; in other words, we would need to contribute funds toward its operation because it would not be expected to make a profit, at least not initially. The money would come from the student activities fund.

8.9

Presenter: Today I'm going to talk about how the jury system works. I'll give you the basic information, and then I'll take questions. So please hold your questions until the end of the presentation.

First of all, in this country, every citizen has the right to a jury trial. What this means is that every citizen also has a duty to serve on a jury. So from time to time, you might be asked to go to the courthouse to report for jury duty.

When you report for jury duty, the first step is jury selection. You complete a questionnaire with your basic info, and then you wait to be called. If there's a trial starting that you might be appropriate for, they call you in for a short interview. You answer questions from the attorneys on both sides. Then the attorneys choose twelve people that they believe will make a good jury for this trial.

After the jury is chosen, the trial begins. The jurors listen to all of the evidence and hear all of the witness statements. When that's done, the jurors are sent to the deliberation room to discuss the case and make a decision. That's called a verdict.

Deliberation is the most interesting part for the jury. They discuss all the evidence that was presented and listen carefully to everyone's opinion. Finally, they arrive at a decision that they can all agree on. Then they go back to the courtroom, in front of the judge and the attorneys and everyone else, and announce their verdict.

I'll stop there for the moment. Any questions so far?

Student 1: Yes. How long do most trials last?

Presenter: Oh yes, good question! Most trials last between two and five days, although some run for longer. Any other questions? Yes?

Student 1: What if you are on a trial that lasts a long time? You can't go to work. Can you lose your job?

Presenter: No. An employer must keep your job open for you for the length of your jury service.

Student 2: Are jurors paid for jury service?

Presenter: Most courts will pay jurors a small fee. If you work for a large company, you may get paid time off for jury service, so you can still get paid from your work. But not all employers can do that, and they are not required to, at least not in the U.S. Does that answer your question?

Student 2: Yes, thank you.

Student 3: My brother lives in Australia, and he says the system is different there. Is that true? Do some countries not have jury systems?

Presenter: I'm sorry, I don't know the answer to that. My presentation is really only on the jury system in the United States.

Student 4: Is a jury always twelve people? Or are there some situations when a jury can be smaller?

Presenter: I'm not really sure about that. But I can find out and let you know.

Student 4: Thank you.

Presenter: Any more questions? Yes, in the back, do you have a question?

CREDITS

The authors and publishers acknowledge the following sources of copyright material and are grateful for the permissions granted. While every effort has been made, it has not always been possible to identify the sources of all the material used, or to trace all copyright holders. If any omissions are brought to our notice, we will be happy to include the appropriate acknowledgements on reprinting and in the next update to the digital edition, as applicable.

Text Credits

Graph on p. 24 adapted from "OECD v Non OECD CO_2 Emissions 1965 through 2013." Copyright © Robert Rapier 2014. Reproduced with kind permission of BP Statistical Review of World Energy; graph on p. 132 (bottom) adapted from "Data and Analysis of Freelancer Demographics, Earnings, Habits and Attitudes" by Ed Gandia, *Freelance Industry Report,* August 2012. Copyright © International Freelancers Academy 2012. Reproduced with kind permission; Text on p. 173 adapted from "Do You Have a Collaborative Work Style?" by Laura Hills. Copyright © Greenbranch Publishing 2013. Reproduced with kind permission.

Photo Credits

Key: T = Top, C = Center, B = Bottom, L = Left, R = Right

p. 12: Cultura RM Exclusive/Peter Muller/Getty Images; pp. 14–15: Stringer/AFP/Getty Images; p. 27: ARIF ALI/Stringer/AFP/Getty Images; p. 34: Ariel Skelley/Blend Images/Getty Images; pp. 36–37: dreamnikon/iStock/Getty Images Plus/Getty Images; p. 40 (L, C): Anadolu Agency/Getty Images; (R): Laurie Rubin/Photographer's Choice/Getty Images; p. 46: bdStudios/iStock/Getty Images Plus/Getty Images; pp. 58–59: Ute Grabowsky/Photothek/Getty Images; pp. 80–81: Visual China Group/Getty Images; p. 97: Hybrid Images/Cultura/Getty Images; p. 100: PeopleImages/E+/Getty Images; pp. 102–103: Dustin Bradford/Stringer/Getty Images Sport/Getty Images; p. 106: alvarez/E+/Getty Images; p. 115: VisitBritain/Grant Pritchard/Britain On View/Getty Images; pp. 124–125: Adam Rose/Disney ABC Television Group/Getty Images; p. 136: Antonio_Diaz/iStock/Getty Images Plus/Getty Images; p. 141 (photo a): Brand X Pictures/Stockbyte/Getty Images Plus/Getty Images; (photo b): Klaus Vedfelt/Riser/Getty Images; (photo c): ONOKY - Eric Audras/Brand X Pictures/Getty Images; (photo d): Reza Estakhrian/The Image Bank/Getty Images; p. 144: Chris Ryan/OJO Images/Getty Images; p. 145: Eyecandy Images/Alamy; pp. 146–147: ookinate23/iStock/Getty Images Plus; p. 150 (photo a): Peter Dazeley/DigitalVision/Getty Images; (photo b): Comstock/Stockbyte/Getty Images; (photo c): Lisa J Goodman/Moment Mobile/Getty Images; (photo d): piotr_malczyk/iStock/Getty Images Plus/Getty Images; (photo e): BSIP/Universal Images Group/Getty Images; (photo f): Mint Images/Getty Images; (photo g): Valentin Casarsa/DigitalVision/Getty Images; (photo h): John Millar/The Image Bank/Getty Images; p. 156 (T): alexey_ds/iStock/Getty Images Plus/Getty Images; (C): JIM WATSON/AFP/Getty Images; (B): cmannphoto/iStock/Getty Images Plus/Getty Images; p. 166: SolStock/iStock/Getty Images Plus; pp. 168–169: Pacific Press/LightRocket/Getty Images; p. 172: Michael Cogliantry/The Image Bank/Getty Images; p. 175: Mariana Eliano/Cover/Getty Images; p. 179: GOH CHAI HIN/AFP/Getty Images; p. 182: Boston Globe/Getty Images; p. 188: FS-Stock/iStock/Getty Images Plus/Getty Images.

Front cover photographs by (man) Dean Drobot/Shutterstock and (city) vichie81/Shutterstock.

Video supplied by BBC Worldwide Learning.

Video stills supplied by BBC Worldwide Learning.

Illustrations

pp. 41, 113: Oxford Designers & Illustrators; p. 109: Proceedings of the National Academy of Sciences; p. 137: Mark Anderson.

Corpus

Development of this publication has made use of the Cambridge English Corpus (CEC). The CEC is a multi-billion word computer database of contemporary spoken and written English. It includes British English, American English, and other varieties of English. It also includes the Cambridge Learner Corpus, developed in collaboration with the University of Cambridge ESOL Examinations. Cambridge University Press has built up the CEC to provide evidence about language use that helps to produce better language teaching materials

Cambridge Dictionaries

Cambridge dictionaries are the world's most widely used dictionaries for learners of English. The dictionaries are available in print and online at dictionary.cambridge.org. Copyright © Cambridge University Press, reproduced with permission.

Typeset by emc design ltd

Audio production by CityVox New York

INFORMED BY TEACHERS

Classroom teachers shaped everything about *Prism*. The topics. The exercises. The critical thinking skills. The On Campus sections. Everything. We are confident that *Prism* will help your students succeed in college because teachers just like you helped guide the creation of this series.

Prism Advisory Panel

The members of the *Prism* Advisory Panel provided inspiration, ideas, and feedback on many aspects of the series. *Prism* is stronger because of their contributions.

Gloria Munson
University of Texas, Arlington

Kim Oliver
Austin Community College

Gregory Wayne
Portland State University

Julaine Rosner
Mission College

Dinorah Sapp
University of Mississippi

Christine Hagan
George Brown College/Seneca College

Heidi Lieb
Bergen Community College

Stephanie Kasuboski
Cuyahoga Community College

Global Input

Teachers from more than 500 institutions all over the world provided valuable input through:

- Surveys
- Focus Groups
- Reviews